Political Communication and Social Theory

Political Communication and Social Theory presents an advanced and challenging text for students and scholars of political communication and mass media in democracies. It draws together work from across political communication, media sociology and political sociology, and includes a mix of theoretical debate and current examples from several democratic media systems. Its wide-ranging discussions both introduce and contest the traditional scholarship on a number of contemporary topics. These include:

- comparative political and media systems
- theories of democracy, representation and the public sphere
- political party communication, marketing and elections
- the production of news media and public policy
- media sociology and journalist–source relations
- celebrity politics, popular culture and political leadership
- new media and online democracy
- national-global politics and international political communication
- foreign policy-making, war and media
- the crisis of public communication in established democracies

At the same time, *Political Communication and Social Theory* offers a fascinating investigation of the causes of crisis in established political and media systems. In today's democracies, trust in politicians, state institutions and mainstream media sources has dropped to new lows. The traditional business model that sustained journalism is failing and nations are struggling to respond to the existing global recession and impending environmental and resource crises. Drawing on interviews with over 100 experienced politicians, journalists and civil servants, Aeron Davis explores how the varied political actors and communicative processes, at the centre of UK democracy, may or may not be contributing to such crisis tendencies.

Aeron Davis is a Reader and Director of the MA in Political Communication in the Department of Media and Communications, Goldsmiths College, London. He is the author of *Public Relations Democracy* (2002) and *The Mediation of Power* (2007).

'Aeron Davis' eloquent study of political communication and democracy in the age of digital media skilfully blends social theory with a wealth of 'insider' accounts from senior politicians and journalists to produce a classic text. Richly sourced with contemporary case studies, *Political Communication and Social Theory* analyses the global 'crisis' confronting journalism, media and democracy, and offers essential and compelling reading which sets a new benchmark for political communication scholarship.'

Bob Franklin, *Professor of Journalism Studies, Cardiff School of Journalism, Media and Cultural Studies, UK*

'Aeron Davis's brilliant new book offers up clear-eyed, critical analyses of social theory, deftly applied to real-world case studies of politics and journalism in action. He doesn't just review the literature, he transforms it with new ways of thinking about media capital, elite networks, online democracy, and the organizational iron cage. I can't imagine a more engaging, lucid, and original tour d'horizon of political communication, nor a more convincing testament to the dangers – and opportunities – facing contemporary democracies.'

Rodney Benson, *Associate Professor of Media, Culture, and Communication, New York University, USA*

'Aeron Davis's book could hardly be more timely: it examines the delicate question of the links between democratic politics and media systems in the UK at a moment of great change in both. But it is more than timely: it sets the UK experience into a wider comparative and theoretical framework, and is consistently rigorous in its theoretical analysis and deployment of evidence. It will be valuable not only to students and researchers, but to practitioners in the media and in the political system.'

Michael Moran, *Professor of Government, University of Manchester, UK*

Communication and Society

Series Editor: James Curran

This series encompasses the broad field of media and cultural studies. Its main concerns are the media and the public sphere: on whether the media empower or fail to empower popular forces in society; media organizations and public policy; the political and social consequences of media campaigns; and the role of media entertainment, ranging from potboilers and the human interest story to rock music and TV sport.

Political Communication and Social Theory

Aeron Davis

Routledge
Taylor & Francis Group

LONDON AND NEW YORK

First published 2010
by Routledge
2 Park Square, Milton Park, Abingdon, Oxon OX14 4RN

Simultaneously published in the USA and Canada
by Routledge
270 Madison Ave, New York, NY 10016

Routledge is an imprint of the Taylor & Francis Group, an informa business

© 2010 Aeron Davis

Typeset in Baskerville by Taylor & Francis Books
Printed and bound in Great Britain by
TJ International Ltd, Padstow, Cornwall

British Library Cataloguing in Publication Data
A catalogue record for this book is available from the British Library

Library of Congress Cataloging in Publication Data
Davis, Aeron.
  Political communication and social theory / Aeron Davis.
    p. cm. – (Communication and society)
  Includes bibliographical references and index.
  1. Communication in politics. 2. Mass media–Political aspects. I. Title.
JA85.D38 2010
320.01'4–dc22
                              2010002732

ISBN10: 0-415-54712-1 (hbk)
ISBN10: 0-415-54713-X (pbk)
ISBN10: 0-203-84729-6 (ebk)

ISBN13: 978-0-415-54712-3 (hbk)
ISBN13: 978-0-415-54713-0 (pbk)
ISBN13: 978-0-203-84729-9 (ebk)

For Helen Davis and Neville Davis

Contents

List of tables

Preface and acknowledgements

This book is, in part, an advanced textbook on political communication, media and politics in democracies. In part, it is also a wide-ranging study of the strengths and weaknesses of the systems of public communication in UK politics.

In textbook terms its ten chapters cover several common topics that might be included in a standard, one-term course on political communication or media and politics. It includes useful literature surveys on a range of topics, discussions of core theory, and current examples from many established democracies. As an advanced text, it also seeks to stretch the traditional disciplinary boundaries of the subject. The chapters thus attempt a greater synthesis of work from across the disciplines of politics, media sociology and political sociology; hence the book's title. Political communication offers a firm foundation for the book, with its focus on formal political institutions, processes and actors. Media sociology brings an emphasis on social theory and puts greater stress on the production of news media, other actors and forms of communication. Political sociology has a wider interpretation of what constitutes 'the political' and suggests alternative ways of investigating and analysing social processes within political spaces. Thus, all the chapters that follow stick to the traditional territory of political institutions, politicians, news media and public communication, but also draw on a range of sociological and media scholarship to help frame discussions. Accordingly, individual politicians, and those who work closely with them, are treated as actors operating in social settings. The term 'communication' is interpreted here rather more broadly, to include forms that are interpersonal, organisational, mass media, digital, cultural and symbolic.

Chapter 1 looks at *comparative political and media systems*, locating both political science and media sociology traditions within a *democratic theory* framework. **Chapter 2** discusses contrasting *ideal* visions for, and practices of, communication in representative democracies. In the process, it explores alternative models of the *public sphere* and their relevance to 'actually existing democracies'. **Chapter 3** covers *election campaigning* and the *professionalisation* of *party communication*. It suggests that changing electoral conditions and party structures have shaped and *disciplined* a new wave of party leaders, typified by the rise of *David Cameron*. **Chapter 4** looks at the parallel *production processes* of *policy* and *news* within the working *cultures of the new capitalism*. Its point being that the very working conditions of politicians and journalists impact upon aspects of the democratic process. **Chapter 5** revisits the literature on *journalist–politician relations*, investigating how interpersonal communication not only influences news content, but also plays a role in the *social construction* of *micro-level politics*. **Chapter 6** explores the *symbolic-cultural* forms of communication between celebrity-like politicians and citizens. For this it develops the concept of *media capital* as it is generated within and external to a *political field*. **Chapter 7**, concerned with how *digital media* are influencing politics and media, records a series of paradoxical shifts which are both improving and weakening public communication systems. **Chapter 8** attempts to define the territory and associated debates on *international political communication* as they emerge alongside *globalisation*. It draws on a mixture of *network theorists* and *economic sociologists* to offer an alternative account to that offered in the *global civil society/public sphere* literature. **Chapter 9** looks at foreign policy-making, *media and war*, and develops a theory of political *embedding/disembedding* of transnational elite networks. This is followed by a focused case study on the lead up to the invasion of *Iraq in 2003*. **Chapter 10** engages with the extensive literature on the *crisis of public communication* and political engagement in democracies. This also pulls together the themes and findings of earlier chapters.

At the same time the book is also concerned to explore the notion of political and media system crisis, perceived or real, in established democracies; the 'crisis' theme has been a concern of practitioners, journalists and scholars in mature democracies for some time. However, at the end of the first decade of the twenty-first century, faith in the political actors and institutions at the centres of democracy is particularly weak. The near collapse of the global financial system and a recession comparable to the 1930s Depression have severely weakened the economic foundations of many democracies. Such a system of politics seems ill-equipped to manage impending crises caused by global warming, as well as food, energy, and other natural resource shortages. The traditional business model that sustained journalism is also failing as citizens turn away from political news, and advertising rapidly migrates elsewhere. Trust in politicians and governments continues to decline, hitting a new low in British politics following the 2009 expenses scandal. The complete failure of Copenhagen, quickly left behind by 24 hour news, typifies all of these trends. The crisis theme now seems as pertinent as ever.

The core case study example used to investigate this topic is that of the UK. The latter parts of each chapter are thus concerned to explore how the varied communicative processes, involved in UK politics, might be contributing, or not, to such crisis tendencies. They do so, in the main, by focusing on those actors and social processes operating at the institutional centre. These sections draw on interviews with over 100 experienced politicians, journalists and civil servants, as well as official reports and studies. Although the case discussions scrutinise the British experience, most of the themes and problems are of concern to many contemporary democracies.

This book will appeal, first and foremost, to higher-level undergraduates, postgraduates and scholars in the fields of media and communication, politics and political communication, journalism, and political sociology. It is designed to be 'core' or 'highly recommended' reading for courses on political communication, and politics and media. The book will also be of interest to political economists, and cultural anthropologists and sociologists interested in elite cultures and power. Lastly it may well appeal to those who work in or close to the fields of politics, journalism, policy-making, advocacy and campaigning.

I owe multiple thanks to many people and institutions. I begin with the organisations which provided financial support for the research reproduced in these chapters. These include a Nuffield small grant (award number SGS/32887), the Leverhulme/Goldsmiths Spaces of the News Project, and Goldsmiths Media and Communications Department. Thanks go to: Blackwell and the editors of the *British Journal of Politics and International Relations*, for the reproduction of much of (2009) 'Evaluating Communication in the Parliamentary Public Sphere', Vol. 11, No. 2, pp. 280–97 (chapter two); Taylor and Francis and the editors of *Journalism Studies*, for the reproduction of much of 'Journalist–Source Relations, Mediated Reflexivity and the Politics of Politics', Vol. 10, No. 2, pp. 204–19 (chapter five); Sage and the editors of *New Media and Society*, for (2009) 'New Media and Fat Democracy: The Paradox of Online Participation', Vol. 11, No. 8, pp. 1–19 (chapter seven).

I would like to thank the many participants who agreed to be interviewed. Those who were especially helpful, insightful and/or generous with their time include: Donald Anderson, David Blunkett, Adam Boulton, Tom Bradby, Colin Brown, Rob Clements, Frank Doran, Neil Gerrard, Gary Gibbon, Paul Goodman, Philippa Helm, Alex Hilton, Michael Jack, Gerald Kaufman, Neil Kinnock, Julie Kirkbride, Martin Linton, Andrew MacKinlay, Robert Maclennan, John Maples, Estelle Morris, David Normington, Peter Oborne, John Pullinger, Peter Riddell, Angus Robertson, Clare Short, John Sills, Paul Staines, David Stevens, Hugh Taylor, John Thurso, Polly Toynbee, Philip Webster, Michael White, Ann Widdecombe and Carole Willis.

For taking on this project and guiding me through it many thanks go to Natalie Foster and all those involved at Routledge. The many friends, colleagues and external advisors, who have read and commented on specific chapters, given me useful advice and/or moral support along the way, include Peter van Aelst, Rod Benson, Olivier Baisnee, Jean Chalaby, Nick Couldry, Rosemary Crompton, Will Dinan, Matthew Eagleton-Pierce, Bob Entman, Bob Franklin, Julie Froud, Peter Golding, David Hesmondhalgh, Bong Hyun-Lee, Anu Kantola, Risto Kunelius, Peter Lee-Wright, David Miller, Mick Moran, Angela Phillips, Michael Pickering, Mike Savage, Gareth Stanton, Daya Thussu, Frank Webster, Karel Williams and Tamara Witschge. I am indebted to Pat Moloney and the Department of Politics and International Relations at Victoria University, Wellington, for giving me a friendly institutional base for completing this manuscript. I am also very grateful to the people of Otaki and Waitohu School who welcomed my family and me during the final months of writing. Many thanks to Emily Seymour for all her assistance at Goldsmiths and her work with me on the Cameron case study in Chapter 3. Above all, I am hugely apprecia- tive of James Curran, Natalie Fenton and Des Freedman, for reading and com- menting on large parts of the book, as well as covering for me, and being such supportive colleagues/friends. Last of all, I must, of course, mention my lovely family: Anne, Hannah, Miriam, Kezia, Kelly, Helen and Neville.

Aeron Davis
December 2009

Chapter 1

In search of the 'good' democracy

Comparing political and media systems

Introduction

What political and media systems are likely to produce a 'good' democracy? This first chapter attempts to navigate a way through this debate via an examination of cross-country comparative work. Such a discussion, of necessity, also highlights the conflicting democratic norms and practical considerations that push interested parties towards very different conclusions. The intention here is to identify, not just the alternative systems on offer, but also the interpretive frameworks which inform any evaluative process. Such a schema then enables one to place the UK's own institutions and systems in relative context.

The chapter is in three parts. The first introduces the literature on comparative politics, media and political communication. It discusses the many varieties of democratic political and communication systems that currently exist as well as identifying the contrasting normative ideals that underpin those systems. The next section briefly outlines the 'crisis' of democracies debate and links it to the preceding discussion. Finally, it locates the component parts of UK democracy in relation to the existing, practised alternatives on offer.

Comparing political and communication systems

Comparing the comparisons: the highs and lows of comparative work

Before setting out a comparative framework it is worth briefly looking at the strengths and weaknesses of this form of research. In Livingstone's words (2003: 478): 'Cross-national comparisons are exciting but difficult, creative but problematic ... attacked as impossible and defended as necessary.' Starting with the 'necessary', first, comparative work both informs one of the alternative systems that exist and sheds new light on one's own system. Most social science research focuses on one national system and, consequently, its theory, interpretive frameworks and conclusions are limited or biased by this. Comparative research, in part, pushes against these limitations, can help develop more abstract universal theory, as well as challenge universalist claims based on national samples.

Second, comparative work also has a practical, normative dimension. It enables one to identify, classify and focus on specific structures, systems and practices that are either 'most similar' or 'most different' (Przeworski and Teune, 1970) in two or more countries. This allows researchers and policy-makers to learn about and hypothesise, in relation to alternatives, and then test and legislate accordingly (see discussions in Livingstone, 2003, Hallin and Mancini, 2004, Hague and Harrop, 2007: ch. 5).

While comparative work has been a feature of political science research for several decades, similar work on political communication and media systems has been sporadic. Two texts, with very different approaches and methods, conveniently book-end the literature. At one end comes Siebert et al.'s *Four Theories of the Press* (1956) which sought to impose a four-fold typology on the world's media systems. Despite several alternative studies and classifications in the intervening years (e.g., Merrill, 1974, Picard, 1985, Curran and Park, 2000a), the field was really re-ignited by Hallin and Mancini's (2004) *Comparing Media Systems*. This developed a tripartite typology ('polarized pluralist', 'democratic corporatist', 'liberal') to describe the systems of 16 advanced democracies. While these works seek to develop clear classificatory models, within which nations are firmly placed, other texts (e.g., Swanson and Mancini, 1996, Gunther and Mughan, 2001a) adopt a different approach. These present collections of detailed, individual national studies, and then attempt to come to more generalised conclusions based on the repetition of specified phenomena. The number of nations selected is usually dictated by the chosen research method. At one end, studies choose large numbers of nations and apply and correlate several series of measures (Lijphart, 1984, 1999, Inglehart, 1997, Norris, 2000, 2004, Dalton, 2004). At the other end, researchers chose to focus on only a few countries and in depth at a particular element of a system, such as journalist practices, news contents or audience consumption (Donsbach and Patterson, 2004, Esser, 2008, Curran et al., 2009). In each of these cases, quantitative data sets are compared and contextualised within comparative discussions and debates. Normative questions are tested. Are 'majoritarian', two-party or 'consensual', multi-party electoral systems more effective and democratic? Does a free-market-based news media or a public-service-based and regulated system better serve citizens in democracies? Is a 'partisan-advocate' or 'professional-objective' journalist culture more desirable for a fourth estate media?

All these studies offer valuable insights. However, they, along with all comparative studies, have to navigate many practical issues and cannot avoid certain pitfalls. First, comparative researchers, however cosmopolitan in intent, still interpret and frame research through their own nation-state eyes. Country-influenced parameters and values are hard to avoid, and typologies may be crudely imposed on alien systems. Second, researchers have a tendency to adopt certain norms and apply ideological biases in their data collection and interpretations. Thus, on both these counts, Siebert et al. (1956) have frequently been accused of having a 'cold war' mentality and pushing a 'modernization' agenda that placed Western democracies above other systems (Nerone, 1995, Curran and Park, 2000b). This charge is still levied at contemporary Western-based studies (Zhao and Hackett, 2005, Hardy, 2008).

Third, methodological problems abound. Using the nation state as the de facto unit of measurement and comparison is flawed, quite simply because there are so many dimensions and variables to take into account. Finding correlations, as many comparative researchers do (Lijphart, 1999, Norris, 2000, 2004, Dalton, 2004), is not that statistically meaningful when only two or three dozen countries are compared, or when there are multiple independent, causal variables. Qualitative work is also limited as only a small number of countries can be practically compared and detailed country-specific knowledge is required. Slight differences in selection, sample, definitions, translations, etc., can have significant consequences for findings (see Inglehart, 1997, methods appendix, Livingstone, 2003). Thus Benson and Hallin's (2007) and Esser's (2008) comparisons of French and US news content offer quite different interpretations of their relative journalistic cultures. Fourth, with the spread of globalisation (see Chapter 8), the notion of an autonomous nation state is itself an increasingly debated concept. Nation-state boundaries are becoming harder to define and there seems an increasing degree of political and media system convergence (Swanson and Mancini, 1996, Hallin and Mancini, 2004). Such elements introduce another layer of complexity and additional set of caveats into comparative work.

Despite these many concerns all the positive arguments for comparative research continue to be valid. Accordingly, this chapter now proceeds to outline the particular elements and classificatory systems applied to political and media systems across a range of studies. To narrow the parameters it focuses on 'established democracies' and, like the studies it draws upon, relies more on data from wealthier, Western systems. Like these studies, normative schema, and discussions of which systems produce 'stronger' forms of democracy, remain a central feature.

Comparing political systems

All large, modern 'liberal democracies' are, in effect, representative democracies or 'deformed polyarchies' (Dahl and Lindblom, 1953). According to Hague and Harrop (2007), eighty-nine of them can be distinguished and separated from the fifty-four 'illiberal democracies' or forty-nine 'authoritarian regimes' that currently exist. Representative, liberal democracies are to be distinguished from other regimes by basic criteria that include (see Dahl's original definition, 1971): free and fair elections, the right to vote, freedom of association and the right to join or lead a political organisation, an independent media providing free expression and alternative information. Beyond that, representative democracy comes in many forms. In theory and practice there is always a compromise between competing ideals as well as practical circumstances. Individual rights sit uncomfortably alongside ideals of equality and community. States must act with authority and efficiency but also with public legitimacy and respect for individuals. A series of checks and balances on state power need to be in operation but these should not overly hinder new legislation and delivery. Across nations (and periods) attempts to balance such ideals and practical requirements have resulted in a plethora of political, economic and public communication systems.

Studies of comparative political systems have noted several key differences. One regards the balance of power between the head of government, the executive, the legislature and judiciary. In some systems, parliaments have rather more influence over the executive-driven legislative process than others. In Sweden, parliamentary committees are able to substantially alter government proposals but such committees have negligible influence in the UK Parliament. Some states have a constitutional court and/or allow for judicial review of new legislation. 'Judicial activism' is a regular feature of the German, Canadian and US systems but non-existent in Sweden and the UK. Moving further away from the three 'estates' of government, concerns are with how much power is devolved to regional or federal-level institutions, and how autonomous is a country's central bank, civil service and other institutions. The US appears to locate substantial power in the office of the President yet, at the same time, much legislative and economic power is also held by Congress, the Supreme Court, the Federal Reserve and individual states.

Another system's reference point regards the electoral system and the issue of fair representation. The most common systems are 'majoritarian', first-past-the-post and proportional representation (PR). Examples of the forty-seven majority voting systems include the UK, US, India and Canada. This system directly links individual politicians to their constituencies or states and, in most cases, is dominated by two major parties with one party taking control of government. However, such systems discourage smaller parties, exclude minority groups and return parties that are disproportionate to the overall vote. In the UK majoritarian system, one party has almost always gained a majority of MPs but never more than 43 per cent of the vote. In the US, all states, whether large or small, still get two representatives in the Senate. Examples of the 70 PR systems include Brazil, Israel, Finland and the Netherlands. Here, voting procedures ensure that the seat distribution in a parliament reflects the wider popular vote and, most often, encourages several parliamentary parties and coalition governments. Finland has had an average of 5.24 'effective' parties, and Israel 4.55 since the Second World War. However, proportional representation often results in weaker constituency-representative links and is also associated with indecisive coalition governments. There are several variations on, or combinations of, the majoritarian and PR systems, notably in Germany, Mexico, France, Japan and South Korea (figs. in Lijphart, 1999: 76, Hague and Harrop, 2007: 187). The question of representation also stretches beyond the procedural to include elements such as gender, class, ethnicity and religion. No system is, or can be, truly representative here but some are more socially reflective than others (see collection in Norris, 1997). For example, 47 per cent of Sweden's and 44.5 per cent of

South Africa's lower chamber representatives are women, as opposed to 19.5 per cent of the UK's, 16.8 per cent of the US's and 11.3 per cent of Japan's (Inter-Parliamentary Union, 2009).

Each of these factors clearly influence normative evaluations in comparative work. Lijphart (1984, 1999), for example, makes a strong case for arguing that 'consensus' systems of government are democratically stronger than 'majoritarian' ones such as the UK 'Westminster Model'. Consensus systems, typified by Switzerland and Belgium, tend to produce multi-party legislatures, coalition governments, use PR electoral systems, have stronger legislatures, and encourage the devolution of state power to other institutions and regions.

However, the formal procedures and institutions are only one means of assessing the strength of democracy in contemporary states. Several scholars choose to evaluate a democracy on the basis of whether it encourages more 'minimal' or 'maximal' (Crouch, 2004) forms of participation. In more 'maximal' democracies, civil society and the levels of public participation are stronger, and politics is more inclusive and deliberative (Pateman, 1970, Fishkin, 1992, Putnam, 2000, Dryzak, 2002). Two obvious indicators of participation are the number of votes citizens can take part in and levels of voter turnout in elections. The post-war turnout in Austria has varied between 80 and 97 per cent, and in Italy, between 81 and 94 per cent. In the UK it has been lower, between 59 and 84 per cent and dropped lower still in Japan, the US and Canada. The US can claim to have one of the highest per capita numbers of elected officials (some half a million) but also one of the lowest voter turnouts of any mature democracy. Similarly, participation can be measured in terms of levels of political party membership and party identification. At the start of this century, 18 per cent of Austrian voters, 10 per cent of Finns and 4 per cent of Italians were members of political parties (Hague and Harrop, 2007: 238). Participation also includes membership of interest groups and other forms of activity, varying from joining union strikes and public demonstrations, to contacting political representatives and signing petitions (see Norris, 2000, Putnam, 2000, Pattie et al., 2004). Of 57 countries surveyed in the World Values Survey (2005–8), 37.5 per cent of French, but only 10.2 per cent of Japanese, said they had attended a lawful demonstration.

Several of these political system factors are listed across twelve selected democracies: Finland (Fi), France (Fr), Germany (G), India (In), Italy (It), Japan (J), Mexico (M), South Africa (Sa), Sweden (Sd), Switzerland (Sz), the United Kingdom (UK) and the United States (US). The selection includes representatives of Hallin and Mancini's (2004) 'polarized pluralist', 'democratic corporatist' and 'liberal' systems, and several examples of Lijphart's 'majoritarian' and 'consensus' style political systems. It also includes four non-Western nations, three of which are classed as 'new' democracies, as well as a range of different-sized nations. Table 1.1 notes the following factors, each of which relate to points in the discussion so far: 1) population size of a country, 2) Freedom House's democracy rating, 3) the electoral system, 4) whether governments are

Table 1.1 Comparing political systems

	Fi	Fr	G	In	It	J	M	Sa	Sd	Sz	UK	US
1 Population size (millions)[1]	5↓	64	82	**1,166**↑	58	127	111	49	9	8	61	307
2 Freedom House rating[3]	1	1	1	2.5	1	1.5	2.5	2	1	1	1	1
3 Majority, PR, other electoral syst[2]	PR	TRS	MMP	MJ	PR	MMM	MMP	PR	PR	PR	MJ	MJ
4 1 Pty (O) or Coalition (C) govts[3,4]	C	Mix	C	C	C	Mix	O	O	O	C	O	O
5 Parl (Pm), Presd (Pr), Mixed (Mx)	Pm	Mx	Pm	Pm	Pm	Pm	Pr	Pr	Pm	Mx	Pm	Pr
6 Fed system (N, Mix, No. of units)	Mix	Mix	16	28	N	N	31	9	N	26	N	51
7 Index of exec dominance of parlm[4]	1.24	**5.52**↓	2.82	2.08	1.14	2.57	n/a	n/a	4.77	**1.0**↑	**5.52**↓	**1.0**↑
8 Strength judicial review index 1–4[4]	1	2.2	4	4	2.8	2	n/a	n/a	2	1	1	4
9 Last election turnout (%)[2]	65	60.4	77.7	57.7	80.5	67.5	58.9	77.3	**82**↑	**48.3**↓	61.4	60.7
10 Attended lawful demo (%)[5]	10.3	**37.5**↑	30.8	19.4	36	**10.2**↓	16.3	12.8	31.4	28.1	16.6	15.1

Notes

1 CIA, July 2009 Estimates.
2 IDEA, 2009. Proportional Representation (PR), Mj (Majoritarian), Mixed Member Proportional (MMP), Two Round System (TRS), Mixed Member Majoritarian (MMM).
3 Freedom House, Freedom of the World Ratings, 2009.
4 Indexes from Lijphart, 1999: 110–11, 132–3, 226. 1 is low executive dominance or low strength of judicial review.
5 World Values Survey, Fifth Wave, 2005–8.

predominantly one-party or coalition, 5) if it is a presidential, parliamentary or other system of government, 6) whether or not there is a federal system of states, cantons, etc., 7) Lijphart's (1999) index of executive dominance of parliament and 8) his assessment of the strength of a country's judicial review process, 9) the nation's last election turnout for a parliamentary election, and 10) the proportion of citizens attending a lawful demonstration. In each measure, when clear, the extremes or best (↑) and worst (↓) scores are marked.

Comparing media systems within a political framework

Comparisons of media systems in democracies share a number of the same normative and interpretive frameworks of political science. Political philosophers from the seventeenth, eighteenth and nineteenth centuries (e.g., Paine, Jefferson, J. S. Mill, Locke) to the twentieth (e.g., Lippmann, Dewey, Dahl, Habermas) have allocated the press and public media a central role in democracy; something acknowledged in many constitutions and human rights declarations. Accordingly, a set of normative 'ideal' media and public communication functions in democracies have emerged (see Keane, 1991, Norris, 2000, Curran, 2002, for discussions). These include providing: a source of pluralist and 'objective' information widely available to all citizens; a check ('watchdog role') on the activities of powerful institutions and individuals; an arena for rational deliberation and debate on the issues and policies affecting society; and the means by which a wide range of citizens and interest groups may put forward their views. However, as with political systems, ideals are in conflict and practical limitations are constraining. It is also hard to position media in a society as it hovers between the state, market and civil society.

This last point takes us to the most commonly debated issue in comparative media systems work – that of whether the funding and/or regulation of public communication should be predominantly state- or market-led (Hardy, 2008). For Siebert et al. (1956) democratic media were to be classified as either 'social responsibility' (state) or 'libertarian' (market). For Curran and Park (2000b) nations exist along a scale between 'regulated' (state) and 'neo-liberal' (market) models. As market advocates argue, the institutions and actors of the state cannot be held to account if they have too much influence over media. For others, active state regulation and/or financial support appear necessary conditions for a professional, autonomous media to develop (Gunther and Mughan, 2001b, Norris, 2004). For critical scholars, market-dominated media do not fulfil their ideal democratic functions (McChesney, 1999, Freedman, 2008).

Regulation of media in the US, throughout the twentieth century, has been market-led, equating free speech and individual liberties with minimal state interference (see McChesney, 1999). The US has never had an established public service broadcasting (PSB) presence and PSB channels capture less than 2 per cent of the audience. In contrast, European countries have had a traditionally strong PSB presence. In 2006, in the UK, PSB channels gained 51 per cent of audience share. They retained over 40 per cent of the audience in many other nations including Germany, Denmark, Spain and Italy (figs. in Hardy, 2006: 234–35). In some cases (e.g., Sweden, Norway, Austria, France), countries have also offered a variety of subsidies to their press (Murshetz, 1998).

The degree to which states intervene to regulate media (in terms of ownership limits, content and advertising restrictions, licence allocation, censorship and libel laws, and rules on political campaigning) is also significant. The deregulated US market has enabled just a few conglomerates to dominate across all media and communication sectors (Bagdikian, 2004). When it comes to campaign regulation, the US is one of the few democracies not to give free broadcast time to political parties and the only limits on political advertising are those imposed by available budgets. In the UK and other European countries, there are clear (if slipping) limits set on ownership. Approximately half of the established Western democracies, including the UK, France, Switzerland and Denmark, have banned political advertising from broadcasting. Most other nations clearly regulate it (see Hardy, 2008, Norris, 2000: 153). Some countries, such as Switzerland or Portugal, also ban publication of opinion polls during election periods.

Two further features of media systems, particularly highlighted in the comparative work of Hallin and Mancini (2004), are national variations in journalist cultures and modes of news consumption. In several 'Mediterranean' nations, including France, Spain, Greece and Italy, there was a high degree of political partisanship and 'press-party parallelism' (see also Mancini, 1991, Chalaby, 1996). Journalism was more elite-oriented, closely tied to parties and governments, often written by political actors and intellectuals, and full of opinion and polemical rhetoric. Among countries across the 'North Atlantic', including Canada, the US and UK, wider press circulation and a strong 'professional' model of reporting developed relatively early. Content aimed to be 'neutral', 'objective', 'balanced' and fact-based (debatable in terms of the UK press). Several studies have identified further differences in the practices, professional ideals, presentational styles, 'hard'-'soft' news balances, and types of news source used (e.g., Donsbach and Patterson, 2004, Benson and Hallin, 2007, Esser, 2008, Curran et al., 2009).

News consumption habits also vary considerably across nations. Literacy rates, per capita wealth, and political history, have each influenced whether, and to what degree, a news medium is taken up by a country. As Hallin and Mancini (2004: 23, 64) observe, countries that had relatively low levels of newspaper circulation in 2000, such as Spain (13 per cent), Greece (eight per cent) and Italy (12 per cent), also had low literacy rates a century before. The reverse is true in many Northern European countries with high circulations such as Norway (72 per cent) and Sweden (55 per cent). Television and internet use is high in all economically-advanced democracies. However, in many poorer democracies, such as Brazil, Mexico or South Africa, a large proportion of news consumption is via radio (see comparative table in Norris, 2004: 133–44). Radio is more likely to be a choice where poverty and low literacy levels are common. At this point it should be noted that media access is not the same as news consumption, a common faulty assumption of many statistically-based comparisons. According to Norris (2004), US citizens have the highest levels of media access in the world. The US scores clearly above Denmark, Finland and the UK. Yet, in Curran et al.'s (2009) study of these four countries, actual levels of news consumption and 'hard news' knowledge are shown to be significantly lower in the US.

Several of these measures are indicated in Table 1.2. They include: 1) Freedom House's freedom of the press score, 2) Curran and Park's classification of a nation's media, 3) whether political advertising on television is banned or not, 4) the percentage of political news stories featuring women, 5) the UNDP's educational development rankings, 6) levels of newspaper readership (not sales), 7) television sets per 1,000 of the population, 8) percentage of internet users, and 9) levels of public confidence in the press.

Democratic norms, values and 'quality'

We now have a number of means of classifying and evaluating political and media systems according to certain normative values. Political and media systems may be better or worse in terms of promoting individual freedoms, systems of representation, sets of checks and balances, or encouraging participation and deliberation. However, several of the above authors also judge the health or 'quality' of democracies based on other national indicators.

One such common set of measures is linked to the economic wealth of a nation. This is noted in such things as per capita GDP, ease of 'doing business', and rates of growth, inflation and unemployment. By such measures most established democracies score fairly highly (give or take the odd global recession). In 2009, Singapore and New Zealand topped the World Bank 'Ease of Doing Business' rankings. Sweden was 18th and France 31st. Connected to wealth, but more person-centred, is the UNDP's (UN Development Programme) Human Development Index (HDI), combining life expectancy, education levels and living standards. Norway, Australia and Iceland top the 2009 rankings. Other measures highlight the issues of equality and welfare state provision. Recorded data here include levels of public health expenditure, measures of financial inequality and relative poverty, and female representation at the senior levels of politics and business. So, for example, South Africa has the highest measures of financial inequality but one of the highest levels of female representation in its parliament (CIA, 2009, IPU, 2009).

Increasingly, per capita levels of CO_2 emissions, energy use and environmental waste are seen as significant measures. Here the US is clearly the worst polluting nation with 19 metric tons per capita. This is compared with Germany's 9.7 or India's 1.3 tons per capita. Finally, another set of measures record public values. What levels of trust do populations have in governments

Table 1.2 Comparing media systems

	Fi	Fr	G	In	It	J	M	Sa	Sd	Sz	UK	US
1 Freedom of the Press Score, 2008[1]	9↑	22	16	35	29	21	51↓	28	11	13	18	17
2 Curran/Park classification 2000,[2]	DR*	DR	DR*	AN*	DR	DN	AN	DR	DR	DR*	DN	DN
3 Political TV ads banned?[3]	Y	Y	N	n/a	N	N	N	n/a	N	Y	Y	N
4 % of political news with women[4]	15	n/a	16	15	7↓	24	n/a	16	28↑	15	15	21
5 Education Development Rank, 2008[5]	1↑	12	31	142↓	22	33	81	98	15	39	28	19
6 Newspaper readership % 2004[6]	43.1	16.3	26.7	7.1	13.7	55.1↑	n/a	3↓	48.1	42	29	19
7 TV sets per 1000, 2003[7]	679	632	675	83↓	490	842	277	195	966	582	1105↑	876
8 Internet users % 2009[8]	82.9↑	67.7	67.1	7↓	50.1	74	24.6	9.4	80.5	75.8	79.8	74.1
9 Confidence in the press [9]	−33.6	−22.9	−41.3	41.6	−49.8	49.2↑	0.2	21.8	−33.8	−29.4	−72.5↓	−52.2

Notes

1 Freedom House, Freedom of the Press Index, 2008 (lowest is most free).
2 Curran and Park, 2000b. Democratic Regulated (DR), Authoritarian Neo-Liberal (AN), Democratic Neo-Liberal (DN). * = Author's Interpretation.
3 Norris, 2000: 153.
4 GMMP, 2005. The percentage of politics/government news stories featuring women.
5 UNDP Human Development Index, 2008, rank out of 176 countries.
6 UNESCO, 2004.
7 EarthTrends, World Resources Institute.
8 Internet World Stats, 2009.
9 World Values Survey, fifth wave, 2005–8.

and other institutions? How happy do they count themselves? According to the World Values Survey (2005–8), South Africans have a net positive level of trust in government of 41.5 per cent, and the Swiss a score of 34.4 per cent, but Germans give a net negative score of −53.1 per cent. 58.5 per cent of Mexicans and 50.8 per cent of Britons say they are 'very happy', compared to just 12.9 per cent of South Koreans or 19.9 per cent of Germans.

Several such indicative measures of the health of democracies are included here in Table 1.3. These are: 1) per capita GDP income rankings, 2) the World Bank's 'Ease of Doing Business' grading, 3) the Human Development Index rankings (combining GDP, education levels and life expectancy), 4) the Gini Coefficient measure of national inequality, 5) the percentage of women representatives in the lower legislative chamber, the World Values Survey responses relating to 6) confidence in government, 7) confidence in the judiciary, 8) per capita CO_2 emissions, 9) levels of 'happiness', and finally, 10) each country is scored from one to 12 on these nine indicators, the scores totted up, and an overall ranking is then given from 1 (best) to 12 (worst).

In search of the ideal democracy

Where does the discussion lead us in terms of the search for the 'ideal democracy'? Which political and media systems are most conducive to its development? Looking back at Table 1.1, on political systems, Switzerland, Finland and Italy appear to have the most consensual-representative systems. They use the PR electoral system and are the most likely to have coalition governments. However, in terms of checks and balances, it is the US system which appears strongest. Executive dominance of the legislature is low and the strength of judicial review is high. It also has a strong federal system. When it comes to citizenship participation it is Italy and Sweden that score best in terms of having higher recent electoral turnout and proportion of citizens having demonstrated. Across each of these measures the UK scores rather poorly amongst the established democracies. Italy scores rather well.

Looking at Table 1.2, on media systems, Finland clearly comes out in front. They actually top the world rankings of 'freedom' (Freedom House) and education (UNDP), as well as topping this table in internet usage and scoring high on newspaper readership. Sweden follows closely. Both of these are classed as 'democratic regulated' (Curran and Park, 2000a) or 'democratic corporatist' (Hallin and Mancini, 2004). Italy, amongst the older democracies, scores fairly poorly on this table. Unsurprisingly, as wealth is a significant factor here, so do India, Mexico and South Africa. Looking at Table 1.3, Sweden comes out clearly in front overall, followed by Switzerland, Finland and the UK (each clearly separated from its closest rivals). The next six, of the US, South Africa, France, Japan, Mexico and Germany, are all bunched fairly closely in aggregate scores. Italy and India are equal last. Across the three tables it is Sweden, Finland and Switzerland which perform well most consistently.

Table 1.3 Evaluations of democracy

	Fi	Fr	G	In	It	J	M	Sa	Sd	Sz	UK	US
1 Per capita GDP (PPP) ranking[1]	20	23	21	130↓	27	24	55	79	15	7	19	6↑
2 Ease of Business grading[2]	16	31	25	133↓	78	15	51	34	18	21	5	4↑
3 Human Dvlpm Index ranking[3]	12	8	22	134↓	18	10	53	129	7↑	9	20	13
4 Inequality Index No. (Gini)[4]	29.5	32.7	27	37	32	38.1	47.9	65↓	23↑	33.7	34	45
5 % of women in Lower Hse Parlm[5]	41.5	18.2	32.8	10.7↓	21.3	11.3	28.2	44.5	47↑	28.5	19.5	16.8
6 Confidence in government[6]	28.3	-41.6	-53.1↓	9.8	-47.2	-37.9	-20.5	41.5↑	-22	34.4	-32.5	-23.6
7 Confidence in justice syst6	64.6↑	-19.7	15	37.8	3.2	64	-24.6↓	32.9	48.6	43.8	19.4	14.7
8 Per capita CO_2 emissions (tons)[3]	12.7	6.2	9.7	1.3↑	8.1	10.1	4.1	8.6	5.6	5.6	9.3	19.0↓
9 % 'very happy'[6]	29.6	36.4	19.9↓	29	18.5	29.2	58.5↑	42.9	43.1	42.2	50.8	34.4
10 Overall aggregate rank (1–12)	3	=5	10	=11	=11	8	9	=5	1	2	4	=5

Notes

1 International Monetary Fund, 2008 (Index of 181 countries).
2 World Bank Group, 2009 (Index of 183 countries).
3 United Nations Development Programme, Indexes, 2006 CO_2 Emissions, 2009 HDI (Index of 182 countries).
4 CIA, 2009, data from 2005–08.
5 IPU, Inter-Parliamentary Union, 2009.
6 World Values Survey, fifth wave, 2005–08.

However, like all comparisons, several measures are fairly arbitrary, in terms of their selection and weighting. Many results may vary considerably across periods, specific survey forms and analytical approaches. Other factors, such as country size, age of democracy, and overall wealth, mean countries are unfairly being compared. Thus, it may be concluded that Sweden, Switzerland and Finland each use PR systems, are 'consensual', and have 'democratic regulated' media traditions. However, they are also the smallest countries studied, are fairly wealthy, and are long-established and stable nations.

The crisis of politics and communications in established democracies?

This next section briefly introduces the 'crisis' of established democracies literature (see Chapter 10). If comparative work seeks to identify the ideals and systems which are most appropriate for democracies, the crisis literature addresses these same concerns but from another direction.

The 'crisis' debate, although far from being new, has produced a substantial body of work in the last two decades. Most agree that some form of crisis, be it one of public perception or something more substantive, has beset many established democracies. The figures and trends have been noted, to a greater or lesser degree, in all the system-types described (see Norris, 2000, Pharr and Putnam, 2000, Putnam, 2002, Dalton, 2004, Hay, 2007). The most overt sign of this is in the long-term decline in voter turnout since the 1960s. Dalton and Wattenberg (2002: 263) calculated that the median change in voter turnout, from the 1950s to the 1990s, was 10 per cent across the nineteen OECD democracies for which time-series data existed. New turnout lows were reached in Japan in 1995 (44.9 per cent), in the US in 1996 (49 per cent), and in Canada in 2000 (54.6 per cent). Measures of crisis go further than voter turnout. Dalton and Wattenberg (2002: 264) found that, on average, only 38 per cent of the publics of these nineteen countries had confidence in their national government. 32 per cent had confidence in their press and just 22 per cent in their political parties. Putnam (2002: 406) noted that membership of political parties had dropped from 14 per cent, in the 1970s, to less than 6 per cent in the 1990s.

This turning away from core political institutions challenges the legitimacy of democracy itself and is potentially very damaging. However, from the vantage point of 2009, the crisis of democracies seems more than just one of public disavowal. First, the global economy is in its worst recession since the 1930s depression era. The problems of the financial collapse will take many years to work their way through as large global trade and economic imbalances, huge debt levels, and financial black holes remain. The neo-liberal market model that has propelled democracies for several decades is unstable. Second, democracies have not found answers to a number of other major crises that are fast approaching. These include: global warming, energy dependence on fast-depleting fossil fuels, drastic forthcoming global water and food shortages, rising inequality, and an ageing and increasingly unhealthy population. At the end of the first decade of the twenty-first century, democracies are in crisis, both perceived and substantive.

The causes of crisis literature can be divided between those works which focus on the core political institutions and actors of society, and those which look elsewhere; or 'supply-side' and 'demand-side' explanations (see Hay, 2007). Amongst this latter camp, the spotlight is turned most frequently on the public itself. A tradition, traced from Almond and Verba (1963) onwards, looks at 'political culture', civic society and citizenship. Key, amongst contemporary studies, is the work of Putnam (1993, 2000). Putnam argues that, for a range of reasons, citizens are less inclined to join and participate in local associations, be they political, civil or merely social. This loss of social capital, in turn, reduces 'trust' in others and in political and other institutions. Another prominent line of work here is more overtly critical of citizens themselves. Inglehart's thesis (1990, 1997) argues that mature democracies have produced wealthy, more educated and demanding publics. They have developed postmaterial values, including a loss of deference towards authority, and have unreasonable expectations of the state. In fact, for Inglehart, and others such as Norris (1999b, 2002) there is no crisis to speak of. The public is indeed better off in terms of its wealth, education, and living conditions. Crises are cyclical not long-term, and attached to particular institutional and party performances rather than democracy per se.

Other works also look to a variety of causal explanations beyond institutional politics. One of these turns optimistically towards the growth in interest groups and social movements in the last decades of the twentieth century. Both inside (Inglehart, Norris) and outside the crisis literature (e.g., Castells, 1997, Della Porta and Diani, 1999, Albrow et al., 2008) interest groups are viewed as a positive alternative to party politics. Politics and participation are simply being reconfigured for the twenty-first century. Globalisation is another means by which politics is being reconfigured, although here assessments are usually more pessimistic. The power of nations to exert influence over larger political and economic issues appears to be waning. Global economic forces have come to control or influence capital flows that are far in excess of those managed by nations (Reich, 1991, Strange, 1996, Crouch, 2004, Cerny et al., 2005). An increasing amount of state politics is also bound up with inter-governmental and transgovernmental systems (Slaughter, 2000, Held, 2002). Accordingly, it thus becomes clear to many that voting in national elections may have little impact on the major problems of the day.

An alternative set of literatures has focused more directly on those institutions and actors operating at the centres of national political power (supply-side explanations). Most obvious amongst these is the literature comparing political systems (see above). The indication is that some types of system may be more prone to crisis than others. Another system-based thesis looks at the strategies of government and the larger role of the state in society generally. There is a convincing argument to be located across the work of Rhodes (1997), Burnham (2001) and Hay (2007) which highlights the problem of political 'depoliticisation'. This states that, since the 1970s, public discourse (political, academic, institutional) has encouraged politicians to cede power to non-democratic organisations and actors. Governments accordingly have created more independent institutions and quangos, tied themselves to sets of operational rules and international legislation, and supported the establishment of transnational institutions. Consequently, the levers of power and resources of government are increasingly put in the hands of institutions and experts who operate with little transparency, public accountability, or engagement with ordinary citizens.

Crisis literature has also focused more directly on the part played by modern political parties and politicians. Over several decades, parties have had to adapt, to significant population shifts and the rise of the mass media (Swanson and Mancini, 1996, Blumler and Kavanagh, 1999, Dalton and Wattenberg, 2002, Gunther et al., 2002). Both trends have eroded the traditional links between parties, and their members and core voters. In response, parties have become 'electoral-professional' in nature, in ways that help them to win elections but further alienate their publics. Major parties have converged ideologically on the centre ground and have become more reliant on external experts from business and media (Entman, 1989, Heath et al., 2001, Meyer, 2002, Crouch, 2004). Professional campaign strategies are focused on a few marginal seats and swing voters and, instead of communicating policies, promote negative attacks, spin, and personality-centred politics (Hall Jamieson, 1996, Herman and Chomsky, 2002, Franklin, 2004, Dinan and Miller, 2007). All of this leaves voters and members feeling ignored, excluded, and ignorant of the policy debates as well as the differences between parties.

The last target of crisis literature is the news media and journalists. Much of the well-known crisis literature either hardly mentions or dismisses the media altogether as a contributory factor (Inglehart, 1997, Norris, 2000, Dalton, 2004). This denial finds ample support amongst many media scholars who argue that media effects on audiences are minimal (Lazarsfeld et al., 1944, Blumler and Katz, 1974, Morley, 1980, Gauntlett, 1998, Norris et al., 1999). However, there is also a sizeable literature which does pinpoint the media as a major source of crisis. Many record that political coverage, whether driven by campaign strategy or media logic, has become full of 'soundbites', 'horse-race' stories, negative and confrontational reporting, political personalities and scandal (Hallin, 1994, Hall-Jamieson, 1996, Delli Carpini and Williams, 2001, Franklin, 2004). Since the large majority of people learn about politics through the mass media, political understanding and behaviour is likely to be filtered and distorted accordingly. Indeed, there are a number of more sophisticated studies which demonstrate a range of minor effects, such as agenda-setting, framing, demobilisation, and partisan reinforcement (Gerbner et al., 1984, Iyengar and Kinder, 1987, Jhally and Lewis, 1992, Capella and Hall-Jamieson, 1997). In aggregate, these can have a significant influence on how people understand and respond to politics.

Conclusion: locating the UK case

This chapter concludes by summarising where the UK, the central case study of this book, is specifically situated. Lijphart (1999) identifies the UK political system as the most 'majoritarian' of the democracies he looked at. As a democracy it does score rather poorly on the measures used in Table 1.1. Executive dominance of the Parliament and local government is high and judicial review is non-existent. Despite many recent constitutional reviews and changes, such as Scottish and Welsh devolution, the UK system has not departed radically from Lijphart's description. In terms of 'crisis' indicators, voting and political trust levels are lower than most comparable established democracies. In the UK new post-war lows were reached in 2001 and 2005 as turnout dropped from 76 per cent average to around 60 per cent. By 2002 only 1.5 per cent of the UK public were members of parties and only 16 per cent stated they felt strongly affiliated to a party (Heffernan, 2003). Hansard's (2009: 3–4) more recent audit of political engagement found that only 53 per cent of the public said they would definitely vote in the next election. In the last '2–3 years' nine per cent said they had contacted a politician, and three per cent had donated to/joined a political party. In September 2009, following the MPs' expenses scandal and economic slump, only 13 per cent of the public said they 'trusted' politicians to tell the truth (Ipsos-MORI, 2009).

In its press freedom and educational levels the UK scores slightly below average amongst wealthy, established democracies. Levels of newspaper readership and internet usage are better than average here and TV ownership is very high. In terms of media regulation it shares a mixture of public service/regulatory and free-market/neo-liberal elements. Its national broadcaster, the BBC, often draws international praise. However, levels of trust in its journalists generally are extremely low comparatively. In the last World Values Survey (2005–8) only 13.8 per cent of the public trusted the press; the second lowest rating of the 57 countries surveyed.

Lastly, it has a relatively high per capita GDP and is more market-oriented and business-friendly than most. It has more average or below average scores when it comes to measures of equality, environmental waste and confidence in its governing institutions. It is a richer but less equal democracy that, despite high levels of cynicism about its government and press, has many 'very happy' people. The effects of a prolonged recession and new government may well produce rather different opinion survey data in 2010.

The chapters that follow, although self-contained discussions, can each also be related back to the crisis themes outlined here. Because they focus on political institutions and actors they naturally say more about the 'supply-side' than the 'demand-side' causes of crisis. Chapter 2 is concerned with political systems of representation and the transfer of 'public- and will-formation' into legislation. Chapter 3 investigates the transformation of parties and how that has affected politician-member/citizen exchanges, concluding with a detailed case study of the rise of David Cameron. Chapter 4 looks at how the working conditions of politicians and journalists affect their relations with others and the production of national news and legislation. Chapter 5 investigates how the personal exchanges, between political journalists and MPs, affect micro-level politics within parties and parliaments. Chapter 6 explores the symbolic forms of communication between politicians and publics and suggests that an increasingly media-oriented politics is having a destabilising effect. Chapter 7 looks at how new media have influenced political exchanges, media outputs and public engagement. Chapter 8 discusses how globalisation affects nation-state politics, communication and participation. Chapter 9 delves into the communication around war and focuses specifically on the invasion of Iraq in 2003. Chapter 10 concludes the book with a more detailed discussion of the crisis literature and, along the way, incorporates the wider findings and themes of the book.

Chapter 2

Citizens, political representation and parliamentary public spheres

Introduction

This chapter looks closely at the issue of communication between citizens and states. In so doing, it navigates a path between supporters of 'liberal', limited, rational choice models of representative democracy and advocates of greater 'republican', participatory democracy. Having introduced the participants and parameters of this debate, the chapter then focuses squarely on the output of Jürgen Habermas. Habermas, through an evolving body of works, has come to plot his own alternative path between these two traditions.

After introducing Habermas's original 'public sphere' conception (1989 [1962]), and its influence in the field, the chapter then explains Habermas's more recent analytical approach. This sets out a quite different description and set of evaluative norms with which to observe political communication in contemporary democracies. In this he describes a 'centre–periphery' model, in which multiple public sphere forums formulate and relay opinions from 'weak' publics to the parliamentary centre. It is at this centre that such inputs are absorbed and deliberated upon, by 'strong' publics and according to public sphere norms, to then be transformed into publicly-legitimated law. A parliament operating in a mature democracy, in effect, is now to be treated as the most significant public sphere component of a linked network of public forums. Such a model places greater emphasis on communication within interest groups and associations in civil society, within the institutions of parliamentary bodies, and the communicative links between them. This, in turn, has strong implications for the way media and communication, operating in democracies, are documented and assessed.

The chapter then applies this framework to an investigation of the British parliamentary public sphere operating at Westminster. The study is presented in two parts. In the first, it concludes that the UK Parliament at Westminster, in several respects, operates rather better according to public sphere norms than the public sphere described in Habermas's earlier (1989) accounts of eighteenth- and nineteenth-century England. However, clearly such a conclusion does not match with general public perceptions of institutional politics. The second part therefore engages with the reasons for this disparity and offers two explanations for it. The first regards the impeded transfer of that public 'opinion- and will-formation' from parliament to government. The second relates to the faulty means of 'critical publicity' by which the process of governance is relayed back to ordinary citizens via the mediated public sphere. As such, even if the UK Parliament is legitimately linked to, and adequately deliberates on, public 'opinion- and will-formation', it fails to transmit that, either upwards to government, or downwards to its citizenry.

Citizens, politicians and public communication spheres

Between direct, participatory and limited representative democratic conceptions

The question addressed here is how should a democratic public communication system best function in order to link publics to their political representatives and governments? In large part, the answer depends on a preceding question: what part can or should publics play in today's large, complex, representative democracies? As Stromback (2005) notes, different ideal models of democracy present varied normative implications for the evaluation of media. All agree that public communication systems, be they mass media-based or other, serve vital functions in democracies. However, beyond certain minimum requirements, necessary for the linking of politicians and citizens, baseline norms for assessing media and communication vary considerably.

Democracy and public communication have become inseparable. With the parallel developments of democratic state-building and mass printing, so several political philosophers in earlier centuries (e.g., Paine, Jefferson, J. S. Mill, Bentham, see Keane's overview, 1991) awarded print media a key role in democracies. Clearly, the ways the state establishes legitimate authority without recourse to violence, how political leaders are best selected, act according to the public will, and are regularly held accountable for their actions, involve public communication. Accordingly, such public communication functions came to be enshrined in many national constitutions and charters of human rights. With the expansion of the state, electorate and mass media, in the twentieth century, however, the role of public opinion and media in democratic polities became more complex.

Arguably, the debates that have consequently emerged can be framed in terms of disagreements about how modern democracy best functions vis-à-vis issues of representation and participation. For many (e.g., Dahl, 1961, 1989, Kateb, 1992), representative forms of democracy, in spite of their many flaws, are the only practical options for large, complex societies. Decision-making may be in the hands of the few but, ultimately, benefits can be far greater for the many. For others, ideal democracy requires more inclusive participation on every social and political level and, accordingly, good democratic processes should encourage that (MacPherson, 1965, Fishkin, 1992, Dryzak, 2002). Such opposing positions ultimately feed into views on the value of public opinion and the expectations of public communication systems. The public disagreement between Lippmann (1925) and Dewey (1927) typifies this division. Lippmann, despite his more positive aspirations for democracy, had a sceptical view of journalism and public opinion. Journalism was driven by expert and political elite opinions, and general publics were too disinterested and/or unqualified to challenge this state of affairs. Dewey, while conceding to many of Lippmann's points, argued forcefully for greater individual-level participation in everyday politics of all kinds. Journalism was capable of, and should be reconfigured towards, the promotion of citizen participation rather than passive consumption.

These positions are still clearly detectable today. There are several who argue that contemporary media do well enough in their contributions to modern, representative democracies (Norris, 2000, 2004, McNair, 2006, Schudson, 2006). Despite their acknowledged flaws they still succeed in being critical of governments, pluralistic, and able to serve varied audiences and information needs. It is simply impractical to measure them against a direct democracy model that cannot exist. Critics cast doubt on these claims (McChesney, 1999, Herman and Chomsky, 2002, Curran and Seaton, 2003, Bagdikian, 2004, Entman, 2004), while also pushing for improvements closely related to direct democratic ideals. More public media and information, quality of information content, access and participation, each need to be fostered. Habermas's work is centrally situated in terms of these debates.

For many scholars of public communication systems, Habermas's most substantive contribution is his *The Structural Transformation of the Public Sphere* (*STPS*, 1989 [1962]). In this, his identification of the emerging 'public sphere', and its significance for the evolution and sustenance of democracy, offers much conceptually, historically and normatively. The book is essentially in two parts. The first documents the historical evolution of bourgeois public spheres of communication, operating between states and private individuals; first in Britain, and later in France, Germany and elsewhere. The earlier emergence of such spheres, established through the circulation of printed works (newspapers, pamphlets, journals) and recognised discussion forums (coffee houses, clubs), worked to establish a wider sense of public opinion on issues of the day. The ideals on which these spheres operated were instrumental in challenging the legitimacy of the older ruling orders and the authoritarian practices of the state. These ideals reduced the significance of social status, opened up subject agendas, attempted 'rational deliberation' with a view to locating what was in the best interests of the wider 'public good', and encouraged discussions to be subject to 'critical publicity'. In effect, political and communicative power were shifted away from the monarchy, nobility and church, and towards the emerging bourgeoisie and, later, provided impetus for the development of citizen-based forms of democracy. The second part of the book, inspired by Habermas's Frankfurt School influences, describes the decline, or 'refeudalisation', of these public spheres in the nineteenth and twentieth centuries. The spread of the modern welfare state encroached upon, and squeezed out, the autonomous public sphere. Mass, commercialised media made it a more corrupt and anarchistic space in which rational debate was replaced by self-interested rhetoric and passive consumerism.

Many of Habermas's key conceptions, if not his terminology, had already been absorbed into critical studies of media, politics and political communication before the English translation of *STPS* (1989) was produced. The book itself was thus readily absorbed into, as well as directing, many mass media-oriented discussions of public opinion, state power and legitimacy. Several challenged the historical accuracy and idealised account of the earlier public spheres (see collection in Calhoun, 1992, or summary in Goode, 2005). However, they also declared that, in spite of its flaws, *STPS* offered a clear and robust set of conceptual terms and normative ideals with which to measure the health of modern public communication systems. Indeed, in the 1990s, after the fall of communist states, and amidst the prevailing postmodern academic agenda, Habermas's work acted as a conceptual beacon for those with a continuing interest in questions of media and democracy.

Much of the work that has followed has taken two divergent pathways, choosing to engage with either the first or second part of the book. The first has taken a starting point that looks back at those idealised elements of the earlier bourgeois public sphere, particularly its inclusive democratic values. Thus, several have attempted to assess the direct, participatory and deliberative potential of public communication spaces at the local, transnational and digital levels (Coleman and Gotze, 2001, Dahlberg, 2001, Sparks, 2001, Coleman, 2005, Polat, 2005, Wikland, 2005). The second pathway has focused on the mass media; the assumption being that this is what constitutes the most significant component of the public sphere in large, modern democracies. For many, earlier public sphere ideals are used to assess and/or prescribe changes to current mass media systems (Dahlgren and Sparks, 1992, Hallin, 1994, McNair, 2000, Curran, 2002). Other work here has chosen to take issue with Habermas's overly-pessimistic account of twentieth-century mass media and culture. They have also questioned his over-emphasis on inclusive, rational and participatory public dialogue in an era of large-scale, representative democracy. For these scholars (Thompson, 1995, Hallin, 1994, Dahlgren, 1995, Kellner, 2000, Crossley and Roberts, 2004, Goode, 2005, Schudson, 2006, Butsch, 2007) mass media may still make positive as well as negative contributions to the contemporary public sphere.

However, at base, many such engagements with *STPS* suffer a fundamental flaw; one that is often alluded to in several of the more sophisticated accounts mentioned. This involves applying a set of political and communication ideals, derived from eighteenth- and nineteenth-century political circumstances and philosophies, to twentieth- and twenty-first-century polities. Parliaments, electoral systems, institutions, and a thriving civil society have all evolved to reshape democracies and, consequently, public spheres and their relationships to the state (Calhoun, 1988, Fraser, 1997, Curran, 2002, Garnham, 2007). In effect, the use of ideals, identified in *STPS*, to evaluate contemporary communication environments relies on a set of now questionable assumptions.

The first of these is that direct, participatory democracy is the evolutionary end point to aspire to in democracies. However, direct democracy has never existed outside of small, usually exclusive and exclusionary, collectives; a description which applies to both the ancient Athenian polis and eighteenth-century bourgeois public sphere. Thus, representative forms of democracy appear, as yet, to be the only practical models to use in large, complex societies. Indeed, it is because representative forms of democracy are the only viable models to use in large, complex societies, that many noted political sociologists have turned their attention to the central part played by mass media (Calhoun, 1988, Thompson, 1995, Fraser, 1997). Second, there is a tendency to treat the state as a single monolithic force, and to merge the three estates (executive, legislature and judiciary) into one. In contemporary polities the three estates are expected to divide and balance state power (even if many would argue that evenly balanced systems are rare (see Chapter 1) or the three estates share too many similar interests). Third, there is a continuing assumption that there exists a general, unitary public sphere that occupies a space between private citizens and the state. Of course, civil society has since evolved a plethora of organisations, associations, institutions and communication forums. These (counter) public spheres frequently have contrasting memberships and 'public good' requirements. They may remain distanced from *the* 'public sphere', instead choosing to remain at the local level and/or directly engage with state institutions (Ely, 1992, Fraser, 1997). By the time the English language version of *STPS* was published Habermas was already aware of these deficiencies :

> The presumption that society as a whole can be conceived as an association writ large, directing itself via the media of law and political power, has become entirely implausible in view of the high level of complexity of functionally differentiated societies. The holistic notion of a societal totality in which the associated individuals participate like members of an encompassing organization is particularly ill-suited ...
>
> (Habermas, 1992: 443)

At the same time he was not satisfied with the directions public sphere and related democratic theory were going. For him, accounts initiated media and communication-oriented discussions on the basis of two contrasting but problematic views of democratic systems. In the first, representative and mass-mediated forms of democracy are seriously flawed. Solutions require much higher levels of formal political participation and deliberative engagement which, to date, have proved impractical. In the second, representative and mass-mediated forms of democracy are an accepted, if flawed, reality. However, this approach, despite its critical stance, is based on and gives credence to a rather limited model of democracy, public debate and participation. In this, citizens weakly relate to a unitary, mediated public sphere (or linked spheres), are vaguely (mis)informed and participate minimally in politics on the national scale. For Habermas (1996) these accounts, however critical, fall into either an idealist, 'republican' advocacy of direct, participatory democracy, or, a limited, 'liberal', rational choice model of representative democracy. Both fail to engage with the shape and direction of politics in 'actually existing democracies'.

Actually existing democracies and parliamentary public spheres

By the 1990s, Habermas had spent several decades exploring the central questions and ideals associated with *STPS* but in relation to contemporary democracies generally and post-war German politics specifically. In 1992, while in dialogue with his *STPS* critics, he was already formulating an alternative model for evaluating the communicative links between citizens and polities in democracies. In this the normative basis of his enquiry was broadly similar:

> The question remains of how, under the conditions of mass democracies constituted as social-welfare states, a discursive formation of opinion and will can be institutionalized in such a fashion that it becomes possible to bridge the gap between enlightened self-interest and orientation to the common good.
>
> (Habermas, 1992: 448–49)

Thus, although his political concerns and normative ideals had changed little, his account of 'actually existing democracies' in practice and the means to evaluate them had. In *Between Facts and Norms* (*BFN*, 1996), he then proceeded to outline a description of how contemporary democracies operated and how, ideally, they should operate. Several authors (Von Schomberg and Baynes, 2002, Goode, 2005, Garnham, 2007) indeed trace his lines of thought on these issues from *STPS*, via *The Theory of Communicative Action* (1987) to *BFN* (1996).

In *BFN* what is described is a 'two-track' system that channels the multiple spheres of civil society through to legislative bodies which then deliberate and produce law. Acknowledging his conceptual debts to Bernard Peters and Nancy Fraser, a core–periphery model with 'strong' and 'weak' publics is described. Civil society is made up of 'weak' publics which identify issues, agendas and solutions through local, deliberative and non-deliberative forums, both formally and informally. Parliamentary bodies, made up of political representatives, then formally deliberate on these issues and their solutions according to established procedures and rules. The law-making and its enforcement, which follows, is thus legitimated, being tied to 'public opinion- and will-formation'. In this two-stage 'procedural concept of democracy' (Habermas, 1996: 308), 'Deliberative politics thus lives off the interplay between democratically institutionalized will-formation and informal opinion-formation … like social power, political influence based on public opinion can be transformed into political power only through institutionalized procedures.'

Clearly elevated in this account is a more complex and institutionalised system of civil society and its links to proceduralist state complexes. Here, far less emphasis is put on individual relations with 'the public sphere' or indeed the generalised, mass-mediated public sphere itself. Instead, far more is put on citizens participating in multiple, overlapping spheres, in which shared interests and values are identified informally, to be channelled more formally to the parliamentary centre:

> The core area as a whole has an *outer* periphery that ... for different policy fields, complex networks have arisen among public agencies and private organizations, business associations, labour unions, interest groups and so on ... [which] belong to the civil-social infrastructure of a public sphere dominated by the mass media. With its informal, highly differentiated and cross-linked channels of communication, this public sphere forms the real periphery.
>
> (Habermas, 1996: 354–56)

At the same time, at the heart of this model, much greater weight is put on legislative assemblies, their constitutions, administrations and law-making. Now, parliamentary bodies are to be viewed as the most significant component of the contemporary public sphere. For as Fraser explains (1997: 170–71):

> the issue becomes more complicated as soon as we consider the emergence of parliamentary sovereignty. With that landmark development in the history of the public sphere, we encounter a major structural transformation, since a sovereign parliament functions as a public sphere *within* the state. Moreover, sovereign parliaments are what I shall call *strong publics*, publics whose discourse encompasses both opinion formation and decision-making.

If we take this alternative model of democracy and political communication as our starting point where does that leave critical enquiry? What should scholars be looking at and what normative ideals need to be applied in any evaluative process of media and communication in 'actually existing democracies'? Communication-oriented research needs to be done on those intermediary spheres that engage 'weak publics' at the 'periphery', on those 'strong publics' at the 'centre', and the links that form between them. In terms of investigating 'strong publics' at the centre, Rehg and Bohman's (2002) interpretation of Habermas's schema offers four specific evaluative criteria: i) a vibrant and inclusive public sphere with inputs into legislative bodies, ii) the composition of legislative bodies must be representative of society, iii) there must be 'real deliberation' within parliament, and iv) there must be parliamentary mechanisms to ensure equal deliberation of participants and that self-interest and external power is appropriately countered. Dahlberg (2001) and Wikland (2005) sum-marise in greater detail the ideal conditions under which deliberative forums are able to support 'rational critical debate' beyond the mere aggregation of opinions. These include: 'reciprocal critique of normative positions', 'reflexivity', 'ideal role-taking', 'sincerity', 'discursive inclusion and equality', 'autonomy from state/economic power'.

The UK parliamentary public sphere

Communicative action in the UK parliamentary public sphere: a positive evaluation

Habermas's 1996 account and these research parameters were used to investi-gate communication processes in and around the UK Parliament. The actors, practices and institutions contained within were assumed to operate as the core public sphere component of Habermas's two-track model of democracy. The overall conclusion, based on interviews with over 100 Westminster-based actors, is that the UK Parliament in the twenty-first century, in many respects, operates far better according to public sphere norms than the bourgeois public sphere of eighteenth-century England. There are many shortcomings in what exists. However, as a political institution, open to a wide variety of public inputs, and enabling rational and reflexive deliberation on those inputs and possible legislative solutions, it is rather successful.

There are some quite immediate flaws in terms of politicians neither being close to demographically representative of citizens, in terms of gender, class and ethnicity, nor autonomous from their parties (see Chapters 1 and 3). Thus Rehg and Bohman's second and fourth evaluative criteria remain unfulfilled. How-ever, despite these clear obstacles, Parliament, in many ways, offers much to foster and facilitate the type of ideal procedural and normative conditions equated with public sphere norms. This begins with the physical conditions and institutional structures, especially those developed during recent waves of modernisation. The new Portcullis House offers a large central courtyard area full of cafés and restaurants and ringed by meeting rooms and offices. In the public areas many MPs are to be seen meeting visitors or colleagues and then discussing issues in the open café areas. During parliamentary sessions, at the main entrances (Portcullis House, St Stephens) daily lists of public meet-ings and venues are displayed and large numbers of visitors are to be seen queuing up. Although Westminster remains exclusionary in several respects, there is also a strong impression of a vibrant, communicative café culture, similar to that described at the centre of Habermas's (1989) earlier bourgeois public sphere.

During interviews with MPs two key themes were explored: the information links between MPs ('strong publics') and those at the periphery ('weak publics'), and the cognitive and deliberative conditions under which MPs came to conclusions about political issues. Forty-five of the MPs were asked 'What are your main sources of information when it comes to informing yourself about, and deciding where you stand on, policy and legislative issues?' Eleven types of source were mentioned, six by half or more of respondents. The top six were: News Media, Party Whips/Briefing Material, Interest Groups, Party Colleagues, the House of Commons Library, and Constituents/the Constituency.

Further analysis of the responses and questioning of interviewees at the time revealed more details. External information sources, outside Parliament, were used more frequently than internal, party ones. The Constituents category was most often identified first, closely followed by the News Media. Both were seen as a means to identify and select issues to follow up; i.e. agenda setters. What came through repeatedly was how important, above all else, constituents and constituency information/opinion were regarded by back-bench MPs when it came to setting their policy priorities.

> As a back-bencher, the issues you become involved in, either superficially or in-depth, can be anything and everything. But your focus is on those matters which are of greatest relevance to the constituency … the biggest employer in my constituency is BAE Systems so, anything to do with military aerospace, then I'm straight into the detail of that in case it's going to have an immediate effect on employment opportunities in the constituency.
>
> (Michael Jack MP)

At a later stage in the interview just over half of MPs were asked how they gauged 'public opinion'. Three-quarters of respondents replied through direct contact with constituents and activities in the constituency. Further discussion about their information gathering and evaluation processes often gave the impression that party loyalty did not mean MPs simply followed the party line unthinkingly.

Table 2.1 Information sources used by back-bench MPs for evaluating policy/legislation

	Information source	Total (45)	Priority (1st / 2nd)	Capacity
1	Media	**24**	**11** (2)	General, not detail
1	Party whip/briefs	**24**	5 (4)	Specific voting
3	Party colleagues	**23**	**9** (3)	Specific
3	Interest groups	**23**	5 (4)	Specific
5	HoC library	**22**	5 (4)	Specific
6	Constituents/local	**21**	**12** (1)	General & specific
7	Own knowledge	12	4 (7)	General & specific
8	Internet	11	4 (7)	General & specific
8	Academic/res/advisers	11	0 (10)	Specific
10	Externl/personl netwks	10	3 (9)	General & specific
11	Govt material	7	0 (10)	Specific

Party line, when in conflict with obvious constituency needs and desires, was the most frequently mentioned dilemma for MPs when deciding how to vote:

> for most of us, we are content that our colleagues get it right and therefore we follow into the lobby like sheep in whichever direction the Whip's pointing us ... There are issues where you do go against the grain of your constituency but it's not a thing you want to do too often because then you don't get re-elected.
>
> (John Thurso MP)

Clearly, evaluating the responsiveness of politicians to their constituents, when based primarily on interviews with politicians, is problematic. The finding does however tally with other independent studies (Healey et al., 2005, Power Report, 2006). These have noted that individuals who have attempted exchanges with their local MP are much more likely to be positive about their MP than about politicians and institutional politics generally.

The other main information sources noted (Interest Groups, the House of Commons Library, Colleagues, Party) were all more likely to be mentioned in terms of specific policy information-gathering terms. In each case, there was a strong sense of trying to get information that was considered expert, objective and from multiple, politically-balanced sources. When dealing with interest groups there was a general assumption that such sources took partial positions and that this was countered by gaining a pluralist mix of groups and evaluating the group alongside its information and arguments:

> Say on Trident, I got lots of stuff from shop stewards who want to see more submarines built at Barrow-in-Furness. At the same time I'd have informa- tion from CND. They don't want nothing built in Barrow of that sort ... If they're making an argument, I use my own wits to assess the merits of the argument. If it's factual information I seek, I tend to seek corroboration of one sort or another ... In other words I'm not going to take somebody's word for anything.
>
> (Peter Kilfoyle MP, former minister)

A further attempt was made to assess the institutionalised deliberative process at the group level in terms of the ideal criteria listed above. As an institution, the parliamentary public sphere is organised around a plethora of formal and informal committees and groups, supported by extensive clerical and research services. For example, in 2004–5, 44 government bills and 95 private members' bills were discussed at 421 standing committee meetings. There were 1,286 select committee meetings and an average of 16 EDMs (Early Day Motions) tabled each day (all figs. HoC, July 2005). The research focused in particular on the conduct of select committees. A quarter of MPs, including nine current and recent committee chairs, were asked further questions about the selection of information sources, committee procedures and the group deliberation process. Four senior clerks, experienced in select committee work, were asked the same questions.

Procedures for all of these committees were very established. All committees were fairly autonomous, being able to set their own enquiry agendas and time-lines. In terms of information sources there were three key categories mentioned by all: Clerks, Interest Groups and Academic Experts/Research Institutes. Half also mentioned the importance of one's own general expertise in an area and the importance of external site visits. Clerks acted as intermediaries between the two, drawing up lists of potential advisers, interest group representatives and experts, as well as putting together the source information supplied.

All interviewees spoke very positively about their experiences on select committees. For many it was an educative experience with members given first-hand access to experts in the field as well as more tangible visits to sites on the ground and individuals involved. They also spoke of the unusual 'luxuries' of time, administrative support and relative political autonomy. The general atti-tude towards information gathering came across as pluralist, deliberative, expert-oriented and evaluative. Witnesses were presumed to take a certain stance and their evidence evaluated and questioned on that basis. Opposite stances were consciously sought out for balance. In almost all cases there was also a strong sense of many 'ideal' forms of communicative action taking place, including: 'discursive inclusion and equality', 'reflexivity' and a 'reciprocal critique of nor-mative positions'. This seemed apparent in the way committee agendas were agreed and enquiry issues were deliberated on:

> when we came to enquiries, I asked colleagues on the Committee what they thought was important and to make their case ... the consensus one, was the one we did ... And genuinely I pride myself that over the eight and a half years that I chaired the [Foreign Affairs Select] Committee, there were only two reports which were not unanimous ... The Committee then might have three or four long sessions discussing amendments raised by members of the Committee, and there may be votes, and we do our very best to reach a consensus.
>
> (Donald Anderson, Labour MP, Committee Chair)

Many of these observations and interviews tally with Philip Cowley's work (2002, 2005, see also Power Report, 2006). For Cowley, the popular image of passive back-bench MPs, simply following party orders, presents a distorted pic-ture of the day-to-day deliberations and negotiations that take place during the legislative process. Much is altered before voting takes place. Rebellions, of varying sizes, are a frequent occurrence. In the 2001–5 Parliament he lists forty-seven occurrences where over fifteen Labour MPs defied party policy and government whips. Fourteen of these involved between 40 and 139 MPs defying the party.

Thus, in many ways, the Westminster parliamentary public sphere of the twenty-first century is a significant advance on anything described by Habermas as existing centuries before. This conclusion is reached because for many (including Habermas) the account of the public sphere described earlier was idealised and based on limited historical accounts. The bourgeois public sphere excluded a majority of the public, was frequently irrational and was entirely ad hoc in its social organisation, choice of subject matter and deliberations. In the intervening centuries, the conditions for 'democratically institutionalized will-formation', centring on Parliament, have been firmly established. Clearly there are several shortcomings. But as a system the UK Parliament is very much oriented around public sphere ideals in both its institutional formation and the cultural norms and values adopted by the politicians within.

Communicative breakdowns in the UK parliamentary public sphere model

Obviously, this glowing assessment of the UK parliamentary public sphere would seem bizarre to the many who have documented the strong decline of support for the formal political process (see Norris, 2000, Dalton, 2004, Hay, 2007, and Chapter 10). According to Cowley (2005: x) 'one of the paradoxes of modern British politics is that we currently have the most accessible parliamentarians we've ever had – and probably the most professional and hard-working, too – and yet we hold them in lower esteem than ever'. Indeed, the majority of interviewees questioned recognised the existence of some form of public crisis of confidence in UK politics; something further exacerbated by the 2009 MPs' expenses scandal. This being the case either the above assessment is wrong or there are other fundamental problems with the UK parliamentary system of government.

The study also attempted to explore the causes of this disparity. Several explanations have been put forward in other works (see above references). Two in particular emerged during the interviews and found support in related public studies. The first of these revealed that there is a pronounced separation between parliament and government in terms of communication with the periphery. Parliaments may be very good at centrally absorbing opinion- and will-formation from weak publics at the periphery but governments may not. If government is the dominant partner in the legislative process that follows this is a potentially significant flaw.

It is also a problem apparent in the UK case. The UK Executive, as a source of opinion- and will-formation, operates on a different basis to the UK Legislature. This begins with the physical, social and cultural environment. MPs who become government ministers take up an office in their Whitehall department. Civil servants and fellow departmental ministers replace back-bench party members as colleagues:

> when you're a backbench MP, or you're in the opposition, physically, your working life revolves around the Houses of Parliament. The minute you get

to be a minister physically, geographically your life revolves around the department ... the people you mix with everyday are not your own people, they're civil servants ... I really felt that quite strongly when I became a minister.

(Baroness Estelle Morris, former Cabinet Minister)

Sixteen of the interviewees with senior ministerial experience were also asked about the information sources they used in developing policy and legislation within their departments. All sixteen stated their main source was civil servants and all sixteen prioritised them as the first or second most important source. Other information sources were mentioned but rather less often.

Unlike parliamentary clerks, who took an intermediary position between politicians and periphery sources, civil servants were primary information sources. Government departments had large numbers of internally-employed expert personnel that were likely to be at the centre of the policy process: The Cabinet Office had 1,410 full-time staff, the Treasury 1,130, Defra, 3,950, Health, 2,290, Transport, 2,120 (all figs. ONS, 2007). Opinions on the quality and balance of that material were mixed but all admitted a high level of dependence on it:

the bulk of the information and briefing material I received was from the official briefings ... Certainly, for instance, when I arrived at the Department of Health as Health Secretary there was briefing material this deep ... No wonder people never got a grip on an issue if their information system was like that.

(Frank Dobson MP, former Cabinet Minister)

What also became clear was how internally oriented ministries were. Instead of general news consumption ministers and senior civil servants tended to be given daily clippings files consisting of coverage of their own department and

Table 2.2 Information sources used by government ministers for evaluating policy/legislation

Information source	Total (16)	Priority (1ˢᵗ/2ⁿᵈ)	Capacity
1 Civil servants	**16**	**16**	Specific
2 Media	8	0	General, not detail
3 Cabinet colleagues/manifesto	7	4	Specific
3 Academic/res/advisers	7	4	Specific
3 Interest groups	7	1	Specific
6 Own knowledge	6	4	General & specific
7 Govt. material/existing legisln	5	0	Specific
8 Externl/personl netwks	4	1	General & specific
9 Constituents	2	0	General
9 Other	2	0	General & specific

related remits. 'Collective cabinet responsibility' and time constraints meant that ministers rarely strayed into other policy territory. The picture that emerged, from both politicians and civil servants interviewed, was one where government ministers adopted policy directions from manifesto commitments and senior party leaders/advisers. Thereafter it was civil servants that were the predominant information sources. The inputs of external sources, such as interest groups, experts, constituents and general media, came later and were greatly reduced. Interviews with civil servants took place at ten departments; only two (Health and Children, Schools and Families) gave responses suggesting that external inputs were a regular and institutionalised feature. Again, such findings tallied with other recent studies of Whitehall (Marsh et al., 2001, Smith, 2003). These suggest that, despite many outward-facing reforms, policy is still dominated by department civil servants and limited sets of interest group representatives in 'fairly closed networks'. These observed civil service cultures that, while following norms of integrity, neutrality and objectivity, also regarded the public as ignorant, and 'public opinion' as being of minor concern to the policy process. Thus, the level of connection between government departments and the periphery of 'weak' publics varies but certainly appears rather weaker than that encountered in Westminster.

These differences become more significant when one looks at the power relationships between a government and its legislative assembly. For Scheuerman (2002: 69) commenting on *BFN*, this indeed is the crux of the problem: 'Most parliaments today continue to rubber stamp decisions that have been made elsewhere, by the upper division of the state bureaucracy' (a point acknowledged by Habermas, 2002). According to Lijphart (1999) the UK system, in contrast to more 'consensual' systems such as Switzerland, Finland and Italy, is amongst those democracies which have the highest level of 'executive dominance'. As more recent studies note (Marsh et al., 2001, Brazier et al., 2005, Cook and Maclennan, 2005, Power Report, 2006), attempts at modernisation since 1997 have managed to improve the efficient running of Parliament while failing to address the key issue of power imbalance. The UK Legislature is thus less able to transmit public opinion- and will-formation from the periphery through into the legislative process.

The second explanation for the public perception of crisis in the UK parliamentary public sphere relates to the failure of its Legislature to adequately convey its deliberative processes back to the periphery. In the UK case, the critical mass media eye has come to focus on government and political party competition rather than parliament. The work of most MPs, as constituency representatives and deliberative actors within Parliament, has become minimised. In effect, the Legislature and its law-making processes have become largely omitted from the mediated discourse about politics more generally. Parliamentary process is itself not publicly revealed (open to 'critical publicity' in Habermas's terms). Over time this symbolically delegitimises parliamentary activity and, consequently, contributes to public cynicism and distrust of politics per se.

The conditions of this state of affairs became increasingly apparent as the research progressed. Parliament, as an institution distinct from government or individual political parties, has always attempted to restrict journalists and shield its activities from the outside media (see Reid, 2000). Since the 1980s news organisations have been less inclined to cover Parliament in mainstream news fearing lack of consumer interest (Negrine, 1998, see also Barnett and Gaber, 2001). As Negrine noted, throughout the twentieth century there has been a steady decline of parliamentary print news coverage. By the mid-1990s, no British Daily paper offered a section dedicated to debates and speeches in Parliament. These failings have been identified by a number of recent inquiries within Parliament (HoC, 2004, HoC, June 2004, HoC, Dec 2005) and the Hansard Society (2005). The 2006 Commons Business Plan (HoC, Dec 2005: 20) identified, as 'a primary objective', the need to improve information to the public and to establish the identity of Parliament 'as distinct from government', a body that is 'holding government to account' and 'welcoming to citizens'. The reports recommended a range of strategies to improve public information outputs such as the employment of dedicated press officers to promote the work of Parliament itself. At the time of the research, only a handful of such posts existed (none did before 2000).

In contrast, it was also clear that the machinery of political publicity is driven by government departments and the competing leaderships of the main political parties. In 2006, for example, the Prime Minister's Office employed twenty-four 'information officers', the Cabinet Office thirty-five, and the Treasury thirty-one. The larger government departments, such as the Home Office or Department of Health, had over 100 such staff (figs. in COI, 2006). Party leaderships also employ teams of public relations staff and/or special advisors with communication skills. Consequently, the public projection of UK politics by political actors is directed by the goals of government, the civil service and the competing political party leaders. The majority of MPs may spend much of their time interacting with constituents, and engaged in positive deliberation over policy and legislation, but that is not the symbolic image of politics projected.

Interviewees frequently voiced frustration at the long-term failing of Parliament to promote itself and its activities, as well as general media disinterest in reporting policy matters and deliberative processes. A majority of politicians and officials expressed their concerns in this area and/or condemned the general shape of news coverage of Westminster:

> the unmentionable is the disillusion of both people here, and people outside ... the overall strategy here, is to make people aware of the role of Parliament, that Parliament isn't just a legislation factory for the Government, it is also a watchdog of what the Government does, and indeed a challenger of what they do.
>
> (Robert Wilson, Senior HoC Clerk)

I don't think there's a terribly strong interest in the media for policy debates you know. Newspapers are about news and policy isn't really news. It's events that are news, so policy comes into the news when the consequences of policy create a news event, such as we've seen with the failure to deport foreign prisoners.

(Greg Clark MP)

Interestingly, approximately half the twenty political journalists interviewed admitted similar levels of frustration at their role in this. They regretted the fact that their editors pushed for personality- rather than policy-oriented stories. Others, even if uncritical of journalism per se, saw their role in terms of reporting politics rather than policy: i.e., party competition, conflicts and personalities involved in politics. Policy analysis was something left to specialists in other news sectors:

We've contributed, the media have probably contributed by giving more attention to those kind of personality-driven stories than highlighting the policy stories, focusing on the good work, maybe that politicians do at Westminster and in their constituencies. That may well have contributed to the sort of general public malaise about politics.

(Philip Webster, political editor)

Ultimately, media and citizens (at the periphery) have a significant input into the parliamentary public sphere but this is not reciprocated. Instead, strategic communication emanates from state apparatus and political parties which, coupled with news media values and practices, exclude and mask the positive deliberative policy process within parliament itself. Coverage also fails to apply 'critical publicity' to the processes of information-gathering and deliberation at the stronger centres of legislative power in the civil service and government departments. In consequence, whether or not the legislative process is sound, its symbolic presentation fails to convey to the public the elements of legitimacy that do exist.

The UK is not alone when it comes to declining parliamentary news coverage and the focus on party personalities in conflict. Such trends have also been noted in the US where half the states no longer produce a newspaper that covers Congress (Patterson, 1994, Hallin, 1994, Delli-Carpini and Williams, 2001, Entman, 2004, Pew, 2009). Studies of French news content (Negrine, 1998, Benson and Hallin, 2007: 11) suggest similar declines and imbalances. In the 1990s, the ratio of 'Executive/judicial' to 'Legislative' sources cited was almost 2:1 in the US and 6:1 in France.

Conclusion

At the heart of this chapter is a desire to move critical debates about politics, communication and citizenship into new territory. This means engaging with 'actually existing democracies', contemporary media environments, and what that means in terms of evaluating media and public communication processes.

Ideas and arguments have been applied to the UK Parliament which, to all intents and purposes, constitutes in institutionalised form the core component of the contemporary public sphere. Applying the evaluative schema directly to this sphere it was found to operate surprisingly well. Political representatives at the centre are very well connected to those at the periphery, individually, via media and through interest groups. The UK electoral system encourages MPs to have regular, direct dialogues with their constituents and to be sensitive to local opinion. Institutionalised procedures, as well as the cultural norms of participants, then encourage deliberative forms of dialogue and evaluation. Public opinion- and will-formation lies at the heart of the UK parliamentary public sphere.

The process falls down for several reasons. Two are identified here. First, the UK Executive is both too powerful, in relation to its Legislature, and less linked to the public periphery. Thus, public opinion- and will-formation is not necessarily adequately transferred into legislative outcomes. Second, even when the legislative process operates 'legitimately', such a process is not publicly visible. Government and competing party communication strategies dominate the mediated symbolic presentation of politics to the detriment of parliamentary processes. Since political systems must not only operate legitimately, but must be observed to operate so, this adds to the public perception of crisis in UK politics.

Chapter 3

Professionalised parties, the electoral mechanism and the new wave of party leaders

The rise of David Cameron

Introduction

This chapter is focused on the transformation of parties and politicians as they adapt to changing electorates and campaign environments. In contemporary politics, traditional links between parties and voters, based on socio-economic and ideological ties, have declined. Mass media has become central to elections. Parties, accordingly, have evolved, first into 'mass' or 'catch-all' parties, and then into 'electoral-professional' parties. Modern parties now rely less on traditional party organisations and ideologies, and more on centralised management structures and the inputs of a range of external 'professionals' from marketing, media and elsewhere. The questions are: have such developments made parties more responsive to electorates or less, and how has the process of professionalisation influenced parties and politicians themselves?

Debates have focused on how recent waves of party professionalisation have affected news contents and citizen engagement with politics. For critics, electoral coverage has been contaminated, turnouts have declined and public cynicism has risen. The professionalisation of party politics is part of the problem. For advocates, alternatively, the professionalisation of parties has made them more communicatively adept and more sensitive to public opinion generally. Declining turnouts and memberships have other causes.

This chapter aligns itself with critics but pursues an alternative line of argument. Employing the ideas of Max Weber and Michel Foucault, it contends that the very processes of professionalisation work in ways that socially detach political leaders from wider society. As party leaders have 'rationalised' their parties, in order to impose themselves on new campaign environments and electorates, so parties and conditions, in turn, have 'disciplined' and separated their leading politicians. Consequently, we have a modern class of party leaders who are more proficient at winning elections and attuned to elite policy networks but, at the same time, are less connected socially to general publics.

The chapter is in three parts. In the first, the literature and debates on party professionalisation, and their impact on news content and electorates, are reviewed. As argued here, a key impact of professionalisation has been the reshaping of parties and leading politicians themselves. In the second part the argument is tested by looking at the personal characteristics of MPs of the front-benches of the two main UK parties. This is followed by an extended case study focusing on the rise of David Cameron as he unexpectedly gained the leadership of the Conservative Party in 2005.

Elections and political party transformations: from 'rational choice' to 'rationalisation'

Party–citizen links, elections, and the professionalisation of relations

In democracies political parties and elections are key system components for communicatively linking citizens to states. Parties provide the organisational means for representing particular interests in society and developing publicly-linked policy. Elections enable voters to choose which parties and policies they want and legitimate governments. New administrations are then expected to transform policies into legislation (see accounts in Dalton and Wattenberg, 2002, Webb, 2007). Media and communication are, of course, central to these processes.

However, over the course of the twentieth century, electorates, media and parties have all evolved significantly. Consequently, the communicative links between parties and citizens have shifted too. Three particular transformations are recorded. First is the changing shape of electorates (see Inglehart, 1990, Dalton and Wattenberg, 2002, Gunther et al., 2002). A mixture of socio-economic shifts, increased mobility, and changes in religion and ethnicity have eroded the traditional ideological and regional links that existed between parties and voters. Second has been the advent of mass, broadcast media, from the 1950s onwards, in most advanced economies. Coinciding with the evolution of 'mass' parties, television changed the organisation of party campaigning itself (see accounts in Maarek, 1995, Rosenbaum, 1997, Blumler and Kavanagh, 1999, Wring, 2005). National television appearances have proved to be far more cost-efficient, in terms of time, money and organisation, than local campaign networks. Third, parties have attempted to adapt to such changing circum-stances. Initially they converted themselves into 'mass' or 'catch all parties' (Kircheimer, 1966), with weaker ideologies and broader policies, designed to appeal to wider citizen bases. Then they became more professionalised. As many studies of political communication (Blumler and Gurevitch, 1995, Swanson and Mancini, 1996, Farrell et al., 2001, Lilleker and Lees-Marshment, 2005) and political parties (Webb, 2000, Heffernan, 2003, Hay, 2007) have noted, large parties everywhere have developed centralised campaign structures and brought in a range of outside professional experts. They have thus become 'electoral-professional' or 'modern cadre' parties in the process.

A number of recorded trends suggest that one or more of these changes is having a negative impact on citizen–party engagement and on faith in the electoral mechanism. In the majority of mature democracies, voter-turnout, party membership numbers, and strong party identification (partisan alignment) have all declined since the 1960s. While most agree that party–citizen links are declining, there is some disagreement as to the causes and whether democracy is substantially poorer overall as a result (see overviews in Norris, 1999a, 1999b, Dalton, 2004, Hay, 2007, and Chapter 10). One area of debate, explored in the rest of the chapter, focuses on the part played by party professionalisation.

For many, professionalisation, in the larger scope, has been broadly positive. The line adopted is strongly influenced by a 'rational choice' perspective, inspired by Anthony Downs's (1957) *An Economic Theory of Democracy*. The framework outlined here, is one in which parties compete in the electoral market place for votes. Voters, in turn, behave as rational market participants (or consumers), making choices according to a personal cost-benefit analysis. The elements of this rational choice thinking are to be found in authors such as Inglehart (1990), Norris (2002) and Dalton (2004). While being dismissive of the professionalisation and associated critiques, they also prefer to focus on the 'rational' reasons citizens choose not to vote or join parties. An increasing proportion of citizens of wealthy countries have a 'postmaterialist' political outlook based on their higher education, personal wealth and critical faculties. They support 'democracy' per se, and make logical choices about not voting for parties, choosing instead to support single-issue interest groups.

An equivalent, party-based, 'rational choice' approach, that has gathered momentum in the last decade, has been developed by advocates of political marketing. Jennifer Lees-Marshment (2001/2008, 2004, Lilleker and Lees-Marshment, 2005) has done most to develop a positive interpretive framework here, with inspiration and/or support from Scammell (1995, 2003), Newman (1999) and others. According to the 'Lees-Marshment model' good (often interpreted as 'successful') parties are those that have made the transition to being 'market-oriented parties' (MOPs). Traditionally, parties were simply sold as product-oriented parties (POPs), but then developed marketing and other promotional practices, becoming more sophisticated sales-oriented parties (SOPs) in the process. In the next phase, MOPs also used such marketing tools as part of the initial policy formation process. MOPs and citizens now both benefit. Parties free themselves from the constraints of ideological dogma and, also, automatically become more consultative and deliberative with citizens. The additional positive is that a party is also better at communicating with the public because of its consumer-oriented messages. Thus, Margaret Thatcher was a 'marketing pioneer' of MOP for the Conservatives in 1979, as was Tony Blair for Labour in 1997. The electoral highs and lows of these two parties are best explained within this framework, as are those of a number of other parties elsewhere (Lilleker and Lees-Marshment, 2005).

This account of mutually-benefitting communication processes also features strongly in the way the promotional industries of marketing and public relations see (or perhaps sell) themselves. Grunig and Hunt (1984) developed an earlier schema very similar to Lees-Marshment's in describing the positive evolutionary stages of public relations, from a mode of propaganda to a 'two-way' form of communication. The American Marketing Association (AMA) states that marketing creates 'exchanges that satisfy individual and organisational goals'. Similarly, the Public Relations Society of America (PRSA) declares that public relations contributes 'to mutual understanding among groups and institutions. It serves to bring private and public policies in harmony.' Such positive industry and academic accounts indeed suggest that the use of such professional occupations may help restore certain key public sphere ideals (Grunig, 1992, Nessman, 1995, see Benson's 2008 critique).

However, party professionalisation has also been held to be a cause of, rather than a treatment for, public disengagement. The rational choice framework, used by its advocates, makes two basic, but rather flawed, assumptions. The first of these is that product consumption and citizenship are the same things. They are not. Consumption is an individual activity whereas citizenship is a communal one requiring wider social engagement. As several admit (Scammell, 1999, Wring, 2005, Lees-Marshment, 2001/2008) there is no simple overlay of the 'marketing mix' and 'four Ps' (product, price, place and promotion) on to politics. Policies are not simple, self-contained products with a definable consumer base. They are complex, evolve over time, impinge on other policies and citizens, and have to be delivered. As Washbourne (2005) argues, the marketing approach does not distinguish between 'wants', 'desires', 'interests' and 'needs'.

Second, those who follow the rational choice line tend to underestimate the 'rational' behaviour of politicians and parties, and overestimate the 'rational' abilities of citizens. It is unlikely that politicians are motivated to enter politics to simply follow public opinion. Similarly, outside professional experts are employed by parties, first and foremost, to win elections and good poll ratings, not engage with citizens. Thus, for critics, campaigning in majoritarian electoral systems, in particular, becomes increasingly focused on small groups of 'swing voters' and marginal constituencies or states (Lilleker, 2005, Savigny, 2005, Wring, 2005). If it only takes a few per cent to change their vote this means that 'rational' parties are likely to disproportionately focus their campaign resources and messages on only 1–2 per cent of citizens.

By the same logic, the way professionalised parties communicate with media is likely to be directed by party rather than public needs. Such strategies lead to media manipulation, negative attacks, spin, symbolic and pseudo politics, because they are effective (Boorstin, 1962, Wernick, 1991, Hall Jamieson, 1996, Herman and Chomsky, 2002, Franklin, 2004, Dinan and Miller, 2007). Coverage, whether directed by party or media logic, becomes full of 'soundbites', negative and confrontational reporting, political personalities, scandal and tabloid-style content (Hallin, 1994, Patterson, 1994, Sparks and Tulloch, 2000, Thussu, 2008). Agendas are narrow, and citizens find it hard to discern the policy positions of parties (Entman, 1989, Delli Carpini and Keeter, 1996, Webb and Farrell, 1999). Deacon et al.'s (2005) study showed many of these trends to be in evidence in the last 2005 UK election. In the best-selling tabloid press the three party leaders alone accounted for 39 per cent of all politician appearances and 60 per cent of direct quotations. They also found that 44 per cent of coverage focused on the electoral process itself ('horse race' issues) and 8 per cent on 'political propriety'. The most important electoral issues, according to polls (MORI, 1997–2009), such as health and taxation, were each covered in only 3–4 per cent of stories.

Citizens, in contrast, cannot possibly be entirely 'rational' in their electoral choices. Evidently, they are not aided by the content of electoral coverage. Most do not have the initial information or expertise to evaluate the multiple policy choices on offer on a range of issues, let alone weigh up how one policy arena imposes on another. It is for such reasons that voters are increasingly likely to vote on the basis of a party leader personality (a cognitive short-cut) rather than a party policy programme. Lees (2005) demonstrated that Gerhardt Schröder's SPD election victory over Edmund Stoiber's CDU–CSU, in the 2002 German election, was secured on the strength of his stronger 'character traits' rather than greater policy support. Knuckey and Lees-Marshment (2005) had the same finding in regard to George W. Bush's Republican victory over Al Gore's Democrats in the 2000 US election.

The rationalisation of parties and disciplining of party leaders

These trends suggest that successful parties have reorganised themselves professionally in an attempt to master the contemporary electoral environment. Most agree, for better or worse, that this has changed the way parties engage with news media and voters. As now argued, such developments have also reshaped politicians themselves and in ways that further weaken the links between parties and citizens.

Max Weber's related writings on political 'Parties', 'Bureaucracy' and 'Politics as a Vocation' offer much to the discussion here (Weber, 1948). For Weber, there is a continuing tension between the needs of autonomous, individual agents, and those of modern organisations employing them. Individuals, no matter how extraordinary, eventually make way for more 'legal-rational' forms of authority and bureaucratic organisation. This friction and ambiguity is particularly acute in terms of political leaders and their tightly organised parties. On the one hand, 'rulers' are 'charismatic', gifted individuals who come to lead governments and publics. His views here were close to those of Michels (1967[1911]) and his 'iron law of oligarchy' interpretation of leadership in political parties. On the other hand, he states that developed parties are rationalised bureaucracies, 'frequently organized in a very strict "authoritarian" fashion'. They have their own organisational goals directed 'toward the acquisition of "social power"' (Weber, 1948: 194–95).

In his lecture on 'Politics as a Vocation', Weber indeed describes the development of the modern state which brings both the efficient organisation of domination and the emergence of a new class of 'professional politicians'. As parties initially develop, leaders are selected from existing professions (Weber, 1948: 100): 'formed partly according to class interests, partly according to family traditions, and partly for ideological reasons. Clergymen, teachers, professors, lawyers, doctors, apothecaries, prosperous farmers, manufacturers.' However, as parties become more extensive and organised, 'of the necessity to woo and organise the masses', so the role of the party 'machinery' and the specially-trained 'professional politician' comes to the fore. Like all established bureaucratic organisations, the particular political skills, forms of knowledge, personal goals and rewards are all determined by the needs of the party. Candidate selection is no longer tied to general occupational experiences, intellectual 'cultivation', or familiarity with forms of democratic (horizontal, less hierarchical) engagement. Consequently, the 'political master' in a state bureaucracy (1948: 232) 'finds himself in the position of the "dilettante" who stands opposite the "expert", facing the trained official'. Personal success will thus be dependent on an ability to realise key organisational goals which, as Weber (1948: 217) readily admits, may well conflict with '"democratic" principles of justice'.

This notion of the process of rule and organisation, in turn, coming to form and determine the qualities of rulers themselves, is also to be found in the work of Michel Foucault. Foucault's writing plots a parallel path in his accounts of the transformation of state authority. Much of his earlier work describes the ways mass societies emerged and how their populaces were ordered and 'disciplined' through the institutions and discourses of professions, such as psychiatry, law and education (Foucault, 1971, 1975, 1980). 'Power/Knowledge' was employed by those above to discipline those below, down through the ever-larger levels of a 'continuous individualising pyramid' (Foucault, 1975: 219). However, unlike Weber, Foucault was critical of the notion of extraordinary individuals who wield power with conscious autonomy outside of larger discourses and practices. Although power runs from the top down, it is contested at every level and influences those above as well as those below. As he states (Foucault, 1980: 156) 'Power is no longer substantially identified with an individual who possesses or exercises it by right of birth; it becomes a machinery that no one owns.'

Arguably, these thoughts were extended in Foucault's later lectures, published posthumously, on the subject of 'governmentality'. In the first of these (1991) Foucault describes how advisory treaties for rulers shifted, in the mid-sixteenth century, from an emphasis on maintaining princely power, to one of describing 'the art of good government'. This resulted (Foucault, 1991: 103) 'on the one hand, in the formation of a whole series of specific governmental apparatuses, and, on the other, in the development of a whole complex of savoirs'. By such means states and their rulers, as they 'disciplined' their subjects, were also 'governmentalized'. As such, modern political leaders and the art of leadership become reconfigured by a series of external, expert 'savoirs', linked both to maintaining power and good government.

In effect, politicians become leaders, not simply because they are 'extra-ordinary' individuals, but also because they fit the skills profile dictated by the modern party machine, electoral mechanism and state apparatus. We might then ask: what are the specific forms of 'expertise', or 'mentalities of government', that contemporary 'professionalised' politicians must possess or acquire to be accepted by parties and electorates? Put another way, what kind of individuals are likely to succeed and become leaders of modern electoral-professional parties?

For one thing, such individuals should not have strong ideological positions and should be prepared to adapt policy to middle-ground public opinion and broad electorates. Indeed, as several have noted, there has been considerable convergence in the ideologies and policy stances of major political parties, particularly amongst left-leaning parties such as Labour and the Democrats (Entman, 1989, 2005, Norris, 1999a, Webb and Farrell, 1999, Heath et al., 2001, Curtice, 2005). Second, leaders should be able to command or manage a rigid hierarchical structure and work well with professional experts and funders from business, marketing and media. This is because, as several have recorded (Swanson and Mancini, 1996, Crouch, 2004, Wring, 2005, Hay, 2007), external professionals and centralised hierarchies have become more significant for achieving party goals than traditional party members and local bureaucracies. Third, successful politicians should have an appealing public personality and be able to project themselves well through the mass media. This makes sense if leader personalities, rather than policy positions, appear more significant to electoral outcomes (Meyer, 2002, Corner and Pels, 2003, Lees, 2005). By the same token there is no advantage gained from having a prior non-political career, particular knowledge/experience of specific policy areas, or contact with local party politics and members.

The professionalisation of party leaderships in the UK

The changing patterns of party leadership in the Conservative and Labour Parties

The reshaping of parties and political leaders, and the testing of these ideas, was investigated in the UK case using two methods. First, thirty-six interviewees (twenty politicians, sixteen journalists) were asked specifically about the qualities politicians needed to possess in order to progress to the senior levels of their parties. The second method involved an analysis of the biographical details of the forty-nine members (excluding Peer appointments) of the Labour Cabinet (twenty-four) and Conservative Shadow Cabinet (twenty-five) of 2007–8. In attempting to test possible shifts in the social profile of (Shadow) Cabinet members over time, comparisons were made between entry years and ages. There were twenty members under the age of 50, most of whom entered parliament during or after 2001, and twenty-nine members over 50, all of whom entered before 2000. There were several distinct differences between the older and younger cohorts as well as more general trends in evidence over the period (see Table 3.1). These differences could be said to be reflective of the new professionalisation and media-orientation affecting parties.

The demographic characteristics of both age cohorts confirm what earlier studies of UK party candidates (Criddle, 1984, Norris and Lovenduski, 1992, 1997a, Childs et al., 2005) have documented; that is that MPs are not demographically representative of their populations. They are predominantly white male graduates from middle- and upper-middle-class backgrounds, with a large number going to private, fee-paying schools and then on to Oxford or Cambridge. Not much has changed here between generations.

However, more significant changes are detectable when one focuses on degree subjects, work experience, and career progression. Looking at the twenty members of the younger generation (see Table 3.1), half did PPE (Politics, Philosophy and Economics) at Oxford, a degree specially developed for aspiring 'future leaders'. Four did law and four history/English. Of the older twenty-nine, eight did law, seven did history/English, five did politics/European Studies, and two did PPE. This shift continues when looking at professions prior to entering parliament. Of the younger generation, eleven have been policy advisers/researchers working for politicians, parties and political think-tanks, and ten have worked in journalism and/or public relations. Looking at the older generation, politicians are more likely to have had careers in business/finance (nine), law (eight),

Table 3.1 Comparative profiles of newer and older Cabinet members in the 2007–8 Labour and Conservative Cabinets

	Under 50s (20)	*Over 50s (29)*
Male/female split	3:1	5:1
Ethnicity	All White	All White
Education, private:state ratio	1:1	1:1
Graduates, Oxbridge:other	3:1	1:1
Dominant university subjects	PPE (10), History/ English (4), Law (4)	Law (8), History/ English (7), Politics/ European Studies (4)
Primary occupations listed	Policy (9), Journalism/ PR (5), Business (3)	Business (7), Law (6), Education (5), Campaigning (4)
Most common occupations experienced	Policy (11), Journalism/PR (10)	Business (9), Law (8), Education (6), Campaigning (6)
Pre-MP career period	7.5 years	15 years
Local councillor experience	1 in 4	1 in 2
Average age when elected	35	38
Average age (years taken to enter Cabinet)	39 (4.8)	47 (9)

university lecturing (six) and trade union/other campaigning (six), something also found in earlier studies (Criddle, 1984, Norris and Lovenduski, 1997b).

The older generation, on average, has also worked twice as long in their profession (fifteen years) before entering parliament than the younger generation (seven–eight years). In addition, they are much more likely to have worked, paid or unpaid, as a local councillor. Two-thirds of those entering before 1990, four-tenths of those in the 1990s, and just under a quarter of those in the current decade had been local councillors. The roots to leadership have also changed and become more centralised and fast-tracked. The older generation entered parliament at an average age of thirty-eight but had to wait just over nine years, until their 47th year, to reach Cabinet level. The younger generation became MPs at an average age of 35 (see Table 3.1) but attained full cabinet status in their 39th year. Those entering Parliament after 2001 took just over three years.

The biographical profile findings were backed up during the interviews. When interviewees were asked specifically about the qualities required for political advancement, over two-thirds of politicians and journalists gave the same three answers. The most frequent of these linked promotion to party networks, alliances and loyalties. Several stated that an important route for aspiring politicians was to work in the office of the party leader, usually as a special adviser, before entering Parliament. The second most common answer given was having good media skills and/or the ability to maintain good relations with journalists. The third was being noticed and seen to perform well in the House of Commons, most usually in the Chamber. Several noted that for Cabinet promotion, 'technocratic' and 'media' abilities had overtaken either 'ideological leaning' or particular prior professional 'expertise' as being significant:

> I don't find MPs as a whole necessarily terribly well informed people actually … these days, it's much more a sort of technocratic political process, which is I think to the detriment of politics … The ethos of Blair and New Labour is technical and media ability rather than knowledge of a subject. More so than any other leader has ever been.
>
> (Jeremy Corbyn MP)

> Twenty years ago … it [the Conservative Cabinet] was largely full of people who'd had serious jobs in the real world before going into politics … so many politicians today have never done anything other than politics. They got elected very young or they became special advisers before that and they're not people who seem to know very much about the real world … They have views that are the views of their party, or they have views of their seniors that are manufactured for them by special advisers and policy wonks … the present leader of the Conservative Party [David Cameron] is somebody who is motivated by a desire to be Prime Minister and not by a desire to fulfil a programme of political conviction.
>
> (Simon Heffer, political editor)

Putting these findings together, it could be argued that the newest generation of political leaders are a more 'professionalised' class of politicians in the Weberian sense. They are more likely to have a degree, purpose made for political elites (PPE), and prior professional experience in policy-making and/or journalism/ public relations. They are more equipped to engage with any policy process but are less knowledgeable about particular policy areas per se. They are mass media oriented. More contemporary leaders, at an early career stage, have emerged from social networks that comprise of existing party leaders, think-tanks and political journalists. Such shifts also suggest that the newer generation are more socially and culturally removed from wider publics. Their links to professional occupations (business, education, unions/campaigning groups and law) and local council politics are rather weaker. They do not seem to have had much of an alternative career beyond the parliamentary political sphere and, in many cases, their only career has been within party politics. They have spent rather less time as local councillors and back-bench MPs before joining the senior levels of their parties.

All of this may make them better attuned to party politics, more adept at campaigning, and more able to engage with a range of outside experts and policy briefs. However, at the same time, their life experiences, links to professions, and experiences of local politics and party supporters all appear to be rather weaker (see also Dalton and Wattenberg, 2002, Crouch, 2004, Hay, 2007).

The curious rise of David Cameron

David Cameron is the archetypal new generation political leader. A case study of his successful election in 2005 demonstrates this and the arguments of the chapter more concretely. It draws on a combination of interview material and newspaper content analysis. Twenty-four politicians and fifteen reporters were asked about their recollection of events during the leadership contest and why they thought David Cameron had triumphed. A content analysis of four national daily newspapers and their equivalent Sunday titles, during the main election period, was also conducted. From 6th May to the 21st October, 813 pieces were looked at, from the *Daily/Sunday Telegraph*, *The Times/Sunday Times*, the *Daily Mail/Mail on Sunday* and the *Sun/News of the World*.

Following the 2005 General Election loss, Michael Howard, the then leader of the Conservative Party, announced his resignation on May 6th 2005, and a delayed leadership election was announced. To win the contest candidates had to gain support first amongst the 198 Conservative Members of Parliament (MPs), whose two ballots would decide the two final candidates. Party members (PM) would then cast the final vote. Over the summer, David Davis, the Shadow Home Secretary, was the recognised favourite to succeed out of more than fifteen potential candidates. At the end of September, five put themselves forward as the official election began in the week before the Party Conference in

Blackpool: David Davis, Ken Clarke, Liam Fox, David Cameron and Malcolm Rifkind. Rifkind then dropped out.

As the official contest began in late September, it seemed that Cameron's hopes of winning were remote. The traditional indicators of support, in terms of political experience, party links and media exposure, were all weak in his case. He was relatively little known to MPs having only been elected in 2001 and then appointed to his first Shadow Cabinet position in May 2005. In contrast, all his rivals had had lengthy careers and worked their way up the party ranks. Fox had been an MP since 1992 and in the Shadow Cabinet since 1999. Davis had been an MP since 1987, a Minister (1994–97), the Party Chairman (2001–3) and then Shadow Home Secretary (2003–5). Clarke had been an MP since 1970, a Minister and Cabinet Minister (1979–97). Cameron also had had the least media exposure. Table 3.2 shows the media mentions of the candidates in the eight selected news titles for the three years prior to the election period. Cameron's coverage was less than a quarter of that of Ken Clarke and less than a ninth of that of David Davis.

Accordingly, most journalists and MPs at the time concluded that Cameron could not win and Davis was likely to emerge victorious. Davis had the most media exposure, a clear lead amongst MPs, and was deemed to be ideologically closest to the mass of ordinary members who would cast the final ballot. Ken Clarke was the most popular amongst general voters and party members but he lacked strong support from fellow MPs and was unlikely to survive the first two parliamentary party ballots. In early September Cameron was only supported by 3 per cent of party members and less than 5 per cent of Conservative MPs (*Sunday Times*/YouGov, 04.09.05, *The Times*/Populus, 06.09.05).

However, everything appeared to change dramatically during the few days of the conference where all five candidates gave speeches. After a very well-received speech by Cameron on 4th October, and a poorly-received one by David Davis the next day, Cameron was suddenly catapulted out of obscurity to become the front-runner. Media coverage enthusiastically backed Cameron while criticising Davis. Between the conference speeches and the second MPs'

Table 3.2 Media exposure, in eight news titles, of the four lead candidates three years prior to, and during the campaign period (6th May 2002–21st October 2005)

	D. Cameron	D. Davis	K. Clarke	L. Fox
6.5.02–5.11.02	17	327	170	132
6.11.02–5.5.03	14	181	215	149
6.5.03–5.11.03	21	213	183	211
6.11.03–5.5.04	26	343	91	124
6.5.04–5.11.04	49	290	56	183
6.11.04–5.5.05	64	444	90	258
Total	**191**	**1798**	**805**	**1057**
6.5.05–21.10.05	524	561	424	279

ballot, two weeks later, 112 pieces in the papers were overtly supportive of Cameron and 52 overtly critical of Davis. By the time of the second ballot, on 20th October, Cameron had gained a strong lead amongst Conservative MPs and was clearly ahead in polls of public and party member opinion. For the next six weeks little changed and, on 6th December, Cameron won with more than two-thirds of the final vote. For many interviewees, who followed the election closely, the outcome was unexpectedly changed in a two day period:

> he was a million to one outsider really, I don't think he had a cat's chance in hell of winning. You know, he was a new kid, new boy and no one knew anything about him. He was a nobody. I mean his has been one of the most stunning political rises ever.
>
> (Tom Bradby, political editor)

Cameron versus Davis, the new versus the old

As argued here, Cameron's success was not as instant or mysterious as many believed. Nor was his rise, as many argue, simply down to sudden media interest and his telegenic appeal. While he lacked the obvious measures of political experience, party support and media exposure, he benefited from several less visible advantages. In fact, Cameron perfectly fitted the ideal profile typical of the new generation of professionalised UK politicians described above. After graduating in 1988, with an Oxford degree in PPE, he spent six years working closely with many of the Party's most senior leaders. This included stints at the CRD (Conservative Research Department), briefing and election strategy work for the Prime Minister John Major, then roles as a special adviser to Norman Lamont in the Treasury and Michael Howard in the Home Office (see Elliott and Hanning, 2007). In effect, although little known in the wider party, Cameron had worked in four of its key power centres and had established social capital at the highest political levels. Similarly, while lacking in media exposure, he had extensive experience in media, PR, and public affairs, and a long-established journalist network. This included media relations work with lobby journalists in his CRD and political adviser roles, and seven years as Head of Communications and then Director of Corporate Affairs at Carlton Communications (1994–2001), one of the dominant UK television companies of the 1990s.

Such networks and experiences proved instrumental to Cameron's advance. His connection to Howard, the 2005 party leader, was important as Howard clearly backed Cameron over Davis (mentioned in forty-four articles by twenty-five journalists in May and June). Howard immediately promoted Cameron and several key allies, such as George Osborne, to the Shadow Cabinet. In delaying the contest by several months he allowed time for Osborne and Cameron to develop their campaigns, wider party links, and media profiles. His core campaign team was drawn from similar party policy and media networks. It included several policy and campaign strategists from his CRD and adviser days (George Osborne, Oliver Letwin, Rachel Whetstone), experienced professional journalists (Ed Vaizey, Michael Gove and Boris Johnson), and Steve Hilton, a public relations expert who worked for Saatchi and Saatchi and on the Conservatives' winning 1992 election campaign. Several interviewees commented on these elements of Cameron's past as well as his present media knowledge and social networks.

Davis, in contrast to Cameron, had had a seventeen-year career in business and then worked his way up the party. He had been an MP for eighteen years, a junior minister for three years, then a senior party figure for four years. He was well known across the party. However, he did not have the policy, campaign and media experience of Cameron, was thought to be a weak public speaker and did not cultivate journalists contacts (Montgomery, 2006, Elliott and Hanning, 2007):

> You can definitely say that David Cameron was part of the media elite in a way that David Davis was not part of that elite. And Cameron was sort of media savvy, fresh faced.
>
> (Peter Oborne, journalist, commentator)

> There was a feeling among the media that they were being intimidated by certain members of the Davis leadership team … it all crystallised obviously around the conference when David made the speech.
>
> (Iain Dale, political blogger, Davis's campaign manager 2005)

Such differences directly influenced the campaign strategies of the two candidates, as relayed in the interview and content analysis data. Through the summer period, Cameron and his team proved to be more adept and active than any other group. David Davis got the most media coverage (561 articles) of the four candidates, followed by Cameron (524), Clarke (424), and Fox (279). However, when compared to the six-month pre-election period (see Table 3.2), it is Clarke and Cameron who have the most significant upward shifts in media exposure. Davis's total coverage for the campaign period was up by a quarter on the previous six months but Cameron had a nine-fold increase. Cameron and his allies were also the most proactive as news sources in terms of supplying information to journalists. Cameron, whether cited as a direct or indirect source, was the most active individual, with 121 source references. He wrote more articles and/or was the subject of an interview piece more than anyone else. Cameron's allies were cited more than any other candidate's, with 104 source references. Davis was personally cited 111 times and his allies 98 times. This activity by Cameron was clearly noticed by those who regularly reported political affairs:

> There had been a number of [Cameron] speeches that hadn't really made it onto the telly … of course, it informs our opinion … so a lot of journalists had been following his progress for quite a while, but hadn't really talked

about it much in their newspapers or on the telly because they hadn't had much of an opportunity.

(Daisy McAndrew, political editor)

Davis's campaign was focused on maintaining his strong support amongst back-bench MPs and appealing to traditional party members. He made little additional effort with lobby correspondents, something noted by some of the interviewees and in some press accounts of the time (e.g., Kavanagh, 28.05.05, Sylvester, 13.06.05, Jones and Helm, 7.10.05). In contrast, Cameron's individual presentation attempted to appeal to the wider electorate beyond the Conservative Party. He made several approaches to left-leaning journalists and publications, and consciously positioned himself as the 'heir to Blair'. All this was reflected in the content analysis. Some seventy articles drew comparisons between Cameron and Blair, with many likening David Cameron and George Osborne to the young Tony Blair and Gordon Brown. While being positioned as a moderniser from the centre-left of the party he offered little in the way of clear policy statements. Several interviewees, as well as much press coverage, regularly referred to him as 'policy-lite' in his public statements (see also Montgomery, 2006). The content analysis also recorded the audiences addressed or mentioned in articles. In Davis's case, sixty-seven pieces mention MPs, sixty-eight party members, but only nineteen general voters. For Cameron, twenty-seven mention MPs, sixty-four party members, and seventy-eight general voters.

Evidently, throughout the summer period, Cameron had done more than any other candidate to increase his levels of media exposure, journalist contact and positioning near the electoral centre ground. At the end of September, what he was still lacking was television exposure and public recognition. His ability to potentially establish a 'para-social relationship' (Horton and Wohl, 1993, see Chapter 6) with the wider public, party members and general voters beyond Westminster, had yet to be tested. Three particular events changed that and encouraged the relatively small parliamentary networks of Conservative MPs and journalists towards a Cameron endorsement. The first of these was Cameron's official campaign launch to journalists on 29th September. The launch was chosen especially to follow Davis's own launch earlier on the same day and contrasted strongly in its presentation and target audience. Days later, Cameron's impact on the elite group of lobby correspondents was becoming evident. William Rees-Mogg (02.10.05) wrote in the *Mail on Sunday* that 'Most journalists thought that David Cameron had a much better launch than David Davis. David Cameron has some of Blair's skills.' The launches were clearly remembered by several journalist interviewees who commented on them without prompting. As one recounted:

we went to David Davis' first, and it was in this traditional wood panelled room with lots of men in suits. David Davis is not intellectually self confident enough to take more than three questions. It was smug and presumptuous ...

And then we went down the road and we went into Cameron's launch, and they'd made some effort with the production and there it was nicely lit, nice stage, young people coming onto the stage saying this is why I support this man … They'd made the whole thing look like a brasserie … on comes Cameron, he talks without notes, and is intellectually and self confident enough to take virtually every question in the room. And everybody felt that difference.

(Gary Gibbon, political editor)

The second, significant event was a BBC *Newsnight* piece, broadcast on 3rd of October, the eve of Cameron's speech. In the piece, Frank Luntz, a political consultant, had organised a focus group of potential Conservative voters. Clips of the five candidates speaking in public were presented to the audience and David Cameron got the most favourable response. One week later, during the conference, the Cameron team sent round DVDs, which included this piece, to all Conservative MPs and several journalists. This in itself drew some favourable commentary (e.g., Hurst, 11.10.05, Aaronovitch, 04.10.05). The third event was the conference speeches where, once again, the mediated performance skills of the five candidates were going to be directly compared. In almost all newsprint and interview accounts, Cameron's speech was deemed to have made a strong impact but was not considered the best of the five. However, several stated that broadcast coverage was particularly enthusiastic about Cameron and fairly negative about Davis the next day.

Over a five-month period Cameron had drawn on his senior political and journalistic networks, and significant campaign, lobbying and media experience, to move from last to first amongst the candidates. The new Conservative political generation had usurped its older, more traditional rivals. The contrast in the profiles, abilities and appeals of the two candidates was summed up by David Blunkett MP:

David Davis did much better on the *Today Programme* that same day than David Cameron, but he undoubtedly flopped in his formal platform speech … And, therefore, the new benchmark was different to the old one. Instead of it being experience, knowledge, hands-on in Parliament, dealing with big issues, gravitas … the new benchmark [was] the presentable, the fresh, the new, the ability to ditch policy and image, and that became then the judgement that had to be made. So, it didn't just change perceptions about the two individuals, it changed the terms under which the leadership campaign had been run.

Conclusion

Cameron, in almost all ways, possesses the ideal profile of the modern, aspiring party leader. Young, white, male, an Oxbridge graduate with a PPE degree, lengthy policy, campaign, media and public relations experience, a network of contacts that includes party leaders and political journalists, and a willingness to adapt ideology to political circumstances. His experience, outlook and contacts fed through to his electoral strategy. The televised speeches, as well as less publicised earlier events, demonstrated that Cameron was far more capable than Davis of generating positive media coverage and gaining the support of centre ground and swing voters. Journalists and MPs picked this up and relayed it to watching party members.

Cameron has continued to campaign successfully and, at the time of writing, is on course to win the 2010 election. As with Tony Blair in 1997, Cameron's ideological motivations and long-term policy goals remain vague. There is nothing in this account that implies that Cameron is any more out of touch with ordinary citizens than any other party leader. But then, there is nothing in his profile or history to suggest that he has any experience or contacts beyond the elite political cadres that currently lead many parties: a wealthy background, Eton and Oxbridge education, and continuous employment within the party–media–public affairs sphere of UK politics.

Chapter 4

The production of policy and news
Liquid politics and the working cultures of the new capitalism

This chapter looks at the daily working practices of MPs, ministers and journalists as they are engaged in the production of legislation and news coverage. Despite their privileges and positions of power, in many ways they operate as skilled, professional 'wage labourers'. Therefore, the changing conditions of work in politics and media are likely to affect how MPs and journalists engage with their publics, and how they produce and report law. This chapter thus outlines two contrasting accounts of work in capitalist democracies and applies such descriptions to political actors.

As described below, like many other employees, journalists and politicians operate in restrictive, hierarchical environments, and are continually expected to be more productive with their time; i.e., to be more cost efficient and produce quantitatively more with less. At the same time, many aspects of what they produce are not quantifiable as they are oriented around human exchanges, information-gathering and public audience connection. Both, accordingly, try to have more human exchanges, and to learn, deliberate and write about more policy issues in an increasingly complex policy sphere. Over time, the expectations and demands have crept up, putting individual resources under strain. In trying to fulfil these increasingly elusive goals, politicians and journalists are adopting new working practices and technologies to cut corners; in effect, appearing to manage the unmanageable. This, in turn, affects information-gathering, understanding and expertise, and human interactions. Such activities are becoming transformed in practice. Thus, politician–citizen engagement, the policy process and political reporting are increasingly more 'liquid' than 'solid', more 'symbolic' than 'substantive', based on 'thin' rather than 'thick' social ties, built on 'flexibility' and 'abstraction' in place of 'craftsmanship' and 'specialist knowledge'. Such developments in turn have implications for the democratic process.

Politics and journalism: democratic ideals meet the iron cage and new cultures of capitalism

It is rare for critical accounts of politics and communication to investigate the working practices of politicians or to treat political actors as workers (not so rare with journalists in media sociology). After all, the 'political class' is considered to be an 'elite' who benefit from the maintenance of capitalist democracy. Status, financial reward and power come with their position. They regulate and legislate for the working lives of others. For a variety of reasons they choose to cooperate with, or are forcefully persuaded by, the powerful forces of capitalism, be it in the shape of free-market thought, vast global financial flows, or corporate CEOs and lobbyists. However, as argued here, such assumptions also miss a key point. Political actors, operating in contemporary, large, complex democracies, are also workers, albeit of a professional-managerial nature. They are 'wage labourers', with all that that entails. Thus their very working conditions affect their ability to represent citizens, engage with publics, and develop new policy and legislation. Regardless of external pressures and influences, or of personal democratic ideals and intentions, the circumstances of working life in politics matter to politics itself.

Two well-developed accounts of how organisational working practices in capitalist democracies guide individuals offer useful guidance here. The first was produced by Weber in his observations of German society around the start of the twentieth century. For Weber, bureaucracy, as a 'superior' form of social organisation, becomes adopted as a dominant feature of advanced social systems. Pyramid-shaped, hierarchical organisations develop, first in a country's military, and then in its commercial, state and welfare sectors. Everyone, from top to bottom, has a position, with identified skill sets and tasks, and moves up or down the established levels. Through such 'rationalised' forms of organisation the production of anything, material or cultural, can become more efficient, calculable, predictable and easier to manage. In time, bureaucracies come to follow their own self-sustaining logic whereby individual behaviours and outcomes are as much governed by the perpetuation of the organisation as by official organisational functions. Ultimately, bureaucracies turn even the most senior people within them into operational parts (Weber, 1948: 228): 'the professional bureaucrat is chained to his activity by his entire material and ideal existence. In the great majority of cases, he is only a single cog in an ever-moving mechanism.' As stated (see Chapter 3), Weber also conceived of the modern state and its governing professions as being increasingly directed by 'rationalisation' and the 'iron cage' of bureaucracy. Politicians, like every other profession, are prone to become 'professionals' operating in party and state bureaucracies.

Many core elements of the traditional 'iron cage' are to be found in contemporary commercial and public organisations of all sizes. For Ritzer (1998, 2004), although the structures and forms of labour have evolved considerably during the twentieth century, key elements of 'functional rationality' are ever present. Hierarchies, Fordist/Taylorist principles of 'scientific management', quantification, and control through non-human technologies continue to be applied. The aims are predictability and cost efficiency, regardless of whether the occupation is manual, white-collar or professional. Modern variations of

'McDonaldisation' are to be found across business, leisure, education, health, religion and, of course, politics and journalism.

A second, contrasting account of organised capitalism has focused on new forms of production and work as they developed from the 1970s onwards (Piore and Sabel, 1984, Boltanski and Chiapello, 2007). At this point capitalism appeared to have reached a political and commercial impasse. Fordist models of production, along with Keynesian economics and expanded welfare states, were deemed the problem. The newer, post-Fordist blueprint of firm management emphasised flexible, faster forms of production, rapid change and adaption, and centralised but flatter hierarchies. Major operations were increasingly sub-contracted out to smaller firms. Workers were persuaded of the changes by the enticements of consumer-oriented production, and by the 'new spirit of capitalism'. This emphasised creative autonomy for individuals and freedom from the old, rigid and repressive structures.

However, as Sennett (1998, 2006), Bauman (2000) and others have observed, one set of individual, iron cage-like restrictions have been replaced by another, more subtle set of controls. The impacts on individuals, firms and societies are very real but also more subtle and less quantifiable in nature. While the old Fordist hierarchies were repressive, they also gave individuals stability, set work identities and, above all, bestowed 'the gift of organised time'. Now, in many areas of working life, the qualities valued in individuals are those of speed, autonomy, 'potential', flexibility, change and adaption. These also mean that employees have greater job insecurity. They have to move jobs and learn new skills with greater frequency. There is no stability and no time to build up institutional experience, 'informal trust' or strong 'social ties' with others.

A common element in these accounts is the rise of the superficial and symbolic (or 'liquid') over the substantive and solid, in terms of social relations and production. As Sennett notes, there is a general weakening of direct social ties. Social relations take time and investment, make difficult management decisions more complicated, and are thus an impediment to the new flexible, ever-moving workforce. Similarly, 'institutional knowledge' and 'craftsmanship', being able to build up experience, skills and to develop something well, are discouraged. In Sennett's descriptions :

> The fragmentation of big institutions has left many people's lives in a frag-mented state: the places they work more resembling train stations than villages ... In a speeded-up institution, however, time-intensive learning becomes difficult. The pressures to produce results quickly are too intense ... so the work-place time-anxiety causes people to skim rather than to dwell.
>
> (Sennett, 2006: 2, 127)

But, at the same time, organisations have to continue to 'look beautiful' to passing investors and citizen-consumers. Companies, public institutions and individuals have to promote themselves and their products as both consistent and reliable, but also ever new and changing, as ordinary and universally appealing, yet also extraordinary (see also Boorstin, 1962, Horkheimer and Adorno, 1977, Wernick, 1991). Thus, greater efforts are expended in the promotional and symbolic aspects of human relations and production.

New information and communication technologies (ICTs) are another common feature of this literature. For technology has enabled and facilitated new forms of rationalisation and market flexibility. ICTs offer greater predictability, cost efficiency, flexibility, quantification, alternative hierarchical management schemes, organisational expansion and forms of non-human control of human activity. Anonymous, computer-mediated transactions are more cost efficient than personal relationships. As Ritzer, for example, states (1998: vii): 'McDonaldization involves an increase in efficiency, predictability, calculability and control through the substitution of non-human for human technology.'

These issues also affect those at the top who, in turn, have to accommodate a variety of alternative bosses, from anonymous international investors to auditors and consumer-citizens. They must themselves appear to be flexible, adaptable, more productive, offer constant change and 'new' ideas. Part of this involves an increasing tendency to employ outside business consultants (Burnham, 2001, Sennett, 2006, Hay, 2007). Such consultants know nothing of the core business or its employees, but are regularly brought in to restructure and promote the institution according to abstract economic and management ideas. Such changes mean that those in official power, politicians and CEOs, live more 'nomadic' existences as they rapidly change position, and also, that power is given up to an array of external, unaccountable experts and organisations. For Sennett (2006), by such means, power becomes disconnected from legitimate authority in contemporary hierarchies. For Bauman (2000: 150) there are no centres of corporate control or stable leaders for workers to focus on: 'capital travels light with no more than cabin luggage ... That new attribute of volatility has made all engagement, and particularly stable engagement, redundant and unwise at the same time.'

Thus, the successful professional, operating in 'the culture of the new capitalism', needs to be: technically proficient, flexible and adaptable, able to learn new skills, regularly change to new work environments, able to sustain weaker social ties, seen to increase personal and organisational productivity, and be able to promote oneself and one's products. As argued below, each of these elements, tied to rationalisation and marketisation, can be found within the professions of journalism and politics. Such personal abilities are not likely to be strengthening the communicative ties between politicians and journalists or between these professions and their publics. Instead, while news outputs, policy production and public political engagement each become quantitatively greater and more 'productive', so they are also becoming 'thinner', 'short-term' in horizon, based on superficial knowledge bases, and more 'symbolic'.

The occupational pressures of politics and journalism: the political and journalistic iron cages of the twenty-firstcentury

Politicians, ministers and the policy process

The occupational structures within which MPs and ministers work have elements of both the old centralised bureaucracies and the new working cultures of capitalism. On the one hand, many elements of political working life are ordered and directed by institutions. Parliamentary parties have become rigidly controlled through their central leaderships. MPs are strictly monitored by the party whips and records kept of each individual, their votes and other activities. Rewards, such as select committee appointments and promotions, are tied to party loyalty. The overriding impression, gained from interviewing politicians, is one of constant pressure to keep up with a fast-moving timetable and sequence of tasks. The majority of these on-site interviews were sandwiched between other appointments. They were frequently interrupted by urgent calls, text messages, calls to vote, and assistants looking for instruction or ushering the interviewee to the next appointment.

However, in many other ways, the work of politicians mirrors those professionals operating in the new, flexible firm. Occupational security is low and, in many cases, lasts only one or two electoral cycles. MPs are constantly moving between their constituency, parliament, and other placements. They have at least six constrating groups they have to engage with: home constituents, the parliamentary party, local party members/workers and personal assistants, funders and allied interests, interest group representatives and think tanks, and journalists. Their occupations involve: rapid information collection in a diversity of subject areas, multiple contacts and exchanges with others, information summaries and presentations, evaluations and decision-making points. In effect, the majority of their time is taken up by human exchanges and information collection on a series of non-linear tasks. Thus, political life is fleeting, nomadic, insecure, multi-task oriented, flexible and encourages the development of numerous weak social ties.

Like much of professional life, personal expectations continue to rise. This means, in effect, more human exchanges and information-gathering on a wider range of topics. The average MP has over 90,000 constituents they may potentially have to deal with. Conversely, party membership is roughly a fifth of what it was in the 1960s and local party support structures have declined accordingly (see Webb and Farrell, 1999). Parliamentary existence is busier still. In 2004–5, MPs had to deliberate and vote on forty-four government bills (ninety-five Private Members' bills were also submitted), to which 7,668 new amendments and clauses were tabled. There were 421 standing committee meetings to discuss these and 1,286 Select Committee meetings, producing 190 reports. Many MPs were also a member of one or more of the 303 all-party groups and 116 country groups (Norton, 2007: 436). An average of sixteen EDMs (Early Day

Motions) were tabled each day and drew over 100,000 signatures (over 150 per MP) in total (all figs. HoC, July 2005). The sense of overload and strain was clearly apparent. All MPs admitted to being inundated with information and requests from constituents, interest groups, officials, colleagues and their party. Many struggled to keep up:

> I'm quite astonished at people who seem surprised when they ask me to do something on a Tuesday evening, and I say 'Look, I'm sorry I can't because I've got to be in Westminster, Parliament's sitting that evening' ... We all run surgeries, fine, and we all do case work, but it's taking over our offices to a degree that we're starting to shut out the politics. So you cease to be a politician, and you start to be a grossly overpaid advice worker.
>
> (Neil Gerrard MP)

> It's sharp end stuff ... For MPs, of course, day one, they've got their pile of post unopened waiting for them to wade through, with no office, no secretary, and then expected to make their maiden speech, if they're a Liberal Democrat, probably appointed at the Front Bench.
>
> (Rob Clements, HoC Official)

The range of parliamentary topics addressed was extremely diverse. With the rising complexities of the 'multi-dimensional policy space' politicians are having to be increasingly flexible in learning about issues, developing and delivering policy solutions, and evaluating alternatives (Webb, 2000, Dalton, 2004, Hay, 2007). Several MPs admitted that they couldn't engage meaningfully with the large majority of the issues and legislation passing through Parliament:

> maybe there's 80 new laws a year and another 200 statutory instruments, and I would guess that out of those you can only ever possibly know really the ins and outs of ten in one year.
>
> (Chris Bryant MP)

> I think the world is faster moving, the expectations are higher ... the Terrorism Bill, we only had 24 hours notice, and we still produced a document of this kind of scale ... We've got an absolutely colossal programme this session. Maybe it's a one off, but governments of all persuasions are quite keen to legislate, and parliamentarians are getting more involved in all kinds of things.
>
> (John Pullinger, HoC Official)

Media, new and old, are also contributing to these rising pressures. There are many benefits brought to MPs by use of ICTs (see Chapter 7). However, ICTs also appear to be increasing expectations, demands, and forms of subtle control. With improvements in transport and communication, MPs are now expected to make more media appearances, travel to their constituencies with greater frequency, and electronically engage with the public more often. All of which means more information to digest, expanded 24-hour and online news media coverage to deal with, and more human interaction; all with no extra resources. MPs are also easier to observe, audit and evaluate by party whips, journalists, interest groups and constituents, each using new media.

Such demands and expectations increased significantly again at ministerial and Cabinet level. Information flows, human exchanges and decision-making processes all multiplied. Politicians were expected to continue dealing with their constituency loads, and attend party and parliamentary meetings, but now also had to take charge of a government (sub) department and make many media appearances. Former Cabinet Ministers frequently mentioned the impossible pressures brought by their positions. Such pressures were echoed by the officials who worked with them:

> It's a real problem, 24 hour news … the department's got five ministers who've been doing different media outlets for fifteen hours that day. The fact is that you don't want to do *Radio Five Live*, between midnight and 2 a.m. as, for heaven's sake, you've been up doing the *Today Programme* from 6 a.m. that morning. It's not surprising.
>
> (Baroness Estelle Morris, former Cabinet Minister)

> They work incredibly hard, ministers. It must be one of the most demanding possible jobs because they just don't stop. Most of them get in pretty early … Then they've got the parliamentary business, political party business, constituency business. And ministers will then go home at night, most of them with a couple of red boxes full.
>
> (John Sills, civil servant)

The speed at which senior officials and ministers move positions appears quite disconcerting. Civil servants and ministers now move on quicker, either upwards or sideways. The average length of time of a Cabinet appointment in the post-war years is approximately two and a half years. In the years of New Labour, the turnover of Cabinet Ministers has got quicker with each term. Since the last election, in May 2005, the average Cabinet post has been just over fifteen months. In twelve years of New Labour (1997–2009) there have been just two Prime Ministers and two Chancellors. However, there have also been six Home Secretaries and Defence Secretaries, eight people in charge of Trade and Industry/Business Enterprise, nine in Work and Pensions, and ten in Transport. Certain individuals have rotated through several Cabinet posts on an almost annual basis. David Miliband had three posts in four years, Peter Hain, five in six years, Alan Johnson, five in five years, Ruth Kelly, six in seven years, and John Reid, seven in seven years. It stands to reason that individuals cannot master such large, complex policy areas in these short spaces of time, let

Table 4.1 Number of Cabinet posts during Labour Government (May 1997–Nov 2009, 150 months)

Department	Chancel	Hm Sec	Forei Sec	Health Sec	Educ S	Transp S	Def Sec
No. of post s 1997–	2	6	4	6	6	10	6
Av. post (months)	75	25	37.5	25	25	15	25
No. since May 05	2	4	3	3	3	4	3
Av. post (months)	27	13.5	18	18	18	13.5	18

Department	Trade/Ind	Treas Sec	Work/Pen	Cult/Med/Sp	Scotland	Wales	N. Ireland
No. of posts 1997–	8	6	9	5	7	6	6
Av. post (months)	18.8	25	16.7	30	21.4	25	25
No. since May 05	4	4	5	4	4	3	2
Av. post (months)	13.5	13.5	10.8	13.5	13.5	18	27

alone manage day-to-day affairs, produce new evaluations, consultations and legislation:

> if anything has suffered, I suspect, in the electronic age, it's probably corporate memory ... I've been here eight years which is very unusual ... there's no one who's been doing Iraq for more than two or three years. I'm the only person ... it's just that the standard tour tends to be two to three years.
>
> (David Stevens, civil servant)

> People who know quite a lot about what they're doing suddenly shuffled into things they know nothing about, for no very good reason ... the numbers of DTI Ministers, the numbers of Europe Ministers for heaven's sake ... chucking Margaret [Hodge] out of Children's when she had created a policy, pushed it through, understood it totally, absolutely her field. 'There you are Margaret, time to get dumped into DWP' ... they [civil servants] just get randomly shuffled about in the same kind of way by heads of department. Knowledge, policy knowledge is undervalued.
>
> (Polly Toynbee, journalist, commentator)

The rapid turnover of executive members, coupled with the pace of media and communication, also encourages a quicker, unstable policy process. Each new appointee attempts to make a mark. The rapid movement of new ministers, policy ideas and legislation, all with short timetables to match, has meant a lack of time to consider, consult and scrutinise the passage of legislation. Indeed, Sennett (2006: 173–74) likened New Labour to a new 'high tech or advanced service business' which became a 'policy factory'.

Clearly politicians cannot come close to adequately fulfilling the ever-increasing demands placed upon them. They can only deal adequately with a limited number of constituent and interest group needs; only hope to gain a moderate understanding in a few of the many policy areas they talk publicly about and vote on; and, if a minister, are limited in the amount of meetings they can accommodate and material they can digest and think about.

Political journalists and news production

Political journalists, like politicians, have working lives that are governed by a mixture of Weberian-style bureaucracy and new, flexible news-making methods (see accounts in Fishman, 1980, Franklin, 2005). News production is very hierarchical, with clear reporting structures, output demands, and fixed deadlines. Journalists are all aware of their place in the Westminster reporting hierarchies, have a series of places and times marked on their 'beats', and are in regular contact with paper editors. As with politicians, my on-site interviews were sandwiched between other appointments and were frequently interrupted by urgent calls and text messages from editors, junior journalists and sources.

However, they are also skilled professionals operating as much outside as within the bureaucratic pyramid. Most of the time they stay within the geographical confines of Westminster. Yet they are frequently on the move, shifting between crowded shared offices, multiple reporting and briefing points, and arranged meeting venues. Their occupational lives are very similar to politicians in that they involve: rapid information collection in a diversity of subject areas, multiple contacts and exchanges with others, evaluations, information summaries and presentations (news texts and broadcasts). The majority of their time is thus also taken up by human exchanges, information collection and reporting in a series of non-linear tasks. Their industry is uncertain and insecure. In 2006 (NUJ, 2006) 31 per cent of journalists were part-time or worked 'flexible hours' and 41 per cent were 'freelance' (there is a large overlap between these groups). Thus, journalistic life can also be fleeting, insecure, nomadic, multi-task oriented, flexible and encouraging of multiple weak social ties.

Political reporting itself, like news journalism more generally, has suffered from the need to become more productive, rational and market-oriented. Over the last quarter of a century, the following trends can be observed with some consistency in the UK amongst other democracies. There is substantially more news space and more news producers than before but also greater competition and fragmentation with fewer consumers per outlet (Tunstall, 1996, Franklin, 1997, 2005, Curran and Seaton, 2003, Davies, 2008). Global competition, market segmentation and entertainment alternatives have meant a steady decline of audience figures and advertising revenues for most single, commercial news outlets. In an effort to remain competitive and profitable, producers have raised prices well above inflation, increased outputs and news sections while simultaneously cutting back on staff. They have also demanded more news copy and in less time from their journalists:

> the news media is highly competitive, it's much more marketised than it was, and there's a lot more of it, notably 24/7 television ... And all of this marketisation of society and technical transformation of communications are both pointed to the same direction: enormously more speed and the need to get your message across rapidly because if you don't somebody else will.
>
> (Michael White, political newspaper editor)

Tunstall (1996) estimated that, between the 1960s and 1990s, individual output had at least doubled. More recently, Davies (2008) concluded that journalists are now having to fill three times as much news space as they did in 1985. Such calculations may be over-estimates as it is difficult to work out how much the use of freelancers or new technologies has filled the gap. However, these and other accounts strongly suggest that more news is being produced more quickly, with far fewer human resources, and under poorer working conditions (see collection in Fenton, 2009). Critics have labelled the new end product 'Newszak' (Franklin, 1997), 'Infotainment' (Delli Carpini and Williams, 2001), 'junk-food journalism' (Ritzer, 2004) and, most recently, 'Churnalism' (Davies, 2008).

A large number of correspondents interviewed described their conditions in ways that tallied with this overview. Several recounted experiences of: job cuts and declining employment security, the hiring of cheaper, junior staff replacements, an increase in output demands, impossibly large amounts of information to gather and read and, above all, the relentless pace of the job. As with politicians, new ICTs, while bringing huge gains in research capacity and communication, had also added to the demands placed on journalists. New media both contributed to information overload and an expectation of more output per individual. Twenty-four-hour news channels and blogs required journalists to re-report in different formats, so reducing their story-producing resources:

> in the old days you had to get up in the morning and read all the newspapers, listen to the *Today Programme* ... Now, in addition to all of that, we also have to keep an eye on websites, blogs of others, just in case stories crop up ... As on the internet what we have to contend with is hugely increased sources of information.
>
> (Ben Brogan, political newspaper editor)

Consequences for policy, news production and public exchange in the new cultures of capitalism

As stated above, the principal activities of both professions involve multiple and intense human exchanges, and regular information collection and production tasks. The problem is, in the organisational 'culture of the new capitalism', gaining a full understanding of a subject takes time, deliberation with others takes time, and human face-to-face interaction takes time. Time is precious. New organisational processes and media technologies are all seductive as a means of stretching time. They appear to enable more information collection and more individual exchanges. However, doing 'more' by such means also mutates those same activities into something quite different.

Politics and policy: pseudo knowledge, the loss of policy craftsmanship and symbolic public exchange

Politicians feel they have to build up minimal levels of policy knowledge on a range of subjects. They frequently need to engage with others, from constituents to journalists, and be able to account for their position and vote on a diverse list of topics. Overwhelmed by the information-gathering and human-interaction requirements of their job, they have adopted many practical solutions in order to cope. One of these is to rely on others (assistants, advisers, officials, the party) to summarise information for them and offer advice and direction. Another is to use conventional media reports or the internet to quickly brush up on a subject. In fact ICTs have made a significant impact on MP research capabilities here. However, in each case, there is a tendency to quickly skim a topic, to build up enough of an understanding to appear knowledgeable during these engagements:

> the MPs might be front bench spokesmen or backbenchers from all parties phoning up and saying look I'm on the radio in five minutes, can you bring me up to date on this … we try to meet deadlines, because Members forget that they've got a parliamentary question to the Prime Minister tomorrow, or they're appearing in committee the day after … And all the time, you know, the old joke, 'when do you want that'? 'I want it today', they laugh in a hollow way.
>
> (Rob Clements, HoC Director of Research)

In effect, these are methods which simply enable MPs to take on the appearance of expertise in an area. This is not substantive knowledge. It is a 'pseudo' (Boorstin, 1962) expertise, that offers a facsimile of technical knowledge and 'competence', enough for fleeting, temporary engagements; a soundbite-level of knowledge for a soundbite news culture. It also offers a false expectation that politicians know and are in charge:

[you are] trying to keep a very large number of issues on the boil simultaneously when you simply don't have the means to do so. The only way you can is if you essentially subcontract your judgement to other people ... I think it increasingly shows where people haven't got a deep understanding of the subject but they're simply parroting pre-prepared lines to take. But that, of course, will earn them more brownie points than people who genuinely try to give a serious answer, because usually serious answers have shades of grey within them rather than absolute black and white, and party managers rather prefer black and white.

(Nick Raynsford MP, former minister)

This loss of substantive policy knowledge and expertise does not just affect the information-gathering and knowledge bases of MPs. In a speeded up political environment, with more interactions, it is also clear that actual human exchanges must take on a new form. MPs cannot fully engage with all their constituents. So they rely on a mix of assistants, conventional and new media to do so for them. Mass media use, developing 'para-social' (Horton and Wohl, 1993) forms of public engagement, is obviously a productive means of symbolically communicating with many voters at the same time. New media also provides a further means of exchange and deliberation with citizens that bypasses normal time and space restrictions. However, the interviews suggested that new media use often made individual engagements weaker and more symbolic in nature too. Many MPs (see Chapter 7) thought that rising email demands meant that they personally could not fulfil the new contact expectations of constituents. Consequently, more constituency exchanges and case work then had to be dealt with by assistants rather than MPs, ironically, through the use of the politician's official email address and website.

The same forms of symbolic rather than substantive exchange occurred in terms of general public consultation and deliberation. Most MPs avoid placing online consultation mechanisms on their websites (Jackson and Lilleker, 2004). At the levels of government, real public dialogue and consultation is a time-consuming process. Although, many of those interviewed were enthusiastic about such processes they also questioned their efficiency and value for money. Such public exercises thus became more about demonstrating an institutional willingness to consult and listen, rather than a real consultation. Thus, the demands for time-efficiency encourage public engagements to be symbolic and promotional rather than substantive in nature (Edelman, 1964, Wernick, 1991):

the rise of email is a disaster for Members of Parliament ... to [continue to] cope with it we would have to employ staff to respond on our behalf, perversely making us more remote from our correspondents, while appearing to be more responsive.

(Peter Luff MP)

many a consultation has basically already decided the outcome by the time
you get to the formal public stage. It's a very strange government that
spends all its time saying 'I've no idea what I want to do in this area. I'm
having a public consultation. Here's all the ideas we can all think of. What
do you think?' I mean that's not how the Department's basically operated.

(David Rowlands, Permanent Secretary)

Clearly, politicians and ministers must appear to know more than they can and
must appear to have more human exchanges than is possible. They manage with
a series of short-cuts, assistants, media and new ICTs. However, in the process of
trying to manage through adopting new practices and technologies, the nature of
those human exchanges and knowledge bases is changing. They develop pseudo
expertise and competence, race through a weakly considered and scrutinised
policy process, and engage and consult in mediated and symbolic rather than
direct and substantive ways.

News production: pseudo knowledge, symbolic personal exchange, and the loss of journalist craftsmanship

Journalists too have had to present a professional veneer that hides the fact that,
most of the time, they cannot possibly produce the kind of journalism they aspire
to. Reporters, every day, must do instant research, gain an objective overview,
and locate a balanced set of reliable sources, on a diverse range of news topics.
Consequently, as media sociologists have observed (Tuchman, 1972, Gans,
1979, Fishman, 1980, Gandy, 1982, Schlesinger, 1987, Tiffen, 1989, Tunstall,
1996), a number of practices have developed for bridging the gap between
expectations and resource limitations. These include set beats, diary stories,
presentation of opinions rather than facts, the use of 'information subsidies', and
the recycling of news within and across formats. Many daily practices are no
more than short-cuts or proxy substitutes for what is required. However, as the
business model underpinning news journalism becomes more difficult to sustain,
so the journalistic iron cage has been further tightened (Davies, 2008, Fenton,
2009, Nichols and McChesney, 2009, Pew, 2009). The professional veneer is
retained in the presentation of news but rather less journalist 'craft' goes into the
production process.

One clear outcome is that journalists have less depth understanding and in
fewer subjects. Established news operations have cut back specialist reporters
in many 'political' subject areas such as industrial relations or international
affairs. Political lobby journalists are expected to cover a greater range of policy
topics. Since they cannot, they instead choose to report on personalities and
conflicts and/or develop temporary forms of pseudo knowledge on many subjects.
Once again, new media has made such activities seem much more achievable. It
is easier to find quick information sources online, monitor other news outlets and
cut and paste from web sites and other news reports. Thus, like politicians, there

is a greater dislocation between the 'pseudo expert' presentation and the increasingly ad hoc, under-researched and unreliably sourced nature of the production process:

> you see a big story breaking on the telly, and you look at the presenter, let's say on a 24-hour news channel. Yes you can see the presenters Googling as they're broadcasting, because they're thinking you know 'shit, Denis Healey, what did he do?' It gives you that thing, and that could be quite dangerous because the web is not a hundred per cent accurate … when you're under those time constraints, the internet is fabulous but it's dangerous as well.
>
> (Daisy McAndrew, political broadcast editor)

Another noticeable trend coming out of the interviews was how much less direct human contact there was between journalists and politicians. Physical movement is time-consuming and general forays into Parliament, which do not have a direct story purpose, are risky. Likewise, senior politicians do not have time to stop for impromptu discussions with passing journalists. Several interviewees on both sides commented on how daily 'lobby' exchanges, a traditional means of newsgathering, were now fairly rare. Instead, journalists pieced together politician-centred stories from website materials and quick mobile conversations. High-level meetings were still arranged but the smaller, multiple, chance interactions were far less:

> They [journalists] don't even try to talk to you, they just watch breaking news upstairs. I pass them every day when I come in. I pass one of the rooms and I see them watching telly and they're banging away on the typewriters, all of them … [before] it would be rare for that Lobby not to include some journalists, and sometimes it could be as many as ten or a dozen or twenty. Now, the only people you see in the Lobby are the fellas in the fancy breeches looking after the place.
>
> (Dennis Skinner MP)

> In the past they [MPs] would have been hanging around, well mainly then in the Members' Lobby or the adjacent areas. Now though, after a vote … they're going back worrying about decisions. It's more individualised, compartmentalised … the ones on front benches, they're much more likely to be going back to their office to work on something.
>
> (Peter Riddle, journalist, commentator)

There was also a sense in interviews that the act of crafting news stories had changed. Stories, more than ever, were generated from political PR handouts, watching other news media, or tracking rival journalists and following the pack. Rising pressures on journalists, to be both time-efficient and not lose out on the big stories, means an ever-greater emphasis on staying at one's desk, and monitoring others. Instead of covering unfolding events, the emphasis has moved to the micro-level politics behind the events, or second guessing future developments:

> Yesterday morning's papers had this grand announcement but the grand announcement is today. Well what's the bleeding point of that? … Newspapers are constantly trying to anticipate policy and have it the day before. But it means they have half the policy, they don't have the whole thing. And then when it comes round to the next day, and the formal announcement's been made, and there's a bloody great document in front of you which you can analyse in detail, they don't cover it because they say we did that the day before. And there's this ludicrous competition between papers that's misleading the readers.
>
> (Gary Gibbon, political broadcast editor)

Ultimately, news stories are still written and imparted with the same author-itative style as before; the same sense of an issue investigated, researched and sourced, and then 'expertly' presented. However, the production processes behind the presentation are far from authoritative. 'Pseudo expertise' rather than depth understanding informs the output. A variety of information subsidies – gifted, purchased or stolen – have been utilised to paper over the ever-larger resource cracks that journalists struggle with. The communicative ties between journalists and a few key politicians remain (see Chapter 5), but are weaker in terms of direct, personal exchanges with MPs generally. Following the herd, cut and pasting PR material or part of a rival's copy, and guessing the future, are all too easy to do. They replace the need for journalistic craftsmanship. These devel-opments are significant because many publicly-reported insights on politics emerge from scrutiny of documents, a depth knowledge of policy fields, and close journalist-source relationships.

Conclusion

In many studies of politics, journalism and democracy, politicians and reporters are themselves held to blame. They are portrayed as lazy, greedy, sleazy and untrustworthy. Indeed, they regularly come at the bottom of polls of professions that people trust (Ipsos-MORI, 1983–2009). This rarely appeared to be the case during my interviews and observations. Indeed, most of those I met appeared to work exceptionally hard and to support core democratic ideals. The less they managed to fulfil them the harder they tried (see also Cowley, 2002, Hay, 2007).

As argued here, the nature of their modern working conditions means that politicians and journalists can never achieve what they or the public expect of them. Political and journalist life is fleeting, nomadic, flexible, multi-task orien-ted, and encourages multiple weak social ties. Their work revolves pre-dominantly around human exchanges and gathering information with a view to reporting and/or making decisive evaluations of political issues. As they have been driven to become ever more productive in these tasks so they have found new intermediaries, practices and technologies to help them. Adopting such means has both assisted and altered their relations, practices and core 'crafts'. The shifts identified here are: the gathering of 'pseudo' rather than substantive forms of expertise, many weak social ties and thin forms of communication and human exchange, speeded-up policy and reporting procedures, and symbolic and promotional exchanges and presentations. All of which, rather imperceptibly, erodes key components of the democratic process.

Chapter 5

Journalist–source relations, mediated reflexivity and the politics of politics

Introduction

This chapter focuses on relations between political reporters and politicians. How the two relate has come to be recognised as a key part of the debate on the news media's effective functioning in democratic societies. The nature of such reporter–source exchanges clearly has a significant influence on the shape of news content and thus public understanding of politics.

Observation and discussion of such relations has most commonly revolved around two analytical paradigms: the first, the *adversarial-exchange* line, has conceived the core issue as one of relative power in which the autonomy of the journalist and 'fourth estate' media is investigated vis-à-vis their sources. If sources are too powerful they undermine media autonomy. The second line is an investigation of *pluralist source conflict*. This seeks to compare how a range of sources seek to gain a media platform for their views and whether news media adequately reflects pluralist opinion in politics and society. Both lines are essentially concerned with how media–source social relations affect news outputs and, consequently, citizens' understanding of politics and society. This chapter, as well as exploring these interpretive paradigms and debates, attempts to develop a third line of observation, discussion and enquiry. This argues that, in the parliamentary political sphere, such journalist–politician relations also play a key role in the *social construction of politics* itself. Over time, reporters have come to act as information and interpretive intermediaries for politicians engaged in micro-level politics. This has further implications for assessing journalism's impact on the democratic process.

When investigating the UK case example, many MP and journalist interviewees confirmed the continuing significance of the first two paradigms and their associated normative concerns. At the same time, responses, especially at the senior level, also suggested that relations played an important part in the 'social construction of politics' itself. Relations and objectives are not simply about exchange or conflict but, also, have steadily become institutionalised, intense and subject to a form of 'mediated reflexivity'. As a result, they have come to serve a number of other cognitive and behavioural functions for political actors operating at the heart of the political process. Politicians, when talking to journalists, in addition to seeking publicity, also try to influence political agendas, convey messages to others and/or pick up multiple forms of useful information. These include knowledge about party rivals and opponents, political moods and points of consensus, and shifting levels of support for political factions and policies. Journalists, consciously or not, have come to play a role in the politics of politics itself.

Journalist–source relations: three lines of enquiry and normative evaluation

The adversarial-exchange and pluralist source conflict frameworks

Media–source relations have been investigated most frequently within the interpretive framework of the 'adversarial-exchange' paradigm. This has looked directly at issues of control and power when journalists and sources meet and, accordingly, how such shifting relations are reflected in news outputs. Politicians seek favourable media coverage by attempting to manage reporters. This objective clashes with 'fourth estate' professional norms which, in the Anglo-American tradition, stress the need for journalist autonomy and a neutral, oppositional stance that holds powerful sources to account. Such antithetical relations have featured in many post-war journalist and 'spin doctor' accounts (Maltese, 1994, Jones, 1995, 2002, Klein, 1996, Gaber, 1998, Kurtz, 1998, Lloyd, 2004, Price, 2005, Woodward, 2006). For many media sociologists, however, the public image of media–source conflict is only part of the story. On a day-to-day basis the relationship is one of uneasy exchange and reliance. Both sides need each other but pursue alternative professional objectives (Ericson et al., 1989, Hallin, 1994, Schlesinger and Tumber, 1994, Blumler and Gurevitch, 1995, Palmer, 2000, Schudson, 2003). Politicians need publicity and journalists need high-level access and story information. Since both sides need to cooperate to fulfil their goals, an ongoing 'tug of war' or 'tango dance' (Gans, 1979) takes place with control shifting from one side to the other. Reporting fluctuates, becoming more compliant or more critical of governments, accordingly.

Consequently, the question of general control has shifted to ask: which side is in control more often and why? In many studies the conclusion is that sources are. As Sigal (1973) pointed out it is political sources which instigate the large majority of stories. This is something confirmed in many studies of political news production across a variety of media systems, from the US, UK and Australia (Glasgow University Media Group, 1976, Tiffen, 1989, Lance Bennett, 1990, 2003, Entman, 2004, Lewis et al., 2008) to Israel, France and Sweden (Darras, 2005, Reich, 2006, Stromback and Nord, 2006). There are several explanations given for this. 'Beat' reporters become dependent on the regular supply of information subsidies supplied by institutional sources (Fishman, 1980,

Gandy, 1982, Tiffen, 1989, Franklin, 1997). Accompanying this institutionalised dependency are a host of other powerful source means of applying pressure, such as controlling access, 'flak', 'spin', 'pseudo events', legal threats and 'embedded journalism' (see variously, Boorstin, 1962, Barnett and Gaber, 2001, Herman and Chomsky, 2002, Miller, 2004). The post-war expansion of the public relations industry, employed predominantly by powerful sources, as well as the professionalisation of party communication, has further weighted the tug of war in favour of sources (Nelson, 1989, Ewen, 1996, Swanson and Mancini, 1996, Davis, 2002, Lewis et al., 2008). Sources, whether by fostering reporter information dependency or more covert means, have more often gained the upper hand and forced journalists into the role of 'secondary definers' (Hall et al., 1978).

However, several accounts question the degree of control sources actually have, with a sizeable group suggesting that journalists and news logics may increasingly be taking control. News values or 'schema', deadlines, and ratings pressures, all serve to limit and shape what journalists take up and how they frame their stories, and often to the detriment of sources (Ericson et al., 1989, Tiffen, 1989, Patterson, 1994, Palmer, 2000). For some (Reich, 2006, Stromback and Nord, 2006), although sources may initially supply information, journalists then take over in terms of following up the story and the final packaging of the raw material. As Esser (2008) noted, the presentation of broadcast journalist reports in France, Britain, Germany and the US means that journalist narrations outweigh political voices by three to one. For others this means sources are increasingly bending to the will of 'media logic' (Altheide and Snow, 1979, Meyer, 2002). The post-war period has indeed been characterised by the rise of soundbite, negative and adversarial reporting of politicians (Hallin, 1994, Patterson, 1994, Esser, 2008). Finally, the damage done to powerful sources, by revelatory pieces and/or the media pack, can rapidly bring down a powerful source, party or organisation (Tiffen, 1999, Palmer, 2000, Thompson, 2000).

The second interpretive model, used to assess the journalist–source relationship in democracies, might be termed the 'pluralist source conflict' paradigm. Whether or not sources have ascendancy, a healthy public media should reflect a wide plurality of opinions and voices and not simply reinforce one-sided source agendas and discursive frameworks.

What has rarely been in doubt is the fact that elite sources dominate the reporting of political as well as most other news sectors. The question is does this necessarily result in a narrow set of sources and content dominating reporting? Earlier, critical accounts argued that it did (Glasgow University Media Group, 1976, 1980, Hall et al., 1978, Fishman, 1980, Gandy, 1982, Miller, 1994, Herman and Chomsky, 2002 [1988]). News reporting reflects the fact that government elite sources, regardless of their differences, work within an ideologically-limited space that constrains political interpretation, story framing and policy choice. At the same time such sources have a range of economic, organisational, cultural and symbolic advantages. These mean that they can continue to be the major suppliers of news material as well as being reported with greater legitimacy and authority.

However, more recent work, while confirming the strength of institutional elite source power, has also reassessed the implications of this. For many, political elites may dominate but pluralist elite competition also features strongly. For Cook (1998) and Davis (2003) such mediated inter-elite conflict has in fact become an institutional feature of political reporting in the US and UK. Politicians leak information, raise policy issues and 'fly kites' in order to undermine and attack opponents at an individual and policy level (Tunstall, 1996, Cook, 1998, Davis, 2003, see also Flynn, 2006, on the Australian example). Such inter-elite conflict is in fact judged to be a key factor affecting the status of such sources and the breadth of opinions sought by reporters. For Lance Bennett (1990), Hallin (1994) and Entman (2004) in the US, in their alternative assessments of reporting of Watergate, Vietnam and other US conflicts, have produced quite fluid accounts based on this. If elites achieve broad consensus then that is reflected in narrow patterns of source reporting. However, when significant elite source differences arise, often as a result of wider social and political events, reporters present a wider spectrum of views and seek out alternative voices beyond the political centre. As Hallin (1994) puts it, the degree of political elite conflict on an issue dictates whether it becomes reported within a media frame of 'consensus' or 'legitimate controversy', or is ignored altogether, being categorised as 'illegitimate political activity'. For several UK scholars (Deacon and Golding, 1994, Schlesinger and Tumber, 1994, Miller et al., 1998, Davis, 2002) elite conflict is frequently reflected in the news media and the 'primary definer' status of such sources fluctuates considerably. On such occasions politicians and their organisations are subject to a loss of legitimacy and credibility to the extent that non-elite sources, such as trades unions and NGOs, may fill the gap (see also Anderson, 1997, and collections in Hansen, 1993, Cottle, 2003).

Beyond the Anglo-American model it is also clear that in many states journalists remain too close to their sources but do so in a system that encourages diversity (Donsbach and Patterson, 2004, Hallin and Mancini, 2004). In several Southern European countries, such as France and Italy, there has been a high degree of 'party–press parallelism', with journalists and politicians closely linked and a strong journalist advocacy tradition (see also Mancini, 1991, Chalaby, 1998). In some Northern European countries, such as Sweden, Norway and Austria, diverse media source representation has been institutionally and economically supported through regulation and subsidies (Sandford, 1997, Murshetz, 1998). In many emerging democracies, such as Mexico or Russia, 'patron-based' or 'clientalist' relationships between journalists and sources are common (Benavides, 2000, Roudakova, 2008); although it should be noted that these are far from balanced, pluralist systems (see Freedom House, 2009). None of these studies would challenge the idea of elite source dominance but, at the same time, each observes that there are occasions when source–media relations do open up and a greater breadth of opinions is reproduced.

Journalist–source relations: mediated reflexivity and the social construction of politics

A third interpretive model, one that is least developed in the media–source relations literature, might be termed the 'social construction of politics' paradigm. The concern here is with the impact of media–source relations on the behaviour of politicians and day-to-day politics within political institutions. In this case, such relations affect democracies because they influence the political centre which, in turn, influences wider society. Several studies have touched on this question hypothetically or tangentially as part of other investigations. These findings, together, contribute to the following speculative account of the part played by journalists in the social sphere of politics.

The 'social construction of politics' paradigm begins by focusing on the social circumstances of the political space in which politicians operate. As Hilgartner and Bosk (1988) reflect, social problems do not simply emerge in general society or out of public opinion. They are 'collectively defined' (Blumler, 1971), usually within specific 'social arenas' including the executive and legislative branches of government. Parliaments tend to be contained within confined social spaces where high levels of personal exchange take place between political actors (politicians, advisers, bureaucrats, journalists and others). Politicians, working in any legislative assembly, are continually engaged in numerous information-gathering and decision-making processes, linked to both policy and internal politics. These include: prioritising daily and long-term policy agendas, identifying political problems and optional responses, setting out and voting on appropriate legislation. These all require that party, constituency and personal career needs are balanced and calculated. All these social processes are indivisible from micro-level politics as they involve negotiating with, and having impacts on, others within the political arena. Social relations thus continually contribute to a series of parallel 'policy networks', political networks and 'epistemic communities' (Haas, 1992). These, through dialogue, exchange and conflict, attempt to locate solutions to policy and internal political issues. In effect, politics in a specified political institutional arena is all about the 'social construction' and negotiation of political agendas, outcomes and hierarchies.

Second, as argued here, political journalists are no longer to be simply regarded as external outsiders who come and go. In many systems, political reporting has become virtually institutionalised and therefore very much part of the social arenas of parliaments and governments. For example, in the White House, on Capitol Hill and in Westminster, journalists have on-site offices, share social facilities with politicians, and have organised political access and regular information supply. Many tend to remain in post for lengthy periods and a significant proportion have been there longer than the average legislator (see accounts in

Fishman, 1980, Hess, 1984, Tunstall, 1996, Barnett and Gaber, 2001, Bennett, 2003). Under such circumstances, journalists become daily presences in legislative assemblies, and journalist–politician exchanges and relations take on a greater social significance. Accordingly, in their regular exchanges, the two sides become intensely 'reflexive' (see Giddens, 1991 and Beck, 1994) in their behaviour towards the other. As the two sides know more about 'the other' so they adapt and find additional uses for their exchanges, and seek greater benefits from their personal investment in these relations. The results are not just an ever-shifting 'tug of war' which results in the 'symbolic' construction of the political in the mass-mediated public sphere (Fishman, 1980, Manning, 2000, Cottle, 2003). They also potentially impact on the social and symbolic construction of the political arena itself. Journalists are thus likely to have become very much a part of the political and policy networks at the centres of legislative assemblies.

As some have observed, politicians, during their daily social interactions with journalists, do indeed make use of, and derive meanings out of, those exchanges. At one level, they utilise their journalist contacts and knowledge of news values and routines to raise issues, test ideas speculatively through the media, and during conflict with opponents. Most obviously, journalists and news content become tools for political conflict within the US and UK political arenas; a point illustrated across the 'pluralist source conflict' literature (see above). Three US studies (Cook et al., 1983, Protess et al., 1991, Baumgartner and Jones, 1993) in fact suggest that, in many cases, reporters are not simply passive reflectors of elite conflict. Politicians and journalists, either through regular dialogue or working in 'coalitions', jointly contribute to some issue agendas and policy debates.

At another level politicians also use these relations to make sense of the policy areas they have to deal with. Journalists may thus contribute to the information-gathering processes of politicians themselves. A few studies have noted how politicians do, at times, look to journalists to provide useful information of an 'expert' nature. Herbst (1998, see also Lewis et al., 2005) observed that political actors regarded correspondents as 'crystallisers of public opinion' on policy issues. Parsons (1989) recorded the importance of financial journalists in discussions on, and shifts in, economic policy. Kull and Ramsey (2000) noted that foreign affairs reporters had become very much part of the 'foreign policy community' that guided foreign policy.

Others have suggested that something rather less conscious, but also more substantive, takes place. Journalists potentially contribute to the shaping of social and cognitive frameworks which, in turn, influence agendas and set the parameters for understanding, dialogue and legislative outcomes. For Baumgartner and Jones (1993), media have fed into the 'policy subsystems' which define the available choice of legislative solutions available. The framing of an issue, such as smoking or the use of chemical pesticides, dictates how an issue is viewed politically and, consequently, if and what type of responses are required.

Cook's (1998) 'new institutionalism' approach argues that, as the three branches of government have become larger and more complex, so news media have come to play a vital intermediary part in cross-government exchanges. So institutionalised has this become that all sides contribute to the formation of a very specific 'bounded rationality'. This both constrains and enables individual politician choices and social patterns in and around the political centre (see alternative accounts in Patterson, 1994, Davis, 2007). Ultimately, not only do agendas and policies rise and fall, so do individuals and political factions. Thus, as Becker (1963) initially posited, and Hall et al. (1978) developed, a 'hierarchy of credibility', in which the 'primary definer' status of individual political actors and institutional positions, becomes established. This is not only via the media to wider society but, also, within the socio-political arena of a parliament.

In effect, it might be suggested that the journalist–source relationship potentially influences politicians and micro-level politics just as it does journalism and news production. Such relations are incorporated into the cognitive and behavioural processes of politicians. Reporters have become one key component of the social and cultural construction of the political centre and the business of politics itself. Thus, the researcher is once again led to ask, but from an alternative vantage point, what are the implications of media–source relations for public communication in democracies?

Journalist–source relations in UK politics

Adversarial-exchange and pluralist source conflict

The study findings here are based on semi-structured interviews with eighty (former) politicians and journalists. The interview material offered ample evidence with which to explore each of the three relationship models put forward. The first part will summarise the findings that support the 'adversarial-exchange' and 'pluralist source conflict' models. The next, larger part will flesh out, in greater detail, the third, 'social construction of politics' paradigm.

When asked directly about 'relations' per se, responses tended to draw out the common 'adversarial-exchange' description documented in many previous studies (Gans, 1979, Schlesinger and Tumber, 1994, Blumler and Gurevitch, 1995, Schudson, 2003). The predominant relationship here was between politicians and journalists working on the local news outlets of an MP's constituency. Most senior politicians (ministers, shadow ministers, committee chairs) were likely to have established additional close contacts with national political and specialist journalists. Over half the politicians asked about their 'relations with journalists', including eleven of the fourteen former Cabinet Ministers, described them very much in terms of a two-way exchange. When asked why they talked to journalists, four out of seven said they did so because they wanted to promote themselves, their party or particular committee, or specific policies to the public/their constituents. A majority of journalists offered a very similar summing-up of relations.

Just under half explained that they needed to make close contact in order to gain 'off-the-record' or behind-the-scenes material. Just under half spoke of the need to establish themselves within their own profession by gaining prestigious contacts and obtaining the kind of inside information that could lead to 'scoops'.

> It's a trade we're in, you know. So we are people pursuing different trades, but we exchange … self interested tradesmen is how I would say the relationship between a politician and a journalist is, and it requires trust, just as if you were doing a cash transaction with somebody for goods that are not actually determined until maybe days later when they appear in print.
>
> (Joe Murphy, political editor)

The adversarial nature of this exchange relationship also came out fairly often. For most interviewees the distinct professional identities of the two sides, and a sense of 'the other', were maintained. All were aware that such exchanges could be mutually beneficial but, equally, that they could bring the two sides into conflict. Thus the terms 'cautious', 'love–hate' and 'trust' came up frequently when describing associations. In fact, over half the journalists and two-fifths of politicians (over half the former ministers) used the word 'trust'. Journalists attempted to maintain 'friendly' or 'civil' relations and a third stated that being seen to be too close to certain politicians would compromise their professional standing with peers and other political sources. At the same time, most politicians, particularly ministers and shadow ministers, were fairly weary of journalists. They were thus likely, with a few individual exceptions, to mistrust reporters or express antagonism towards 'the media' and the 'journalist pack':

> The truth is journalists are out for one thing: a story. You know, they may be your friend, appear to be your friend today but tomorrow they may be cutting your throat because you happen to be the subject of a good story … at the end of the day you don't really have a relationship with a journalist. What you do is you establish basically a series of contacts, because if you have a relationship with someone then it has some obligations. This isn't really a relationship with obligations, it's a relationship with mutual usability.
>
> (Iain Duncan Smith MP, former party leader)

Overall, antagonism and mistrust seemed rather more common between journalists and Labour MPs (the party of government), thus further suggesting that reporters did see part of their function as holding government to account. Over a quarter of Labour MPs talked disdainfully of the media pack and a quarter stated that the news media, as a whole, bred cynicism about the political process more generally. Several said there had been a decline in the ethics and quality of journalism in recent years and several stated that, at times, the press operated unashamedly as an 'opposition'. In turn, half the reporters interviewed talked negatively of the rise of party media management techniques, particularly by the

Labour Government. Several stated that information release was more controlled and that access to ministers was increasingly restricted and monitored (see also accounts in Barnett and Gaber, 2001, Jones, 2002). Criticism of politicians was generally more likely to come from journalists employed in news outlets hostile to the Labour Government.

Thus, in many respects, the adversarial-exchange relationship still seemed the predominant one with journalists seeking to fulfil their fourth-estate professional roles. For most interviewees, most of the time, it was a relationship of cautious cooperation that benefited both sides. At the same time, antagonism and mistrust were common and either side were capable of, and frequently did, damage the other.

Much of the interview material also supported the 'pluralist source conflict' paradigm (Mancini, 1991, Cook, 1998, Davis, 2003). This model came across very clearly when MPs were asked, not about relations per se, but why they chose to talk to journalists. Just over half of the MPs given this question gave answers that suggested a common use of journalist contacts as part of a political strategy. Just under half of the MPs said they attempted to float stories to influence political debate and government policy. The same number said they talked to journalists to push particular views. Such a conflict model was backed up by journalist accounts. Seven of the lobby journalists said that political conflict, within and between individuals and parties, was a key reason MPs talked to them. A third of interviewees from both professions said that lobby reporting was, in line with editorial news values, more oriented towards conflicts and personal dramas.

The most obvious mediated conflict taking place was that between the leaderships of the main parties. However, many back-bench politicians attempted, either in the interests of their constituents or committees, to use their journalist contacts to raise issues and influence the general political agenda. Many MPs offered examples of campaigns they had attempted to use the media for and several reporters presented corresponding accounts:

> I mean one of the few tools in our armoury is publicity ... for example, on the election for the [Labour] Leader and Deputy Leader ... I went onto the Press Association, did a statement, I then telephoned the *Times*, *Telegraph*, *Independent*, *Guardian* and the *Sun* ... because I feel strongly about the thing, I'm going to try and influence it by giving a bit of oxygen.
>
> (Andrew MacKinlay MP)

> Certainly an MP who has a cause that they are trying to get onto the agenda, particularly if they're a backbencher, you will see them seeking to use the media to promote that cause and then action on it.
>
> (Adam Boulton, politcal editor)

However, such activity was most commonplace amongst experienced politicians with twelve of the sixteen (shadow) ministers talking to journalists for such purposes. Not only did senior politicians want to attack party oppositions or raise their own agendas, they often used lobby contacts to undermine other politicians and factions within their own party:

> I think it sometimes became more vicious, like the two courts rather than the two men, and all of it's done through kind of spinning to the media ... Gordon [Brown] never ever spoke in Cabinet to question anything. If there was an issue between Gordon and Tony [Blair] they would always, you know, you'd see it in the media or they'd resolve it individually.
>
> (Clare Short MP, former Cabinet Minister)

Although many politicians used their media contacts in such ways it was also clear that there were significant access inequalities which, consequently, affected the plurality of agendas and frames in play. Twenty interviewees overall talked about the hierarchies that formed and therefore influenced relations. This equated to ordinary back-bench MPs rarely having good access to senior national reporters. The other clear difference was between government ministers and their shadow oppositions. Government ministers had regular, structured access to journalists and, conversely, journalists were far more willing to talk to government than opposition ministers. Clearly, this could potentially restrict the plurality of opinions being reflected in political coverage (Bennett, 1990, Hallin, 1994), particularly if journalists considered the opposition to be weak or uninteresting. Shadow ministers often admitted that getting media attention was most easily achieved by exploiting populist news values which, in turn, could also be self-defeating:

> The relationship is very different in opposition. You want them, you need them. If you want to make news, make an impact, run a campaign, you need their support ... in Government some of the stuff you do is just newsworthy sort of stuff, whereas very little that people do in opposition is actually really newsworthy.
>
> (Frank Dobson MP, former Cabinet Minister)

The social construction of politics in the UK parliamentary sphere

Interviews and observation suggested that, in various ways, journalists have become very much part of the political social sphere at Westminster. Almost all the interviewees had office space on site. Several had been there for more than twenty years and had kept some of their political contacts from the start (see similar accounts in Tunstall, 1996, Barnett and Gaber, 2001). Almost all MPs interviewed also had a very high level of communication with journalists (local, regional and/or national). In all, just over two-thirds of MPs interviewed talked to journalists, on average, once a day. Several, especially senior politicians, might have several journalist conversations per day and, at busy periods, exchanges could be more than hourly. The other third, with two exceptions, talked to journalists once or a few times per week. Consequently, UK politician–reporter relations, regardless of their antagonisms, have evolved to become fairly institutionalised and socially integrated:

> We play football matches, cricket matches against MPs, so you get to know them sort of away from this place. There is a thing called the Parliamentary Golf Society ... working in the same building, being able to go into the members' lobby at certain times and talk to a minister face to face, rather than down the telephone, obviously does make it a different kind of relationship.
>
> (Philip Webster, political editor)

> Most of my colleagues are embedded journalists ... I think that the way in which lobby journalists become manifestations of the political system is quite disturbing.
>
> (Peter Oborne, journalist, commentator)

Over time, and with such levels of personal interaction, the two professions have become hugely knowledgeable about the other and this, in turn, has made relationships extremely reflexive. Just over four-fifths of MPs asked had had formal media training and/or previous experience in journalism or public relations/affairs. Many MP interviewees spoke about the ease of guessing future headlines and slants on the way issues and announcements would be covered. They appeared to have an extensive knowledge of specific publications, reporter routines and news values. Conversely, political journalists had an extensive knowledge of how Westminster, the parties and individual politicians operated:

> when I first came in [1997] ... understanding who was important and who wasn't, you know, who were the senior political editors and correspondents, and who ... needed to be talked to and worked with, and how quickly you needed to be on top of responding.
>
> (David Blunkett MP, former Cabinet Minister)

> I've known them [Gordon Brown and Tony Blair] for 23 years ... they know what to make of me, they know how to handle me, and also, vice versa ... they know where I come from and all that. And over that period you learn about their strengths and weaknesses too.
>
> (Peter Riddell, political commentator)

The combination of journalist institutionalisation, positional longevity, intense exchange and reflexivity, means that politicians have found several uses for their reporter contacts. In many cases, again primarily at the senior level, politicians are likely to actually seek specific presentational or policy advice from political correspondents. Seven reporters, almost all broadcasters, said that MPs and ministers had asked for information on the presentation of a policy or themselves. Certain experienced journalists were also sought out for actual policy advice with some considered to have an in-depth knowledge in key policy areas. Eight (shadow) ministers said they spoke to journalists because they wanted their 'expert' opinion. Eight of the journalists also said that (shadow) ministers had looked for policy advice from them (see related findings in the US in Patterson, 1994, Herbst, 1998, Kull and Ramsey, 2000). Advice was sought either on the basis of having close relations/'friendships' or as part of the professional exchange; i.e., story information for presentational advice rather than publicity:

> If X said 'how would it play in the media?' then I might well have an opinion on it in part because I'm probably trying to persuade them to give me the story ... You know 'If we did this, how would it play?' and I'm saying, 'Well why don't you do it via me?'
>
> (Nick Robinson, political editor)

> I certainly got to know in the course of my political life a good many of the *Financial Times* specialist correspondents, and usually valued their judgements ... somebody like Richard Norton-Taylor was an absolute mine of information about security services ... Somebody like Peter Hennessey was an absolute expert on Whitehall and the structure of government ... And I certainly listened to their views, and might modify my views in the light of their reactions.
>
> (Lord Robert Maclennan, former minister)

As also became clear in the interviews, politicians seek another significant type of 'expert' advice from journalists: knowledge of the micro-level politics of Westminster itself. In essence journalists spend much of their time collecting and exchanging information on 'the political', as opposed to policy, aspects of parliament. A majority of reporter interviewees spoke of the hothouse atmosphere of the lobby, where reporters constantly exchanged information and opinion as they shared facilities and attended briefings and political events. Half of the print journalists talked specifically about trying to gauge the 'political mood' or predominant 'narrative' on an issue or individual at the time. Conversely, several MPs described how there would be sudden bursts of reporter activity and exchange with politicians at key political junctures. Fourteen MPs, almost all Labour, commented on how, during higher-profile political conflict, journalists would move rapidly around trying to get quick opinions and quotes. This vox pop technique would frequently produce a perceived consensus on the politics of a policy or individual. Most of the print journalists spoke of the importance of the journalist 'pack', 'narrative' or 'mood' in influencing both journalism and politics at Westminster. Eleven politicians also spoke about the media pack or mood in similar terms. In effect, lobby journalists continually picked up and circulated information about multiple aspects of the political process itself. As such, they contributed to the rise and fall of political agendas, policies, individual politicians and political factions within the parliamentary political sphere:

> You know, ultimately Westminster is a giant marketplace for political information and political gossip and so we're constantly trading information and passing it on … there's a constant to and fro of information between journalists and politicians.
>
> (Ben Brogan, political editor)

> And people ask your opinion. You ask theirs, you say 'What do you think of this?' or 'What did you make of Blair, Blair's press conference? What did you make of that answer? What do you think?' … So you're constantly in conversation with people.
>
> (Michael White, political editor)

Individual politicians, in turn, sought out such politically-significant information from journalists. A third of the political reporters spoke about MPs and ministers seeking information on some aspect of the political process itself. Similarly, just under a third of politicians, when asked about why they talked to journalists, said they were seeking information about their party, the government or some aspect of Westminster politics. Reporters, who talked constantly to politicians and were experienced political observers, were considered to be good sources of information on the daily events and shifts inside parliament. This might be more general information for ordinary MPs or something more personally significant for (shadow) ministers:

> a 'journalist friend' … would telephone you and say 'So-and-so's stirring it up for you' or they might even say 'I had lunch with so-and-so today and he was singing your praises' … so you've got to steer from them. They were a sort of early-warning system … then you had to weigh that up.
>
> (Lord Cecil Parkinson, former Cabinet Minister)

> the media often know more about what's going on here than MPs do … often journalists will try and be clever and tease information out of you but generally they know stuff … and the reality is it's inevitable that you start becoming friendly and friends with journalists, and they share information.
>
> (Sadiq Khan MP)

At one level, this interaction, combined with actual news coverage, had a potential influence on the policy process. Twenty MPs, including thirteen (shadow) ministers, believed that journalists and the media had an impact on policy and legislative debates. Usually they amplified such political debates, forced greater speed of response and, on occasion, changed policy direction altogether.

> I mean there are certain things that are tipping points, and it's hard to say why … and in a way they're quite important for the policy too, because it's about, will the Government really hold to this line, or is this line tenable? … And so you're looking all the time at the mood, because policy doesn't just sit there in isolation.
>
> (Polly Toynbee, political journalist, commentator)

> the media can reveal what's going on in a policy debate, either before the Government would like it to be revealed or in a way that the Government prefers it not to be revealed. So they can reveal that there are disputes going on … and that can be important when you're coming up to a knife edge vote, and the Government is frantically trying to mollify its rebellious back benchers.
>
> (Danny Alexander MP)

Such conversations and exchanges also appeared to influence the rise and fall of individual (shadow) ministers and party leaders. Just under half the politicians asked, including ten of the sixteen (shadow) ministers, stated that journalists and the media had a role to play in the rise and fall of ministers and in leadership contests. Thirteen journalists also spoke of the role of the reporter network and/ or individual journalists in the movement of ministers. Eleven had similar views in relation to leadership elections. Consequently, journalists both reported on the politics of a policy or individual and, in addition, by circulating opinions and moods, had a role in those political outcomes too:

> you could be talking to, let's say at the moment, a Labour deputy leadership candidate, and the conversation, inevitably, because it's one of the things you're going to be reporting on, comes round to: 'What are their chances?' 'What are people going to be looking for in a deputy leadership candidate?' 'What's the best stance to have vis-à-vis Gordon Brown?' 'You've got to look like the sort of the person who's going to stand up to him.'
>
> (Gary Gibbon, political editor)

> when we had our great leadership crisis back with Iain Duncan Smith, which obviously ended in him losing a vote of confidence, the journalists would ask everybody all the time what they thought … every journo you spoke to, that was the first question they'd ask. And I suspect everybody said 'well, it's terrible, you know, he's going to have to go'. And even if they didn't say anything quite so brutal as that, then their whole body language would … So the journalists could tell and they were very good at reflecting the real mood of the Party.
>
> (Julie Kirkbride MP)

Conclusion

This chapter has identified three interpretive frameworks for investigating and assessing media–source relations in democracies; two established and one relatively under-theorised and researched. Each of these approaches is useful for observing and testing the health of public communication in democracies. The first, the 'adversarial-exchange' model, focuses on the question of journalist autonomy and the media's fourth estate role. The second, the 'pluralist source conflict' model, is concerned with the range of source positions being presented in the media. In the UK case example presented here there was much to support the findings of earlier studies and the continuing core significance of the questions they pose. Although personnel, technology and the 'rules of engagement' continue to shift, politician–journalist relations remain at the heart of political reporting and guided by the same overlapping but conflicting professional objectives. News outputs, in terms of objectivity, plurality and autonomy, fluctuate accordingly.

More interesting perhaps are the findings explored here within 'the social construction of politics' framework. This relates to the part journalists and reporter–MP relations play in the business of politics itself. Relationships are institutionalised, intense and reflexive as both sides have come to incorporate the other within their everyday thinking, decision-making and behaviour. Politicians have thus sought to use their relations for more than mere publicity. They have also attempted to make use of reporters as sources of information about policy, presentation and the micro-level politics of Westminster itself. As a result, journalists have themselves come to act, often inadvertently, as political sources, intermediaries and political actors.

Such findings have additional implications for the well-being of public communication. If journalists have become increasingly influential in their roles, such tendencies could be seen positively in terms of being an extension of news media's fourth estate role. They could also be forcing politicians to look beyond the confines of their self-referencing elite networks and encouraging pluralist diversity. On the other hand, as several point out, the professional and economic objectives of journalists may frequently diverge from public interest norms. Politicians may be setting agendas, choosing and promoting policy solutions and party representatives according to the news values and routines dictated by news producers (Hallin, 1994, Patterson, 1994, Street, 1997, Franklin, 1997, Delli Carpini and Williams, 2001, Meyer, 2002, Walgrave and van Aelst, 2006, and Chapters 4 and 6). Thus a 'media logic' may increasingly be dictating journalist behaviours, their relations with politicians and, consequently, political behaviour. Such influences on the political class may be as detrimental as they are beneficial.

Chapter 6

Celebrity politics, symbolic communication and media capital in the political field

Introduction

This chapter looks at the symbolic and cultural forms of communication between politicians and their publics. In complex, mass-mediated democracies, parties increasingly adopt the promotional qualities of brands, and politicians, likewise, the qualities of celebrities. Like brands and celebrities, parties and politicians must communicate with, and appeal to, large groups of consumer-citizens on a symbolic and psychological, as well as rational level. Politicians thus gain professional status, in part, according to how consumer-citizens actively respond to public representations of themselves. Consequently, the elevation of individual political actors to positions of power is increasingly linked to their ability to generate a positive public profile via mass media (see Chapter 3).

These links, between media, individual celebrity, and symbolic power, have been explored across many research terrains. These variously focus on the innate, charismatic qualities of individual leaders, the requirements of the popular media, the professional manufacture of public personas, and the cognitions and behaviours of semi-engaged citizens. This chapter attempts to develop an alternative means of investigating this phenomenon. It draws on the work of Pierre Bourdieu to develop the concept of 'media capital' and explores its application in the political field. Bourdieu provided a series of analytical tools with which to observe individuals, their movement within 'fields' and wider society, and their accumulation and deployment of cultural as well as economic resources. However, he never investigated the political and media fields using these research tools and did not himself develop the concept of media capital.

The first part of this chapter therefore engages with Bourdieu's writing and attempts to adapt several of his key terms to the topic. Building on this, the second part identifies four forms or components of media capital and the means of their accumulation: 'individualised' and 'institutionalised', 'internal' and 'external' to a field. The final part looks at media forms of capital in terms of their loss, volatility and longer-term influences on political fields. As this speculates, the increasing orientation of political actors towards accumulating unstable forms of media capital, in place of other forms of capital, has had a destabilising effect on the field of politics itself. The second and third parts draw on interview material with UK politicians and journalists to illustrate the discussion.

The rise of political celebrity and the turn to Bourdieu

The politician as public celebrity

The politician as appealing personality and celebrity is not a particularly new notion. Political 'history' is dotted with charismatic leaders who gained national popular support. However, in many modern, representative and mediated democracies, this aspect of political communication now appears almost institutionalised and systematic (see Swanson and Mancini, 1996, Corner and Pels, 2003, Stanyer and Wring, 2004). Several contemporary leaders, such as Vladimir Putin, Silvio Berlusconi and Nicholas Sarkozy, devote extensive resources to the cultivation and promotion of their public images to voters. In competitive presidential and majoritarian type systems, such as the UK and US, personalities often appear to be a more decisive factor in deciding election outcomes than policies and political records. Thus, the 'personal appeals' of Tony Blair and David Cameron are compared favourably to the 'technocratically gifted' but 'uncharismatic' Gordon Brown. Similarly, George W. Bush's personal appeal was earlier deemed significant in overcoming his more experienced Democratic opponents Al Gore and John Kerry.

The accounts and causes of this slow but systematic shift towards the symbolic in politics are varied. Many political (auto) biographies highlight the personal qualities and 'charismatic authority' (Weber, 1948) of successful party leaders. Political leaders rise to the top because they are psychologically superior to others (Mosca, 1939, Pareto, 1935) and because they are able to develop 'parasocial relationships' with their publics (Horton and Wohl, 1993). For others, personalities are necessary creations of political and media systems and, accordingly, are commodities produced by parties and the cultural industries. For several observers of politics (Heffernan, 2003, Crouch, 2004, Hay, 2007), parties have cast off their ideological orientations, and now compete on other levels for increasingly de-aligned and volatile electorates. Political marketing has thus developed to promote personalities over policies and ideas (Boorstin, 1962, Hall Jamieson, 1996, Franklin, 2004, Evans and Hesmondhalgh, 2005). The media, simultaneously, seeks celebrities and personal stories with which to engage their publics. They are therefore willing collaborators in the manufacture of celebrity politicians (Sparks and Tulloch, 2000, Turner, 2004, Evans and Hesmondhalgh, 2005). However such public images of legislators develop, positive public exposure bestows a symbolic power on individuals, to then be converted into political power. Continuing media coverage confers political legitimacy, or a 'primary definer' status, on those already in positions of power. It serves to 'consecrate' the 'already consecrated' (Hall et al., 1978, Miller, 1994, Herman and Chomsky, 2002, Champagne, 2005, Darras, 2005).

What all these works suggest is that politicians, whether via innate personality or institutional manufacture, must communicate with citizens on a more symbolic level. The questions are: can such forms of communication be observed and analysed more systematically?; how do political leaders acquire or lose such symbolic status?; where, exactly, is media to be positioned in these processes?; and, last, what are the consequences for politics of this increased media and celebrity orientation? In seeking answers, the chapter now turns to the work of Pierre Bourdieu and attempts to develop the concept of 'media capital'.

Introducing Bourdieu's conceptual tools to the fields of politics and media

Bourdieu, despite a keen interest in media and politics (1998a, 2005, 2008), never did focused research in this area and did not himself use the term 'media capital' (although see Champagne, 1991). Instead he covered the subject tangentially, for example, as part of discussions of language and symbolic power (1991), in linking political elites to their educational backgrounds (1996), and in his polemical text on television and journalism (1998a). Thus, Bourdieu's work is relatively under-theorised and inconsistent here and has been applied little to work on politics, political sociology and mass media (Wacquant, 2004, Swartz, 2006, Hesmondhalgh, 2006).[1]

In Bourdieu's sociology the key conceptual tools are 'habitus', 'field' and 'forms of capital'. Individuals develop and are guided by their 'habitus', from early childhood onwards, which is mainly determined by their social environment (family, friends, education). For much of their adult existence such environments consist of occupational 'fields', such as art, literature, law, or the social sciences. Sociologically, the 'field' is defined as (Bourdieu, 1993: 162–63) 'a separate social universe having its own laws of functioning independently' but also a 'war of everyone against everyone, that is, universal competition'. Individuals enter into a field and move through the positions offered by that field according to the 'laws' (norms, values, hierarchies) established specifically within that field. In order to enter into a particular field an actor must first possess a certain habitus and the appropriate mix and accumulation of 'forms of capital' (Bourdieu, 1986). While operating there they continue to accumulate, exchange and lose field-specific forms of capital as they move up and down the field's hierarchies.

For Bourdieu, the two most significant forms of capital for individuals to accumulate and utilise are 'economic' and 'cultural'. Economic capital is self explanatory. Cultural capital, in its 'objectified' (cultural goods) and 'institutionalised' (qualifications) states, is transferable. Cultural capital, in its 'embodied state', cannot be bought or sold, but accumulates for the individual through a mix of formal education and social or professional experience. Other forms of capital, regarded as less significant by Bourdieu, are 'social' and 'symbolic'. 'Social capital'[2] is (Bourdieu, 1986: 286) 'the aggregate of the actual or potential resources which are linked to possession of a durable network of more or less institutionalized relationships of mutual acquaintance and recognition'. The term 'symbolic capital' is used more ambiguously across Bourdieu's work. In some cases it is presented as something that simply relays existing symbolic power as an aggregate reflection of other capital forms possessed by powerful institutions and actors (meta-capital). But, elsewhere in his writing, it becomes something to be accumulated as a capital form in its own right by individuals, amongst their peers, within a field, as well as beyond it, amongst citizens (1991, 1998b).

Fields and their participants link socially and communicatively to the wider public through several mechanisms. Bourdieu's position is that all fields themselves operate within the larger 'field of power' (wider society) and that fields vary in the degree of socio-cultural autonomy they have from this. Accordingly, he describes the social architecture of a field as, in part, revolving around an axis of two poles: the heteronomous and the autonomous. The heteronomous pole is where the field, with its participants and outputs, is most outward-looking and connected to the wider social world. The more autonomous pole is least outward-looking and closer to the purer social and cultural elements of the field itself. It is down to a range of 'cultural intermediaries' (Bourdieu, 1984) to link fields and larger society via mass media and other communicative apparatus. These aspects of Bourdieu's work remain relatively under-theorised (see Couldry, 2003 and Hesmondhalgh, 2006, on this point).

How is this discussion transposed on to the contemporary 'political field' and how does the mass media act as the communicative conduit between field and society? For Bourdieu, the 'political field' refers to that of formal, institutional politics, parties and professional politicians (Bourdieu, 1991, 2005). It operates as any other field (Bourdieu, 2005: 32): 'with certain (electoral) procedures, etc., is an autonomous world, a microcosm set within the social macrocosm'. Like all fields, the political field is one of continuous personal and party struggle over position (social, ideological, political). Struggle is also between (Bourdieu, 1991: 189–90, 2005: 30–34): political purists, equivalent to the intellectual avant garde, located at the more 'autonomous pole' of the field, and those seeking broader public appeal, the more 'heteronomous pole', a 'realpolitik' at any cost.

Individual politicians make use of their capital forms in order to win such struggles and progress within political hierarchies. In order to compete, they must continue to accrue and deploy an overall aggregate quantity of 'political capital' which is, itself, made up of other capital forms (economic, cultural, social, symbolic or other). In one key Bourdieu tract (1991: 192): 'Political capital is a form of symbolic capital, credit founded on *credence* or belief or *recognition* or, more precisely, on the innumerable operations of credit by which agents confer on a person.' In other words, political capital is made up of capital forms, which include the symbolic, but this political capital is also conveyed symbolically and bestowed by others. To succeed, therefore, politicians must be able to acquire symbolic capital amongst several audiences, including other politicians, intermediaries and ordinary citizens.

News media and its reporters, as well as linking the political field and wider citizenry, are the primary conduits for the individual accrual, and audience bestowal, of symbolic capital. The accrual of news 'media capital' thus becomes a necessary step in the accumulation of the symbolic and social capital necessary to acquire further political capital in politics. That said, identifying what media capital is is complicated by the multiple roles occupied by news producers. For many in media and cultural studies, news is not seen as a self-contained field but, rather, as part of the production and consumption of the symbolic in wider society. At the same time reporters very much operate within, and become part of, the political fields they report on (Cook, 1998, Herbst, 1998, Barnett and Gaber, 2001, Davis, 2007, see Chapter 5). For others still, journalists are most guided by the norms and practices of the professional field of journalism itself (Bourdieu, 1998a, 2005, Benson, 1998, Couldry, 2003, Benson and Neveu, 2005, Champagne, 2005). Thus, journalists are cultural intermediaries who move between professional fields, newsrooms and publics. This suggests that there is not one but several forms, or components, of media capital which individuals can seek to accumulate in relation to their varied audiences (fellow politicians, intermediaries, publics). These operate within a political field and external to it, and on both a personal and institutional basis.

Identifying the forms of media capital and their accumulation

Media capital forms in politics

Having clarified some key Bourdieusian concepts and relationships, and discussed their possible application to media and politics, the concept of 'media capital' is now ready to be broken down into its distinctive forms. This part identifies four means of distinguishing and classifying media capital and their means of accumulation. The nature of these forms was teased out during interviews with UK journalists and politicians. Summaries and extracts from these are used to illustrate them more clearly. Through this discussion, there is an obvious overlap between symbolic and media forms of capital but, for simplicity, 'media' remains the focus, even if certain descriptions may equally apply to an accumulation of 'symbolic capital'.

One obvious means of distinguishing forms of media capital is between that linked to institutionalised position and that linked to individual personality. Bourdieu (1991) himself identified two symbolic forms of capital in the political field. These he called 'personal' and 'delegated'. 'Delegated', like Weber's (1948) 'legal-rational' form of authority, is linked to recognised official positions. This 'institutionalised media capital' is associated with the position of an individual within a political party or state institution, to be reproduced through media to the wider social world. The alternative, 'personal' or 'charismatic' (Weber, 1948) form is 'individualised media capital'. Individuals may build up personalised forms of media capital with all sorts of performances or associations, reproduced in media over time. Thus, several studies (Boorstin, 1962, West and Orman, 2003, Alberoni, 2006) describe the public communication of an individual politician's 'natural', 'innate', 'heroic' or 'charismatic' qualities. For others (Pels, 2003, Street, 2003, Stanyer and Wring, 2004) politicians must project a 'persona' that combines the familiar and unfamiliar, the ordinary and extraordinary, both impressing an external audience and developing 'para-social relationships' with it. These two forms, individualised and institutionalised, are distinct and a politician may accumulate more of one form or the other. Pym Fortyun's (Pels, 2003) individualised media capital far outstripped his institutionalised media capital during his rise. The opposite may be true in the case of George H. Bush or Al Gore.

The existence of institutionalised media capital seemed to be an accepted norm for both politicians and journalists interviewed (see Chapter 5). There are natural hierarchies of both occupations within the political field. Senior politicians were likely to have an equivalent accumulation of media capital and, consequently, journalists were more interested in them. Elevated politicians also get to choose more established journalists in order to accumulate that capital. Ministers have more contact than non-ministers, government politicians more than opposition ones:

> as someone who's a bit further down the food chain, I've made a point of developing relationships with MPs who, in a sense, are at a similar point. It's obviously good to reach as high up as you can, but it's a fact of life ... it's just how things work.
>
> (Michael Lea, political correspondent)

At the same time there was an awareness of individual political personalities being projected publicly. In discussion with politicians and journalists it seemed that party leaders needed to be able to project a mixture of personal qualities: charismatic, personable, competence and assurance. (Shadow) ministers could succeed by projecting themselves as 'a safe pair of hands', 'competent, intelligent and technocratic'. However, parties also thrived with leaders, or groups of leading spokespersons, who appeared 'of the people', 'charming', 'photogenic':

> Look at Bush, he's very similar to Blair ... this sort of folksy Texan thing that works as a sort of charm thing in America ... politicians who can handle the media come to the fore. So you get Ronald Reagan, Arnold Schwarzenegger, Blair, maybe it explains Bush ... you get the charmer to be the leader, the presenter becomes the decision maker.
>
> (Clare Short MP, former Cabinet Minister)

A second means of distinguishing forms of media capital, in either individualised or institutionalised form, is between that generated within a political field (or network) and that outside it, amongst the public (or 'non-professionals'). Media capital, deployed within the political field, is distinct from, but also related to, that wielded outside it. That produced and wielded outside the field, which is linked to the wider citizenry, is a form of symbolic power, and linked to the meta-capital of the state. As Couldry (2003) advances it might best be referred to as '*media meta-capital*'. That generated within a field, linked to individual political actors, contributes to the total symbolic (or political) capital within that specified political field. As media and journalists have a part to play in the raising of symbolic capital within the political field it might be thought of as a field-specific form of media capital or, in simpler terms, '*internal media capital*'. *A politician may be well liked by journalists, and used as a source or presented favourably, regardless of their low institutional position or of how the public perceive them.*

Politicians, accordingly, are judged differently, in relation to their immediate internal, intermediary or external audiences. How political insiders then judge, and thus bestow symbolic capital on, other politicians, varies considerably from how a wider public judge, and thus bestow it. Such a conclusion is also to be deduced from several non-field oriented studies of politics culture and communication (Ankersmit, 1997, Corner, 2003, Alberoni, 2006, Davis, 2007). For Corner (2003: 72–74), politicians can be seen to 'perform' in two different spheres: 'the sphere of political institutions and processes' and 'that of the public and popular'. Such differences are all too apparent in comparisons of Al Gore and George W. Bush (Knuckey and Lees-Marshment, 2005), Gerhardt Schröder and Edmund Stoiber (Lees, 2005) or Gordon Brown and Tony Blair/David Cameron.

The distinction between internally and externally generated forms of media capital became clear during the research. The news media consumption habits of politicians were quite different from those of the general public. Three-quarters of the sixty politicians were asked specifically about their forms of news consumption. The most common form was broadsheet newspapers, with interviewees, on average, looking at three broadsheet newspapers per day (see also Duffy and Rowden, 2005). When consuming broadcast news it was longer, more depth news programmes, such as the *Today Programme*, *Newsnight* or *Channel 4 News*. The main form of news consumption for the general public is prime-time television news bulletins (Ofcom, 2007) and tabloid newspapers. Several politicians noted that a majority of their constituents were less inclined to consume the elite media outputs, such as the *Today Programme*, which most MPs turned to. Even when they did, the basis of public evaluation might be quite different from that of political insiders:

> I think there's a tendency for politicians to be obsessed with quality newspapers and the *Today Programme*, *Newsnight* or *World at One*, that sort of stuff. But the only people who are reading, listening and watching are people who are political junkies … I think he [Tony Blair] realised that.
>
> (John Maples MP, former minister)

In terms of forms of media capital, what seems to be emerging may be presented with a two-dimensional grid (below). Along one axis there is a division between media meta-capital, generated external to a political field (the heteronomous pole), and that generated within it (the autonomous pole). On the other axis the division is between media capital linked to institutionalised position and that linked to an individual. The means by which these forms of media capital are generated have distinct variations.

The means of media capital accumulation

How are these forms of media capital accrued and recorded? At a simple, quantifiable level they are accumulated through media exposure in terms of number of appearances and circulation size of a news outlet. Clearly, the audience, whether general public, internal field or other, is also significant as media represents or bestows symbolic capital on an individual in relation to a specified audience. Lastly, the more qualitative, discursive and representative framework, implicit in media texts, is a more complex contributory factor.

According to these definitions, externally-generated, *institutionalised media meta-capital* is the most straightforward in terms of its accumulation. There is often a natural hierarchy of political positions that may be correlated with a parallel accumulation of media capital. Thus, as work on media–source relations tends to confirm (Hall et al., 1978, Bennett, 1990, Herman and Chomsky, 2002), political elites automatically come to be the dominant news sources and agenda setters for news. Externally-generated, *individualised media meta-capital* is more elusive; the holy grail that political organisations increasingly look for when selecting leaders and spokespersons. The individual performances and journalist presentation of actors through media become important in terms of conveying the right mix of personal qualities that engage with citizens. Although, once selected, the increasing employment of professional, promotional intermediaries (Boorstin, 1962, Wernick, 1991, Hall Jamieson, 1996, Lilleker and Lees Marshment, 2005) suggests that the political personality presented to the public may, to a degree, be manufactured, focus-group tested and managed.

Two means of internal media capital accumulation with journalists are through an accrual of *journalist-based social capital* and *media cultural capital*. Since politicians and correspondents have intense and regular exchanges, politicians build up their social capital with journalists as they gather contacts and foster good relationships with them during their career. Media cultural capital is based

Table 6.1 The forms of media capital generated by political actors in the political field

	Institutionalised media capital	Individualised media capital
Media capital generated internal to the field		
Media meta-capital generated external to the field		

on an accumulation of knowledge about how news production works and journalists operate. An understanding of what 'news values' are, the beats and routines of journalists, how to construct a 'pseudo event', produce a press release, and conduct an interview, are gained over time by individuals. This comes with political experience, specialist media skills training and, increasingly, from prior professional experience as a journalist or public relations specialist (see Chapter 3). These means of influencing one's own media exposure to the external social world are gained quite independent of an individual's institutional position or telegenic qualities and, therefore, are a way of challenging such determinants.

The importance of accumulating forms of journalist-based social capital and media cultural capital came across in many interviews. Two-thirds of the twenty politicians, asked about the qualities needed for advancement, mentioned the need for good media skills and/or relations with journalists. A majority of the fifty politicians asked about media generally (see Chapter 5), talked of the importance of developing long-term relationships with journalists. Four-fifths of those interviewed had had media training or previous professional experience in media or public relations. Two-thirds of the journalists made similar comments. Half said that one sign of a 'rising star' was a politician's ability to develop and maintain good journalist relations as well as having a good knowledge of news values and routines. Several talked about Tony Blair's obvious media skills, public personality and long-term cultivation of journalist contacts prior to his successful bid for the Labour leadership in 1994. Iain Duncan Smith's contacts, particularly with the *Daily Telegraph*, were considered to have been instrumental in his winning the Conservative Party leadership contest in 2001. Likewise, David Cameron had lengthy media relations experience and had built up many journalist contacts prior to his successful bid for the Conservative leadership in 2005 (see Chapter 3).

> People who have reached the higher levels now were good at generating stories when lower down. For example, Gordon Brown used to put out a lot of stories when he was a junior back-bencher. Alan Milburn and Stephen Byers took a lot of opportunities to put in stories … You also look for who is good in interview. If they are good on camera then it also indicates they must be organised.
>
> (Martha Kearney, political editor)

The other obvious means of accumulating symbolic capital through the media is through public *mediated performance capital*. Politicians are aware of inhabiting an increasingly media-dependent and mediated field. In addition to being key news sources, MPs are frequently the subject of news reports and are also great consumers of news. They both see, and are seen by, their peers through the media lens as well as in person. Mediated performances can thus contribute to the accumulation of each of the four forms of media capital identified and potentially set up a dynamic exchange between forms generated within and external to a political field. This is because political performances are directed towards multiple audiences and, accordingly, are judged (or decoded) in alternative ways by those audiences.

The media-oriented performances, and media-filtered consumption and evaluation of those performances, takes place in a number of settings. These can be classified according to their position vis-à-vis the more 'autonomous' (internal media capital) or more 'heteronomous' (external media meta-capital) poles of a political field. Starting with the most autonomous, the first form of mediated judgment comes in personal exchanges between politicians and journalists, or performances observed by journalists in more private settings (exclusive meetings, briefings, lunches). The second is during performances in public forums (debating chambers, public meeting spaces, conferences) established within the political field.

The third most common answer given by the twenty politicians, asked about the qualities required to rise in their parties, was being noticed and seen to perform well in the House of Commons, most usually in the main Chamber. Two-thirds of journalists asked this question also said they looked at individual performances in the Chamber. The most regular and significant performance event for UK politicians is the weekly Prime Minister's Question time (PMQs) which is reported on national news bulletins and attracts full MP attendance. Several interviewees claimed that William Hague's successful attack on Tony Blair at a PMQ slot had been important in him getting support for his leadership bid in 1997. Menzies Campbell's short-lived leadership of the Liberal Democrats was said to be severely compromised by his poor Chamber performances. As one experienced lobby correspondent explained:

> But performance in the House is what we see ... Prime Minister's Question Time, Chancellor's Question Time ... getting in with a good question in response to a prime ministerial statement, for example. That gets them noticed ... You know, in the end there is no more testing place than the House of Commons Chamber.
>
> (Philip Webster, political editor)

Such appearances were previously recorded, with delay in print, but now are more instantly transmitted in television broadcasts and online webcasts. Consequently, for much of the time, journalists and politicians do not physically attend such media events but, instead, observe, or later review them if present, through these other media. A third form of evaluation comes as politicians and journalists, along with the general public, observe and evaluate others only through media outputs. Split between the 'autonomous' and 'heteronomous' polls of public presentation comes public performance in elite-oriented media programmes. In the UK these include appearances on the *Today Programme* on Radio Four, depth television news programmes such as *Newsnight* (BBC One) and *Channel Four News*, and debate forums such as *Question Time* and *Any Questions?* (BBC One and Radio Four). Moving towards the 'heteronomous' end comes political performance in non-political elite media programmes such as daily news bulletins and documentaries, down to satires, comedy programmes and chat shows. Of course, how the same performances are judged by those inside and outside the political field may vary considerably and, similarly, the basis of performance evaluation shifts with the setting.

MPs generally were fairly conscious of their own public profiles. Two-fifths of those interviewed, often unprompted, made comments about their own local or national media profile and the need to develop and manage it during their career. Half the sixteen former (Shadow) Cabinet ministers interviewed gave first hand-accounts of their party leaders being 'media obsessed' and/or concerned with their own media profile. As one MP explained:

> there's a rather separate issue for any politician, which is about how you manage your own reputation in terms of the media … you don't want to be seen too much as a media tart, and as a rent-a-gob, because you just alie-nate all your colleagues. At the same time you want to be seen to be good on the media, on the telly and radio.
>
> (Chris Bryant MP)

Conversely, several politicians and journalists explained that they watched and evaluated politicians through their media performances. A dozen politicians talked about assessing politicians from all parties when they appeared on elite news programmes and forums such as *Question Time*. Ten said they took note of the comments and assessments of politicians by top journalists, particularly experienced editors and columnists. Two-thirds of journalists also said they evaluated a politician's abilities in elite media, such as the *Today Programme*. Several politicians and journalists recalled that they exchanged opinions with colleagues on individual politicians' performances in parliament and other news media. Thus mediated performances were discussed by mediated 'interpretive communities' of politicians and/or journalists:

> I'm looking to do that kind of *Today Programme* evaluation thing that the political class does, where they form judgements about which colleagues and opponents are doing well, doing badly … same as everyone else in the country, you come to form judgements, a) about the policies, and b) about the people.
>
> (Sion Simon MP)

The interplay and exchange of media capital forms

Although these differing forms of media capital are distinctive, there is also a complex interplay and exchange at work between them. The ability to generate one form influences the accumulation of another. The most public perfor-mances, in the first instance, help accrue *external media meta-capital* beyond the field. However, they also affect the accumulation of *internal media capital* because other politicians are likely to be observing and evaluating the performances of others. This is partly an assessment of political competence and/or significance but, also, partly an attempt to gauge how journalists and citizens might respond. They are thus evaluating the potential of others to accumulate both internal media capital and external media meta-capital. Such potential, in turn, helps people to move into institutionally-recognised positions that automatically bring media coverage (media meta-capital) outside it. Conversely, weak levels of internal media capital may prevent political advancement, limit one's ability to raise symbolic capital and therefore media meta-capital beyond the field.

In terms of *institutionalised* and *individualised forms of media capital*, the perceptions of an individual over time may shift according to changes in the public standing of the organisations and institutions they represent. The reverse is also true. As with agents and social structures, which may have a co-determining evolution, so it is with the symbolic or media capital of individuals and organisations.

On the consequences of rising media capital levels for the political field

As argued, politicians and parties increasingly seek to accumulate varied forms of media capital and in more systematic ways. The question is what are the implications of this greater orientation towards the acquisition of media capital, as opposed to other traditional capital forms, within the political field? This section makes three speculative points. First, it is reasoned that the relative weighting of media capital within the political field is linked to the strength of the journalistic field vis-à-vis the political field. Second, it is argued that the acquisition of media capital forms is problematic for several reasons. Compared to other capital forms they tend to be rather more volatile, unmanageable, and accumulated in artificial and unstable forms. Third, it is suggested that the ability of contemporary politicians to accumulate media and symbolic capital, in greater quantities than their actual political or meta-capital, means that far more is expected of them than they can deliver. This mismatch between perceived and actual power in turn encourages greater public cynicism towards politicians, political institutions, and journalism.

Why media capital is increasing in importance

First, when does media capital become a more significant form of capital for individual politicians to accumulate in the political field? One possible answer is directly related to the relative strengths of the political and journalistic fields. If the political field holds a dominant position over the journalistic field then reporters operate as 'secondary definers' and bestow a 'primary definer' (Hall et al., 1978) status on politicians. The media field privileges political capital, simply reproducing, in symbolic form, the 'meta-capital' of the state. The media, in effect, acts like a central bank for the distribution and exchange of symbolic 'media meta-capital' (Couldry, 2003). In authoritarian political systems, 'statist', or over-regulated, democratic media systems, senior political figures are likely to hold sway and the generation of media capital may be less important for political advancement within political hierarchies. The same may be said where professional journalistic cultures may be more 'partisan' and 'passive' in their relations with politicians, as in France or Italy in earlier decades (Donsbach and Patterson, 2004, Chalaby, 2005, Darras, 2005).

However, if the journalistic field becomes more autonomous, because it is more market-oriented, or government appears weak or divided (see Entman, 2004), then media capital grows in importance. Its unique ability to 'consecrate' politicians, parties and institutions, and so bestow symbolic capital on them, increases the strength of the journalistic field. An accumulation of 'media capital' and/or media meta-capital from the wider social world is then increasingly a prerequisite for politicians and parties to advance within a political field. Such developments are implied in Bourdieu's (1998a, 1999, 2005) more recent work, in which he suggested that the contemporary media had become the 'Trojan horse' of the market. Arguably, the privatisation and deregulation of media generally, in many democracies in the last two to three decades (Hardy, 2008), has given greater political autonomy to news organisations. In turn, politicians have slowly put greater emphasis on accumulating media capital.

Thus, a strong political field results in media reproducing the symbolic meta-capital of the institutions and personnel of the state. A strong journalistic field indicates that media and media capital are more likely to constitute forms of capital in their own right within the political field.

Media capital, volatility, loss and the destabilisation of politics

The greater conversion value put on media capital in politics, relative to other capital forms, may undermine politicians and the political field more generally. While economic, cultural and social forms of capital can, to varying degrees, be accrued actively by individuals, symbolic and media capital forms are dependent on others bestowing them. This means their accumulation and loss are likely to be strongly influenced by competing sets of field-based rules and forms of capital. Thus, as politicians attempt to gain media capital in all its forms they risk becoming driven by 'media logic' (Altheide and Snow, 1979, Meyer, 2002, Davis, 2007).

During the interviews, several respondents indeed commented on how media demands and logics had impacted negatively on the political field. Just under half the politicians, who commented more generally on the media, said that political journalists were far more interested in drama, personalities, wrong-doing and political conflict than they were in productive political activity, constituency work or policy development (see Chapter 2). A third of journalists agreed. Conversely, the need to adapt policies and personalities, in order to gain media coverage (and capital), became apparent in many interviews. Many politicians explained that the gaining of media coverage, by any means, often became an objective in itself and could dictate political decisions:

> leaders of the opposition take media very seriously because it's all you've got ... so you work very closely with them and they are very important to us ... increasingly, in the last 15 years, media has become a very important driver of government activity and policy work ... so government ministers invent another initiative, then another initiative, then another initiative, with no follow through, with no proper execution and with no audit on whether it's working or not.
>
> (John Redwood, former Cabinet Minister)

The demands of media logic apart, many forms of media capital, and their accumulation, are inherently unstable, short-term, and unmanageable. If a politician's aggregate political capital includes a greater proportion of such media capital forms, then political actors are likely to endure more precarious existences. Some forms and means are more gradually accrued, stable and long-lasting. For an individual, accumulation over time may come through regular, recognised personal accomplishments or progression through institutionally-recognised positions (*institutionalised media capital*). It can also come through a gradual build up of journalist contacts (*journalist social capital*) and technical knowledge of media requirements (*media cultural capital*). However, other forms, and means of generation, can offer a short-cut to high office but, potentially, also be more unstable and transitory. An individual may suddenly acquire *individualised media meta-capital* through one-off media stunts, associations, and participation in big news events (Thompson, 2000, Pels, 2003, West and Orman, 2003). Forms of media capital (journalist social and media cultural) may also be 'artificially' acquired with economic capital through the employment of professional communicators (Hall Jamieson, 1996, Davis, 2002, Franklin, 2004, Lilleker and Lees Marshment, 2005). However, such means of media capital accumulation may ultimately be detrimental to individuals in the long term. Stunts and media stories are temporary as politicians may 'command attention' but lose 'legitimacy' (Cracknell, 1993). Similarly, the use of professional communicators causes cynicism amongst journalists and the public (Kurtz, 1998, Jones, 2002, Lloyd, 2004). Professional communicators may 'spin' stories and give false information to media for short-term gain but at the direct cost of carefully accrued, long-term journalist social capital.

Indeed, many interviewees made comments that implied that certain forms of media capital accumulation could be self-defeating within the lengthier political cycle. For example, over-appearance in the media by an individual with little political capital, or in media with little symbolic weight in the political field, can be detrimental. Several MPs said that too many media appearances could have a negative impact with political colleagues and the public. It caused suspicion and left politicians lacking 'gravitas'.

the danger is you can end up like people like Chris Bryant, even old 'Pinky' Powell. Stephen Powell, you know, they're good value for money presumably on more light hearted things, but they devalue their own stock ... as serious politicians. I think amongst their peers and amongst the audience it's difficult to keep that balance between being familiar ... and not being sort of rent-a-quote.

(Peter Kilfoyle MP)

Good media performers could also be left vulnerable to stories based on negative news values, scandal and fast-shifting media fashions. If the journalist 'interpretive community' collectively decides a politician is no longer 'newsworthy', or turns against them, their personal stock of media capital is instantly wiped out and with significant consequences for their total political capital. In several discussions with interviewees, an impression was given that certain ministers and party leaders (Charles Kennedy, Menzies Campbell, Tony Blair) had risen and/or fallen as a consequence of relatively quick gains or losses of forms of media capital. Many talked about the power of the 'press pack' in bringing down figures once a journalist 'tipping point' had been reached. Politicians would be pursued and investigated for lengthy periods and stocks of media capital seemed instantly and permanently lost:

Blair has become such a liability and such a disaster that he can no longer carry a particular policy ... he's a liability to his party and bad news all round ... before he was busted, and a shame that he is, he could still take, every month, a room full of very hostile journalists and leave them gasping at the end of it, unable to think of anything else to attack him with.

(Polly Toynbee, journalist/commentator)

The mismatch between perceived and actual power

Lastly, the emphasis on accumulating media and symbolic capital, over other capital forms, sets up a mismatch between perceived and actual power. As Alberoni (2006) noted, in respect to celebrity power, observability and power may be inversely correlated. For example, over-appearance in the mass media rapidly generates media meta-capital for an individual without accumulating the corresponding levels of internal political and media capital.

Perhaps, at a more fundamental level, political actors (politicians, parties and governments) collectively may have reached a point where their ability to accrue media capital far outstrips their actual political and economic power. This sets up a series of public expectations of politicians and institutions which they cannot possibly fulfil. Politicians are regular lead sources of news but corporate chief executives, senior bureaucrats and heads of transnational institutions are not. Arguably, this has contributed to the long-term decline of stable public support for publicly visible mainstream politics. Shifts in public support for individual political leaders and parties now appear more extreme. During their tenures, George W. Bush and Tony Blair recorded both the highest and lowest post-war approval ratings in the US and UK respectively. This possibly explains why a large majority of citizens in democracies say they support democracy per se while, simultaneously, being cynical about its core actors and institutions (politicians, parties, journalists and news media organisations, see Dalton, 2004, Hay, 2007).

Conclusion

This chapter has initially argued that several elements of Bourdieu's work provide a potentially useful set of conceptual tools for observing 'media capital' as an asset that could be accumulated or converted by individual politicians. This discussion helped establish that there were four ways of conceptualising media capital: in 'individualised' and 'institutionalised' forms, 'internal' and 'external' to political fields. These forms were distinct but could also be inter-related. Their means of accumulation varied accordingly. Highlighted means of acquisition included 'journalist-based social capital', 'media cultural capital', and 'mediated performance capital', recorded in a mix of elite and mass news media outputs.

Lastly, it was argued that, as the journalistic field becomes stronger, vis-à-vis the political field, so the acquisition of media capital becomes more significant for politicians. The growing focus of politicians on the generation of easily-acquired forms of media capital, as opposed to other, more stable and gradually-accrued media and other capital forms, has had a destabilising effect. The mismatch between political and symbolic power wrongly focuses public attention on formal politics while also causing further disenchantment with that politics.

Notes

1 For some important discussions on Bourdieu's applicability in these fields see Benson, 1998, Kauppi, 2003, Benson and Neveu, 2005.
2 Bourdieu's use of the term is distinct from that of others such as Coleman (1988) or Putnam (2000).

Chapter 7

New media and fat democracy

The paradox of online participation

Introduction

This chapter speculates on the internet's wider influences on the shape of institutional politics in contemporary representative democracies. It does so by focusing on the communicative links and patterns of engagement that are emerging between elected politicians and other groups of political actors operating around the political centre. Recent studies are combined with the results of 100 semi-structured interviews with UK-based political actors (politicians, journalists and officials) in an effort to identify developing trends.

Findings suggest that internet-mediated democracy, at least in the UK case, is encouraging two, somewhat contrary political trends. On the one hand, more political actors at the immediate edges of the UK institutional political process are being further engaged in a sort of centrifugal movement going outwards from the centre. However, at the same time, the distance between this fatter political centre and its public periphery is increasing. Mass, off-line news media, which is the dominant source of political information for most, is becoming less informative. Those same online spaces and communicative exchanges, developing around the political centre, are relatively insular and exclusionary. In other words, politics, for those already engaged or interested, is becoming denser, wider, and possibly more pluralistic and inclusive. But, at the same time, the mass of unengaged citizens is being subject to greater communicative exclusion and experiencing increasing disengagement.

These paradoxical tendencies lead to what might be described as a thicker, broader form of elite polyarchy. This is akin to a sort of middle-management expansion of UK politics or a fatter democratic elitist model. While such a shift may be interpreted as 'new' and ICT-driven, it might equally be argued that new media is exacerbating pre-existing political and media trends in mature Western democracies. Internet-enhanced politics may be improving democratic engagement and accountability at the centre but, as yet, is unlikely to be offering a solution to wider patterns of public disengagement from institutional politics.

Evaluating new media's contribution to democratic communication: redirecting assessments from direct, deliberative to actually existing democracies

Digital engagements between politicians and citizens: unfulfilled expectations

Much new media research on politics and journalism has been driven by democratic ideals and ICT potential, rather than the communicative practices of politicians and journalists, operating in 'actually existing democracies' (Fraser, 1997). Whether the starting point is technology, media or politics, a clear normative agenda has driven debate and research on the use of the internet in politics. Existing political institutions and news media are letting down citizens and, at least in part, are responsible for the decline of public engagement with, and participation in, institutional politics (see Chapter 10). A lack of 'democracy', in terms of pluralist access, participation and deliberation, has been the problem for both politics and news. More democracy, facilitated by new media, is the solution.

Early research on the internet's potential for reshaping democracy was clearly influenced by the normative values presented in the works of direct democracy and public sphere advocates (Habermas, 1989, Bohman, 1996, Dryzak, 2002, Putnam, 2000). These argued for more inclusive public participation and deliberative exchange between ordinary citizens and political elites. Accordingly, new ICTs appeared to offer the tools with which to apply the theory. New ICTs offer the communicative potential for greater exchange and deliberation between politicians, journalists and citizens. The internet, in particular, is cheap, easily accessible, offers infinite channels, overcomes barriers of time and space, and is not source restrictive. Thus, Negroponte (1995) and Rash (1997) were amongst the first to argue that the internet offered the potential for a renewal of direct democracy.

At the parliamentary and government levels, a spate of US and UK studies and institutional initiatives (Coleman and Gotze, 2001, Bimber, 2003, Coleman, 2004, 2005, Gulati, 2004, Ward et al., 2005, Chadwick, 2006, Lusoli et al., 2006) have explored the potential for online exchanges between citizens and their elected representatives. These attempted to evaluate the possible conditions for the emergence of a 'civic commons in cyberspace' with 'citizen panels', 'e-consultation and deliberation'. A smaller group of studies have asked similar questions at the political party level (Ward and Gibson, 2000, Ward et al., 2002, Rommele, 2003, Lusoli and Ward, 2003, Gillmor, 2004, Trippi, 2004, Davis, 2005). These asked whether new media could be useful in halting the long-term declines in party membership and levels of member activism. They speculated that new media potentially could reconnect party leaders to ordinary, local members, thus improving accountability as a consequence of better 'intra-party democracy'.

Another series of studies have applied such a research focus to other political forums outside national, institutional politics. These have included investigations of several localised, experimental online forums, involving local officials and politicians (e.g., Dahlberg, 2001, Polat, 2005, Wikland, 2005, Jensen, 2006, Curran and Witschge, 2009), and within the online sites of interest groups, social movements and professional associations (Atton, 2004, Pickerill, 2004, 2006, Kavada, 2005, Dean et al., 2006). Such studies discussed and evaluated these online spaces in terms of their informational and organisational capacities but, also, public sphere ideals such as: horizontal communicative and deliberative structures, ease of access and inclusive participation, openness of agendas and rejection of status, freedom from coercion, rule-based frameworks, free interaction and recognition of difference.

However, to date, early enthusiasm has given way to more sober or pessimistic assessments of the internet's potential for reconnecting political elites (institutional or interest group) to citizens or members. Politicians, parties and government institutions have been slow to adopt online deliberative tools. Instead, new media is more likely to be viewed as an alternative tool for political organisation or service delivery, or be used as an additional one-to-many promotional medium (Jackson, 2003, Gulati, 2004, Jackson and Lilleker, 2004, Chadwick, 2006). Studies of political parties have documented a series of democratic advances. These include the use of websites and email to provide detailed party information, improved organisation and communication, greater linking of ordinary party members to the party, and fund raising. Each of these has been particularly important for smaller, resource-poor political parties such as the Liberal Democrats in the UK. Innovative use of the net has also made a substantial impact on elections, enabling lesser-known and resourced presidential candidates, such as Howard Dean (2004) in the US, and Roh Moo-Hyun (2003) in South Korea, to compete (Ward et al., 2002, Lusoli and Ward, 2003, Rommele, 2003, Gillmor, 2004, Trippi, 2004). In fact, use of the internet was a major part of the successful Obama strategy (2008) in terms of coordination of local campaign activities and a hugely successful fund-raising drive amongst small donors (Anstead, 2009). However, none of these studies has observed more than limited use of online forums for greater external policy inputs or deliberation between ordinary members and party leaders or candidates. Like traditional media, the internet's one-to-many means of communication have proved more expedient than its many-to-many or many-to-one forms in the spheres of contemporary politics.

Similarly frustrating findings have been found in localised political online forums and interest group websites. Most experimental, politically-oriented sites have collapsed. Attracting substantial numbers, and enforcing moderation according to public sphere principles, appears difficult and expensive (Dahlberg, 2001, Dahlgren, 2005, Wikland, 2005, Polat, 2005, Curran and Witschge, 2009). Interest groups have benefited from the internet in the same way that smaller political parties and candidates have. Organisation, information dissemination, internal communication, mobilisation and fund-raising have all improved. However, with the exception of smaller, more fluid grassroots social movements (Pickerill, 2004, Stammers and Eschle, 2005), few established interest groups have encouraged greater deliberation with, and input from, ordinary members. Kavada's (2005) study of Oxfam, Amnesty and the World Development Movement found little to encourage such developments or intention to develop them in the future.

More generally, there appear to be several aspects of the internet which may actually be hindering the very public sphere ideals of public participation and engagement aspired to. Internet use by ordinary citizens is predominantly consumer and leisure, rather than politically, oriented. Internet use for political information is steadily rising in the US but remains some way behind traditional broadcast and print forms (Pew, 2008). In the UK, in the year of the last UK election (2005), only 3.3 per cent of the population used the internet as their main source of political information and only 3 per cent looked at political party websites (Lusoli et al. 2006).

The 'digital divide' is another barrier to increasing political participation (Golding and Murdock, 2000, Norris, 2001, Bonfadelli, 2002, Jensen, 2006, Lusoli et al., 2006, Hindman, 2008). The inequalities in ICT access are large, both within and between nations (see Albrow et al., 2008, Internet World Stats, 2009). Albrow et al. (2008: 280, 286) noted that internet penetration was only 17 per cent worldwide in 2005, reaching 70 per cent in North America but as low as 11 per cent in Asia and 4 per cent in Africa. In addition, many have noted that online political participation is correlated along the lines of education, age, race and, above all, an existing predisposition to participate in real-world politics. For example, Jensen's (2006: 47) survey of participants in the Minnesota E-Democracy Project found that 93 per cent voted in the previous election, 63 per cent were affiliated to political parties, 45 per cent were members of grass roots movements and 74 per cent had consulted politicians or civil servants – all significantly above the average.

Lastly, according to Sunstein (2001) the internet encourages individuals to pick and choose sites in a way that reduces engagement with alternative viewpoints and undermines shared public forums. The consequences are the development of well-organised 'smart mobs' (Rheingold, 2002) and polarised, fragmented interest group ghettos.

All of which suggests that the internet is neither widening nor deepening political participation or engagement between citizens and political leaders. The best that might be said is that interest groups, 'citizen journalists' and others (Downing, 2001, Gillmor, 2004, Pickerill, 2004, Couldry, 2009) may be better placed to organise opposition to politicians and political institutions. Since such developments may also enhance the communicative abilities of those same political and corporate actors, at the centres of decision-making, such gains may be negligible (e.g., Schiller, 1996, Herman and McChesney, 1997, Golding and Murdock, 2000). It is thus easy to concur with a long line of cyber-pessimists in concluding that the internet has had a negligible impact on levels of formal, institutionally-based democracy.

Pragmatic conceptions of actually existing democracies: an alternative evaluative schema

At this point, it might be concluded that the internet's ability to alter communication in democracies, according to the normative ideals of public sphere and direct democracy advocates, appears limited. So does that mean democracy is not being transformed in any substantive way? Not necessarily. Alternatively, it might be argued that the evaluative research parameters being applied need rethinking. Shifts may indeed be taking place but not particularly according to the criteria laid down in much of the aforementioned work. There may well be significant changes taking place in the political information environment, or in the behaviour of existing political actors, which, in less obvious ways, are reconfiguring political communication systems.

The first problem is that much research is conceived within a technologically determinist framework. This puts too much emphasis on technology as a primary, almost revolutionary, driver of social change (see objections of Winston, 1998, Webster, 2006, Lievrouw and Livingstone, 2006). This ICT-oriented approach side-steps the many non-technical (social, economic, organisational) obstacles to such forms of direct, deliberative democracy (see Polat, 2005, Brandenberg, 2006, Dahlberg, 2007, Davis, 2007). This is not to argue against technology playing a part in social and political change. Rather, as recent, strong currents of research on new media and science and technology studies (STS) stress (see MacKenzie and Wajcman, 1999, Livingstone, 2005, Lievrouw and Livingstone, 2006: 4) 'recombinant' and 'social shaping' approaches are key. In these, ICTs are 'more of a mutual shaping process in which technological development and social practices are co-determining'.

Second, many studies are based on measuring qualitative changes in direct and deliberative forms of democracy rather than observing influences on large, complex societies (Calhoun, 1988, Habermas, 1996, Sunstein, 2001) or 'actually existing democracies' (Fraser, 1992). Therefore, evaluations of the internet's impact on institutional and party politics need to be broadened beyond investigating such things as the formal mechanisms of public deliberation. Instead, it should be asked: how might representative democracies in large, complex societies be changing with the arrival of the internet? How might the communication environments and behaviours of those already engaged with institutional and party politics be changing (see Livingstone, 2005, on this point)? This leads observation of change to be investigated in additional directions.

One of these is to move away from the single focus on individual, citizen-to-state communication. In fact, much debate and research about politics and representative democracy, since the early twentieth century, has centred on competing groups, organisations, institutions and networks, and their relationship to the state.

The central concern is whether a healthy pluralist balance of groups exists, as 'empirical democratic theorists' argue (Lindblom, 1977, Dahl, 1989), or whether, as a range of critics conclude (Mills, 1956, Poulantzas, 1975), it does not. A related issue is that of intra-group democracy. Within parties, groups and organisations, rigid hierarchies form and come to be dominated by elites at the top (Michels, 1967[1911]). Representative democracies, more generally, must continue to fend off a tendency to decline into a state of 'competitive elitism' (Schumpeter, 1942); something all too familiar in many current systems (e.g., Crouch, 2004, Domhoff, 2005, Hay, 2007, see Chapter 3). If such issues are central to contemporary representative democracies then perhaps the internet's influence on shaping these dynamics needs closer inspection. Thus, as Dahlberg (2007: 829) suggests, in relation to new media research, 'the public sphere [should] be reconceptualised around both intra- and inter-discursive contestation'.

By the same token new media's impact on mass news media and 'soft' forms of deliberation needs to be included. This is because the majority of citizens in stable democracies only seek to be minimally informed of, or engage with, institutional politics (Hansard, 2004, Ward et al., 2005, Lusoli et al., 2006). As Brandenburg states (2006: 218): 'Public discontent with political elites and representative systems, in general, does not amount to a widespread demand for inclusion in a deliberative system that affords active participation.' Thus, for most of the public their only conscious engagement with institutional politics is through general news media. This, in all its forms, becomes the main 'public forum' for contemporary representative democracies (Calhoun, 1988, Dahlgren, 1995, Kellner, 2000, Sunstein, 2001, Butsch, 2007). The emotional and non-rational may also be significant influences on both ordinary citizens and actors in and around the political centre. As Pickerill (2006) argues, in respect of new media, perhaps one needs to have a broader interpretation of 'deliberation' that includes both its 'hard', formal and 'soft', informal forms.

New media and the thickening of communicative links in and around the UK political centre

Accordingly, an enquiry into new media use in and around the UK political centre attempted to incorporate several of these points into its investigation. It involved observing, interviewing and evaluating politically-active individuals, and their communication processes, as they operated in and around the UK parliament. Research was interested in investigating communicative links and exchanges, both in terms of those taking place between political elites and citizens but, also, within and between groups and factions. It also included a broader interpretation of 'deliberation' to include both 'hard' and 'soft' aspects. In all, semi-structured interviews took place with sixty politicians, twenty-two political journalists and bloggers, and twenty-two officials in parliament and the civil service. Each interviewee was not questioned about democracy or the impact of new media on politics per se. Instead, in line with a 'social shaping' approach, they were asked about the role of media and communication in their daily activities before then asking about how new media had changed the way they personally did things. Aggregated interview results are represented in Table 7.1 and Table 7.2.

Findings here evaluate how the internet might be encouraging democratic shifts in communication around the political centre. As such they focus on the internet's utility in: ameliorating group or faction inequalities in information/ communication resources, the facilitation of intra-group and inter-group exchanges, and the countering of oligarchic tendencies. On each of these points the interview material suggested some positive shifts. Potentially these may be making formal, institutional and party-based politics a little more pluralist, inclusive and accountable.

Table 7.1 Responses of politicians to question a) 'How has the internet changed politics and communication processes around politics?' b) 'How has it changed the way you do things?'

New media application for MPs (38)	*Party-specific activity?*
1 Net as a research tool (24)	Much more Lab/LD, not Con
2 Emails with constituents problematic (21)	More Cons, less Lab, 1 LD
3 Email/net use in political/internal organisation (20)	Half LD, third Cons and Lab
4 Prefer letters/trad. comm forms with constituents (16)	More Lab than Cons or LD
5 Net (e.g. blogs) as tool for MPs/activists (13)	Roughly even
6 E-consultation with public problematic (11)	Marginally more Lab and LD
7 Use of net for customised online news collection (10)	Marginally more Lab, LD
7 Regular email with constituents (10)	Most LD, then Cons, then Lab
9 Parliament/MPs slow to adopt new media (8)	Even
9 MPs admit IT illiteracy (8)	More Lab and Cons, no LD
11 Web information problematic (overload, credibility, etc.) (7)	Lab, 2 LD, no Cons
12 24-hour news/net combination problematic for politics (6)	Just Lab
12 Blogs a waste of resources (6)	Just Lab, 2 LD, no Cons
14 Net changes processes not outcomes (5)	N/A
14 Net can revive direct democracy/ two way comms (5)	N/A
16 Email aggregation of constituents local contact (4)	N/A
16 New media broadens access to parliament and processes (4)	N/A

Table 7.2 Responses of journalists to question a) 'How has the internet changed the way political journalism is done?' b) 'How has it changed the way you do things?'

New media application for journalists (17)
1   Negative view of blogging in general (10)
1   New media used to monitor and cross reference other news media (10)
3   Availability/use of information on party/official sites online (8)
3   Net as a library, fact checker, etc. (8)
5   Trust and 'brand' key issues in choice of sites. Both via offline world (7)
5   24-hour news/new media pressures (competition, speed, space, quality, resources, etc.) (7)
7   Useful organisational/information exchange tool (6)
8   ConservativeHome as key information source on Conservative Party (4)

The internet as a means for obtaining information equality

Starting with the resource question, clearly any political system that seeks pluralist balance is confronted with the problem of economic inequalities being reproduced in information and communication terms (see Goldenberg, 1975, Gandy, 1982). These exist between and within political parties, interest groups and factions, and also affect the professional efficacy of individual candidates and journalists. As such the internet has been seen as a valuable tool that might enable 'resource-poor' political parties (Ward et al., 2002, Jackson, 2003, Lusoli and Ward, 2003) and individual political candidates (Gillmor, 2004, Trippi, 2004) to compete. Thus, the question is: is the internet ameliorating existing inter- and intra-group resource inequalities in and around the political centre?

For a majority of interviewees, the use of the internet to both publish and access political information has been very significant. Many parliamentary and government officials stated that new media has quite simply improved public engagement by making politics itself more transparent and accessible. Following several institutional reviews (HoC, July, 2002, June 2004, Hansard, 2005) extensive amounts of parliamentary material has been published on the web. 'Parliament Live', a new video and audio section of the parliamentary website, now carries live and archived coverage (for twenty-eight days) of all public debates and committee meetings in the two Houses. Parliamentary research papers have been made publicly accessible and downloads have rapidly increased. In 2006–7 there were 1.52 million downloads of Parliamentary policy research papers, 289,000 downloads of standard notes (shorter policy briefings), and 386,000 downloads of fact sheets (HoC, 2007).

Journalists and bloggers also argued that the internet had increased the available space and possible choice of subject matter for publishing political news. Established journalists, using online versions of off-line outlets, could now file additional political reports, offer more background detail and opinion on those stories, and produce extra columns and blogs. Bloggers were free to cover more specialist topics, expand interviews and depth coverage and pursue controversial stories (see similar findings in US studies, Gillmor, 2004, Lowrey, 2006,

Carlson, 2007). Thus the internet has contributed to an expansion of politically significant information, offering what traditional institutions and news media could not:

> the internet capacity on the web, it means that many more of our stories can be made available … stuff, you know, to do with process and constitutional things, perhaps I may write to the online site not to the paper. So there is a crisis there of [off-line] space but that can be compensated for by the online.
>
> (Peter Riddell, political journalist, commentator)

Conversely, it seemed to be clear that all groups of interviewees (politicians, journalists, officials) were benefiting from these additional information sources. When asked how new media had changed their working practices, the most common answer for all was using the internet as a research tool. A clear majority of MPs said they used it to search for information on a regular basis, more than half of these said 'a lot'. Three of the four most common answers given by journalists, when asked about their use of the internet (see Table 7.2) related to its use as a research tool. As many MPs explained, a lack of research resources was a frequent impediment to policy engagement. The internet now enabled them to spend hours, rather than days, in researching topics for political and policy debates.

Interestingly, interview responses, as well as other studies (Ward et al., 2002, Jackson, 2003), indicated that it was the poorest funded of the three national parties, the Liberal Democrats, who were the quickest to adopt internet technologies. All eight Liberal Democrat MPs interviewed were IT literate and most likely to use the internet as a tool for research, organisation and email exchange with constituents. Journalists could also learn more about and engage with party politics and policy (see below). Within parties, lesser-resourced back-bench MPs were more able to challenge policy decisions adopted by their better-resourced party leaders. Typically, as one Labour MP on the Foreign Affairs Select Committee explained:

> For foreign affairs … [I would go to the] Library, internet, not the party on that … I'd dip into sort of [the websites of] the *Guardian*, *Times*, *Telegraph*, you know, and see what has been written … there are serious resource deficiencies here in that the time for research is limited and I do most of it myself.
>
> (Andrew MacKinlay MP)

Digitally-enhanced intra- and inter-party/organisational exchange and deliberation

Another key issue explored was that of the development of online intra- and inter-group communication, exchange and deliberation across political parties and linked constituencies. Starting with intra-party politics, as several have noted (Norris, 2000, Putnam, 2000, Crouch, 2004, Dalton, 2004, Hay, 2007), there has been a long-term decline in party memberships and traditional voter–party alignments. Several earlier studies have explored the internet's potential for increasing membership integration and intra-party democracy in the UK (Ward and Gibson, 2000, Ward et al., 2002, Lusoli and Ward, 2003, Rommele, 2003). Despite some positive developments none recorded any significant success when it came to cross-party or elite-to-member deliberative exchange.

The interview research presented here, and conducted more recently, suggested more significant shifts were now taking place at the party level. In part, this was down to the general take-up and use of ICTs, as more members and MPs used the internet for their daily activities. Within Parliament, internal email traffic has almost quadrupled since 2000 (PICT) and, by 2006–7, a number of parliamentary procedures (e.g., tabling of questions, circulation of Early Day Motions) were increasingly done via the internet (HoC, 2007). This came through in many of the interviews.

Second, the recent emergence of high-profile political blogging and chat-room sites in the UK, oriented around the major parties but not run by them (significant for some years in the US, see Davis, 2005, in particular), also seemed to be part of an important shift here. During interviews with back-bench MPs especially there was a frequent sense of struggling to keep informed about, or contribute to, the policy process and politics within one's own party. Online sites were one increasingly useful means for getting such information about, or participating in, party-wide processes and discussions. Sites like *ConservativeHome* or *LabourHome* were becoming recognised sources of detailed information, analysis and debate on party politics and policy. Others, such as *Guido Fawkes* or *Recess Monkey*, with strong political opinions and gossip, influenced 'softer' forms of deliberation and decision-making. Just as back-benchers looked to such sites so did more senior party figures who were involved in developing party policy or party candidate and leadership selections. Thus, in the view of one former director of the Conservative Party Policy Unit:

> there is a huge community of political blogs that are extremely influential now. *ConservativeHome.com* is a very important one … And blogs like *Iain Dale's Diary* … over the last year or so that has been the big political phenomenon, and no serious analyst of politics could now operate without a detailed understanding of the blogs.
>
> (Greg Clark MP)

Similar views were expressed by the political journalists and bloggers interviewed for the research. Each saw the relevance of these sites for party factions engaged in policy and political differences, with a large proportion of online information and stories coming from inside the same party. Such sites included a mix of 'kite-flying', damaging gossip, rational argument and positive exchanges. As one, more positive account explained:

It's the Cabinet that is the policy making machine of the Labour Party ...
the Labour Party members increasingly need something back for their
membership ... So I wanted to make a space on the internet ... where
anyone could come along and write about Labour politics, or politics in
general, and not feel that their views are unwelcome ... this engagement
across cliques enables people to remind each other of why they're in the
same party.

(Alex Hilton, political blogger)

Overall, the interview material suggested that new media is playing a growing
part in intra-party participation, exchange and deliberation, and in ways that
are more open to back-bench MPs and ordinary party members. However,
where do such developments leave the issue of inter-group communicative
exchange? Increased intra-group exchange might itself be developing at the
expense of inter-group exchange. For Sunstein (2001) and Lovink (2007), individuals are increasingly choosing to avoid public forums, containing mixed
viewpoints, leading to cultural balkanization. Some of these trends are
undoubtedly true. However, the research observed more instances of inter-group
linking than online ghettos.

Those involved in or around the UK political centre regarded it as essential to
both watch and report on their opponents' outputs and all had easy access to
any of these sites. MPs who followed or produced blogs also looked at the
blogs of friendly and opposition MPs. Journalists and bloggers looked at sites
across the political spectrum. The sites of all of the bloggers interviewed
had multiple links to opposing political sites and had even combined to set up a
joint advertising venture. Other studies have observed similar such exchanges
and links (Gillmor, 2004, Jensen, 2006, Quandt et al., 2006, Reese et al.,
2007). Journalists and bloggers, when asked about their online respondents,
all stated that a third or more consisted of individuals with opposing political
views.

Of equal significance, journalists, writing for larger and more varied audiences, made quite extensive use of online information sources (see Table 7.2). As
'general interest intermediaries' (Sunstein, 2001) they drew on a diverse mix of
sites (official and unofficial, left and right) for story ideas and information. For
junior reporters official online sites had become invaluable information sources
which made up for their lack of access to senior political sources. Two-thirds of
the journalists also said they frequently looked at the more popular blogging sites
and, less often, at politician blogs:

it was physically hard to get hold of all these documents. Now you have no
excuse because they're on your screen in front of you. You just have to look
for them and find them. And so the Government websites play a huge part
in what I do.

(Sam Coates, political correspondent)

> Blogs are the equivalent of going to the bar ... *ConservativeHome* is terrific, I
> mean that really is a professional job, where you get quality information ...
> on who's standing in constituencies for the selection processes. What
> used to be a really opaque process, has become transparent, because of
> *ConservativeHome*.
>
> (Joe Murphy, political editor)

The question of how substantial and positive these internet-facilitated shifts are
to representative 'actually existing democracies' remains speculative. However,
what can be argued in the UK case is that the communicative ties between
political participants are thickening. The proliferation of new blogging sites,
chat-rooms and online 'citizen journalism', in providing new political spaces that
are not party controlled, have encouraged a communicative shift at the party
and associated organisations level. There appears to be a sort of centrifugal
movement, outward from the political centre, and more horizontally across
groups and organisations. The insider political process is a little more accessible
and transparent.

New media and the distancing of the popular sovereign periphery

Are there wider consequences of this thickening of the political centre for the
majority of less-interested citizens? Where do such shifts leave those whose
participation in institutional politics varies between total apathy and general
interest/voting? The research here could only answer these questions from the
perspective of those close to the political centre. This suggested that internet-
influenced politics may also be contributing to a general weakening of the communicative links between political elites and citizens. First, new media is further
hastening the decline of traditional mass mediated public spheres. Second, it is
contributing to the exclusionary political 'elite discourse networks' that exist in
traditional, offline politics.

Undermining traditional, offline news production

In terms of the mass mediated public sphere there is long-term evidence of
industry decline in the news media with many non-technological arguments put
forward for this in the UK literature (Franklin, 1997, Barnett and Gaber, 2001,
Davis, 2007, Davies, 2008). These reveal a continuing downward trend in circulation figures, greater pressure to cut costs, recycling of news content and
multi-tasking, and the rise of 'infotainment' at the expense of 'hard' news coverage. Research centres, regulators (Ofcom, 2007) and journalists themselves
have now begun to draw tentative links between the internet's arrival, increased
market pressures, and the quality of journalism. Advertising has been moving
from traditional news suppliers to online, predominantly non-news sites

(Advertising Association, 2007) but, at the same time, online news is being funded out of traditional news-gathering resources. The flourishing of cheap web-based news companies, international competition and news aggregators, such as *Yahoo* and *Google*, have all devalued basic news content. The business model of journalism, which relied on a limited number of news producers and stable advertising, has clearly been breaking down in the last few years (see Freedman, 2009). According to several studies (Cohen, 2002, Singer, 2003, Scott, 2005) this net-linked destabilisation has been some steps ahead in the US. Since 2007, with the global economic recession and rapid collapse in advertising revenues, the profession's long-term decline has suddenly reached a financial crisis point. Big name news producers, both broadcast and print, are on the brink of bankruptcy (Nichols and McChesney, 2009, Pew, 2009). In 2009, Pew (2009) estimated that US newspaper advertising had fallen 23 per cent in two years and nearly 25 per cent of newspaper journalist jobs had gone since 2001.

This came out in interviews. While most of the journalists felt they had gained from the internet, many were also aware of increasing financial constraints, deadline pressures, and an organisational expectation of greater productivity gained via internet use. Reporters were encouraged to spend more time at their desks, constructing news from not always reliable web sources, and less time on traditional news gathering and investigative reporting:

> people are under huge pressure, talk to anyone from the *Telegraph* … At the moment PMQs finishes, George Jones has got to go over and file stuff, and he may even have to do an iPod broadcast as well as something for the blog. And that's all time when you'd normally go straight downstairs and talk to MPs … and there he is stuck in front of his computer writing something that nobody's going to read.
>
> (Gary Gibbon, political editor)

Facilitating online elite discourse networks

Arguably, ordinary citizens are also becoming further disconnected as a consequence of what is taking place in the newly forming online networks around the political centre. This is, in part, because online patterns of political communicative exchange are reproducing offline tendencies. Such trends, whereby political elites frequently tend to look and engage almost exclusively with each other, have been noted in several studies (Herbst, 1998, Davis, 2003, 2007, Lewis et al., 2005). Each has observed the tendency of policy elites (politicians, officials and journalists) to form 'closed information systems' or 'elite discourse networks' that are relatively shielded from the wider public. It seemed from the interviews that, in many ways, new media use has encouraged such patterns.

It emerged that, for users at the political centre, email exchanges and online deliberations with the outside world were problematic for practical reasons.

For each MP who was a constituency email enthusiast there were two more (see Table 7.1) who voiced strong concerns about it. Less than one in ten had engaged with any regularity in forms of wider online dialogue (blogs, debates, etc). In fact, for many civil servants and former ministers interviewed, the wider public had neither the expertise nor interest to participate in the majority of policy processes and outcomes (see also studies by Marsh et al., 2001, Smith, 2003). However, at the same time, for interviewees, the internet had been most useful for organisation and consultation purposes with those they already engaged with. More than a third noted this. Thus, it is no surprise that institutional ICT adoption has been more 'about managerial control and cost reduction' than widening participation and consultation (Chadwick, 2006: 322). As one official explained:

> now everyone can watch it [select committee work] on the website, you know, the web casting, and every public meeting is either in sound or vision … But I think for the moment, that's principally of value to the media and to interested parties like public affairs lobbyists and so on. I'm not sure that, as it were, the general public engages at that level.
>
> (Robert Wilson, senior HoC clerk)

Similar findings became apparent in relation to online journalism and blogging. For both bloggers and blogging journalists there was a strong sense, based on experience of online responses, that their audience was primarily from a privileged, politically-oriented demographic. Paul Staines's (*Guido Fawkes*) actual market data summarised his audience as being: average age 44, richer and from a higher social class than *Financial Times* readers, and with clear clusters from Oxbridge and other top universities, and Whitehall and Westminster (see similar results in Bonfadelli, 2002, Davis, 2005, Ward et al., 2005, Jensen, 2006, Lusoli et al., 2006, Ofcom, 2007). This is unsurprising as the majority of people do not access the online sites of conventional news organisations and political institutions. According to Ofcom (2007), in 2006, only 6 per cent of the UK public got its news from the internet, as opposed to 65 per cent from television. Ward et al. (2005) found that only 2 per cent of people had visited their local MP's website and 5 per cent the parliamentary website in the last twelve months. As Paul Staines and other bloggers explained, they felt they were producing outputs for a relatively specialist group of insiders and 'political junkies':

> Maybe during elections people read political blogs, but mostly it's activists and political junkies … I'm not aiming to write up a story that appeals to, you know, the same readers as the *Telegraph*. I mean, I'm more writing for political hacks and people obsessed with politics. Now I'm narrow casting … about 3,000 hits a day on some of the politics blogs are from parliament.uk and gov.uk.
>
> (Paul Staines, political blogger)

Such insular and cross-referencing networks also seemed to be becoming more entrenched as a result of the internet. When journalists were asked about how new media had changed their practices, the equal first most common answer (see Table 7.2) was its use in monitoring other news outlets. These practices have increasingly come to include the monitoring of bloggers who, in turn, closely follow online journalists (see similar findings in Allan, 2006, Quandt et al., 2006, Reese et al., 2007). According to Reese et al.'s study (2007) 99 per cent of the content of blogging sites was already published material subject to analysis or comment. The picture emerging was one of a conveyor belt of news, information and opinion that rapidly circulates across a select number of top sites. MPs, journalists and other interested individuals choose to go to the websites of a small number of established news producers or well-known bloggers. All watch, contribute to, and may be the subject of, these sites (see also Hindman, 2008, Philips, 2009, on this point). As one blogger explained:

> I wrote a story on my blog about Cherie Blair signing the Hutton Report ... And a few hours later it started appearing on *BBC Radio London*. Then it was on *Channel 4 News* and then, the next day, it was on the front page of three or four of the national newspapers ... that was really the first time that I understood that most of the Westminster Lobby read my blog ... then I found out that I was on the media monitoring list of the Shadow Cabinet. So when I realised that all of the Lobby and half the Shadow Cabinet and a lot of Tory MPs and other MPs read my blog, it was a little bit of a shock.
>
> (Iain Dale, political blogger)

Thus, in several respects, new media has contributed to a weakening of the already fragile communicative links that existed between political elites at the centre and ordinary citizens at the periphery. Clearly, the same political elite tendencies, observed in the pre-internet information environment, are also developing, albeit on a wider scale and in alternative formats, in the new media age. The mass of the public at the political periphery are being further distanced from the political centre. In part, this is linked to the decline in mass media coverage of institutional politics which is, itself, contributed to by the transfer of reporting resources and advertising to online platforms. Partly it is also a consequence of the daily new media uses and practices of those engaged within, or close to, the political centre. Thus, the proliferation of new media sites is not as yet useful for reengaging the mass of citizens who have turned away from party and institutional politics.

Conclusion: thick competitive elitism or 'fat democracy'

Putting these findings together, the following speculative conclusions might be put forward. There does appear to be a significant increase in the communicative links between those in and around the UK political centre. More specialist political information is available to those activists and interested observers than ever before. There are more means of exchange and deliberation of a 'hard'/formal and 'soft'/informal nature. The ability of ordinary party members, journalists and others to engage in such forums is one means of bypassing the restrictions of traditional news media and party-organised communicative spaces. Such developments may encourage greater responsiveness and engagement by party leaders and political elites. However, at the same time, there is a further distancing of the less party-politically engaged mass of citizens. Mainstream news media will devote fewer resources to political coverage because of the collapse of its business model and declining consumer interest. Online spaces and forums may fill the gap but only for those already engaged. The online networks now forming are tightly linked, cross-referencing and self-regarding. As engagements increase at this level so those on the outside, whether through active choice or exclusion, become more removed.

So a sort of fatter, middle-management form of representative democracy is being encouraged with new ICTs. To this extent it might be argued that online trends noted here may be reproducing more general offline trends in the focus and appeal of political parties to members and voters. As others have observed (Crouch, 2004, Dalton, 2004, Hay, 2007, Chapter 3), political parties in mature democracies have increasingly focused their resources on capturing a core grouping of centre-ground, middle-class voters while retaining core supporters. Such strategies involve engaging more with significant stakeholders but at the cost of alienating multiple groups of others. Online politics may be further encouraging these trends.

These larger research-based conclusions relate specifically to the UK case. Although many individual points are supported by studies of journalism, interest groups and politics in other countries, the general picture drawn here may not be reproduced elsewhere. Why, for example, has the internet made a significant impact on elections in the US or Korea but, to date, had a negligible impact in the UK? Variations in political system, traditional media regulation, internet penetration, and geography/population density, amongst other factors (see Chapter 1), may all influence the shape of online politics.

Chapter 8

Politics and communication between the national and the global

Determining the boundaries and significance of 'international political communication'

Introduction

This chapter focuses on the weakly-defined subject of 'international political communication'. Whatever one's views on globalisation and the durability of nation states it is clear that politicians and policy-makers must increasingly engage with transnational actors and respond to global trends and influences. The concern thus becomes to explore the part played by media and communication in these engagements. The questions asked here are: is there such a thing as international political communication?; if so, what form does it take?; and, what part does it play in regard to national and global politics?

One response to these questions has focused on the perceived rise of global civil society and the development of a transnational public sphere. A growing body of literature has recorded the emergence of a set of international political and communicative structures and actors. In documenting such trends observers both detect and positively promote an ideal, future vision of global governance and public communication. However, as argued here, a set of transnational structures and a sense of global interconnectedness may be evolving, but this does not in any way constitute an emerging transnational public sphere. Democratic political and communication systems, those linked to 'public opinion- and will-formation', remain distinctly nation-state based. Instead it is 'cosmopolitan elite networks', international institutions and sites, which make most use of the new global communication apparatus for political and economic purposes. Therefore, investigation of international political communication needs to focus on the communicative practices of these networks and sites and, also, how they relate to national political arenas and publics.

The chapter is in four parts. The first discusses the 'idea' of globalisation itself and whether its multiple strands are steadily eroding the autonomy of the nation state or merely reconfiguring it. It concludes that, regardless of one's analysis, political leaders are increasingly drawn into a series of transnational corporate and governance structures and networks which, in themselves, influence national policy agendas and possible responses. The second part presents the global civil society/public sphere position as it has emerged in response to these trends.

As argued, the positive perceptions of an emerging transnational public sphere are quite misplaced. Part three presents a more critical interpretation centring on 'cosmopolitan elite networks'. Such networks, which generally lack in public transparency and accountability, operate at the heart of the international political communication system. Part four briefly looks at how this state of affairs influences UK politicians and publics in regard to their understanding of, and responses to, international affairs.

Orienting national politics to the international: the death of the nation state?

The slow demise of the Westphalian nation state

Modern (Westphalian) nation states, since conception, have always had to deal with other states and engage with affairs beyond their borders. National security, trade and migration have been of regular concern to national leaders. Over time, a wider range of international issues have emerged that require national political responses, including: competition over finite natural resources and the consequences of environmental degradation; international labour markets, industrial production, trade and finance; transnational flows of media, culture and human migration; international crime, conflict and human rights. A large number of international institutions, transnational corporations and International Non-Governmental Organisations (INGOs) have developed accordingly. The question is, has modern society reached a tipping point whereby even the most powerful nation states are losing their autonomy to the transnational actors and forces of globalisation? If so, what does this mean for the democratic and communicative processes that still remain tied to nation-state frameworks?

Debate about the continued existence of the nation state has wandered over several disciplinary territories. Starting with the issue of political autonomy it seems clear that an increasing amount of state politics is bound up with inter-governmental and transgovernmental exchanges. Held (2002) describes how, since the mid-nineteenth century, there has been a proliferation of international laws and treaties which, in various ways, have come to impinge on or challenge national sovereignty. These, covering warfare, war crimes, human rights and the environment, have merged many areas of state law with international systems of governance. Alongside these treaties have sprung up a rapidly expanding set of International Government Organisations (IGOs) such as the United Nations (UN), World Trade Organisation (WTO) and International Monetary Fund (IMF). This also includes a series of regional organisations, such as the European Union (EU), Association of South East Asian Nations (ASEAN) and Southern Cone Common Market (MERCOSUR), and more exclusive 'clubs' such as the G7 (Group of Seven) and the Organisation of Petroleum-Exporting Countries (OPEC). There has been an even greater proliferation of INGOs such as Oxfam, Greenpeace, Amnesty, and the Red Cross, and including representative bodies for businesses and professional associations. In 1909 there were 37 IGOs and 176 INGOs. By 2000 there were 6,743 IGOs and 47,098 INGOs. In 2001 there were more than 9,000 annual interstate conferences held (Held and McGrew, 2003: 12). In 2005 some 2,800 INGOs had 'consultative status' at the United Nations (Willetts, 2008: 339). In that same year 765 INGOs participated in WTO ministerial conferences. In 2006, 389 INGOs had 'participatory status' in the Council of Europe (Albrow et al., 2008: 324–25).

States have similarly been interlinked with international economic and financial systems. In many accounts (Strange, 1996, Leys, 2001, Crouch, 2004, Cerny et al., 2005, Steger, 2009) a new form of global capitalism, which increasingly restricts state attempts to independently manage their economies, essentially emerged after the global economic crisis years of the 1970s. The 1944 Bretton Woods system of international exchange rate regulation was abandoned, and Keynesian economic policies, which encouraged state economic management, were dismissed. Instead, through the 1980s, neoliberal free-market economics and global financial institutions, such as the IMF and World Bank, both encouraged less state intervention and more international exchange (the 'Washington Consensus'). In many accounts what has since emerged is a new global phase of capitalism propelled by a mix of market ideals, and innovative communication and transport technologies. This next phase has many names and descriptive accounts: 'Turbo capitalism' (Scholte, 1997, Keane, 2001), 'casino capitalism' (Strange, 1986) or 'information capitalism' (Castells, 1996). Each concludes that industrial production, trade, capital investment and currency flows have become more fluid, flexible and transnational and, consequently, have outgrown state economies. One clear manifestation of this is the rapid growth of multi- or transnational corporations (TNCs). In 2001 65,000 multi-national corporations were responsible for $18.5 trillion worth of goods and services and 70 per cent of all trade (Held and McGrew, 2003: 26). In 2004 the 50 largest TNCs each had revenues greater than the GNPs (Gross National Product) of 133 UN Member States (Willetts, 2008: 333).

This combination of transnational influences has had a direct impact on national political, social and economic policy-making. For Habermas (1999), weakened nations have been left with a stark choice: embrace neoliberal orthodoxy, retreat into 'ethnocentric protectionism' or try and chart a problematic and over-compromised 'third way'. For Cerny et al. (2005) governments have most often responded by transforming themselves from welfare states to 'competition states'. Consequently, in many nations, welfare programmes have been cut back, labour laws weakened, and inequality increased. In order to stay competitive in the global market, to attract capital investment and industry, nations have competed in a 'race to the bottom' (in the UK case see accounts in Hutton, 1996, Monbiot, 2000, Leys, 2001, Crouch, 2004, Cerny et al., 2005). As many conclude (Mann, 1997, Rhodes, 1997, Hardt and Negri, 2000, Habermas, 2001, Beck, 2006), such developments are undermining and/or fragmenting national sovereignty. For Rhodes (1997), state political power has been dispersed upwards to supranational bodies, sideways to privatised industries and markets, and downwards to quangos and agencies. There is a shift from 'government' to 'multi-level governance' which necessitates the 'hollowing out of the state'. The state at times struggles to 'steer' let alone 'row'.

For critical media scholars (Schiller, 1969, 1989, McChesney, 1999, Herman and McChesney, 1997, Thussu, 2000, 2008, Bagdikian, 2004), national media, culture and identity seem similarly to be threatened. International flows of news, popular entertainment and cultural commodities now seem to be part of every-day experience. However, these are not free, neutral, multi-directional flows. They are owned and managed by a group of ever-expanding transnational media corporations which are fully interlinked into the global economy and are simply profit driven. They are also predominantly American or Western in origin and facilitate a form of 'cultural imperialism' (Schiller, 1969, 1992, Tunstall, 1979, MacBride Report, 1980, Mattelart et al., 1984, Thussu, 1998, Boyd-Barrett and Rantanen, 1998). Tunstall (1979), Mattelart et al. (1984), and Varis (1988) have traced global media content flows. They found in the 1980s, for example, that a majority of films broadcast in every European state bar France were from the US. Thirty of the top fifty advertising agencies in the world were American. Half of Europe's imported television programming came from the US. Smaller and poorer nations are significantly more dependent on Western, particularly US, imports. For Boyd-Barrett and Rantanen (1998) the issue was particularly acute in terms of international news gathering and dissemination. For most of the twentieth century, four news agencies, from the US, UK and France, dominated the collection and dissemination of international news to national broadcasters. Such discrepancies became the centre of international debate at UNESCO in the late 1970s and resulted in an unsuccessful call for a new world information order (NWICO, MacBride Report, 1980). In effect, international media flows are guided by TNC profit motives and promote Western cultural products to homogenised international consumers, so undermining national identities and citizen interests.

A reconfigured state in a global modernity

However, a large group of sceptics argue that national politics, economics and culture are not being simply eroded by the forces of globalisation. Instead they are being reconstituted. For Held (2002) and others (Mann, 1997, Slaughter, 2000, Keane, 2001, Swank, 2002, Richards and Smith, 2002) this means a 'reconfiguring' of the state is taking place in ways that make it both stronger and weaker. Slaughter (2000) says the state is not in decline but is 'disaggregating into its component institutions', each of which link horizontally with external nation-state equivalents. This 'transgovernmentalism' places the state more centrally in international developments. Mann (1997) argues that some transnational social movements encourage legislation that strengthens nation states. Richards and Smith (2002) maintain that 'multi-level governance' has had a mixed effect on state government but, on balance, the state is merely 'reconstituted' and the core state executive remains 'the dominant actor'.

Others are similarly more equivocal in their perceptions of the encroachment of the global economy. Keane (2001), Gilpin (2001) and Swank (2002) separately argue that states have actively embraced corporations and financial markets. Access to new and flexible forms of global capital have in fact consolidated their ability to manage their economies. Swank (2002) found no correlation between international capital mobility and reduced levels of taxation or welfare state funding. Mosley (2003) also recorded that international investor decisions were more linked to basic economic indicators, like inflation or government debt levels, rather than 'Washington Consensus' principles. As Hay (2007: 144) points out, throughout the twentieth century, state expenditure, as a proportion of GDP, has actually increased in all OECD countries. In 1910 it was roughly 10 per cent but by 2000 had climbed to between 40 and 50 per cent. He continues that levels of FDI (Foreign Direct Investment) have been highest in countries with above average levels of corporation tax, union density, labour costs and regulation. Hirst and Thompson (1996) demonstrate that, in many ways, the world economy was more economically integrated in the two to three decades before World War One. Currently, the majority of TNCs gain most of their revenue from their home country and have more of a regional than global presence in their trading patterns. The global economy is thus more a series of regional trading blocs which have benefited the leading national economies. Most globalisation 'sceptics' do not question the significant, and sometimes negative, influences of large corporations and global markets on national economies. However, the key point frequently made (Hirst and Thompson, 1996, Hoogvelt, 1997, Cerny et al., 2005, Hay, 2007) is that 'economic globalisation' is not an inevitable process that will submerge all states. Rather, it is a Chicago School 'doxa', disseminated by Anglo-American corporations, financial markets, and international economic institutions, that legitimates neoliberal economic policies.

The reconfiguration of states approach is similarly applied by those in media and cultural studies. They argue that flows of international media are increasingly multi-directional and do not in particular reflect the 'centre–periphery' model of the cultural imperialism position (Sepstrup, 1989, Sreberny-Mohammadi, 1996, Rantanen, 2005, Thussu, 2007). In recent decades, Mexico, Egypt, India, Brazil, Hong Kong, China and Japan have all expanded cultural production, exports and investments abroad, variously in film and television production, animation and computer games. Tunstall (2007), three decades after once declaring the dominance of US-based media, more recently concluded that 'the media were American' and now in decline. Others, taking another tack, have also stressed the complex mixture of cultures and ethnicities, within nations and transnationally, making cultural production a less nation-centric occupation than assumed (Lull, 1995, Morley and Robins, 1995, Tomlinson, 1999, Rantanen, 2005). Instead of 'corporate dominance' and 'cultural imperialism' accounts record 'counter-flows', 'hybridisation', and 'glocalisation'.

What does this all mean for democracy and public communication in a globalised world? Political communication theory and debate has traditionally conceptualised democracies and public communication within the framework of the nation state (Habermas, 2001, Fraser, 2007). Whether state sovereignty is being fundamentally compromised or merely reconfigured by the forces (real and imaginary) of globalisation, nations are increasingly internationally oriented. Political, financial, media and environmental systems all stretch and interlink beyond national boundaries. Climate change, international financial regulation, nuclear proliferation, war and instability in the Middle East, rising energy prices and food shortages, are all transnational issues being discussed in 2010 with some urgency. Even if national sovereignty retains its place, as state politics is further linked to external polities, networks and publics, traditional forms of democracy become compromised.

The emergence of international governance, global civil society and the transnational public sphere?

An evolving global public sphere

Taking an alternative starting point, scholars from several disciplines have sought to observe and/or set out guidelines for new, international forms of governance and public communication. As Beck (2006) argues, the way forward requires moving beyond state-centric 'methodological nationalism' to conceptualise and encourage an alternative 'cosmopolitan vision' of global governance. This begins by establishing a set of common principles that involve all world citizens. For Habermas (1999) and Fraser (2007) these include a commitment to 'normative legitimacy' and the 'political efficacy of public opinion' underpinning political action. For Held (2003), the guiding principles should be 'inclusiveness', 'equality', 'autonomy' and 'impartialist reasoning'. Thereafter, there is a split (see McGrew's overview, 2002) between those who focus on reform and/or reconstruction of international institutions ('liberal internationalism' or 'cosmopolitan democracy') and those who seek a radical, more bottom-up approach ('radical democratic pluralism' or 'deliberative/discursive democracy').

Out of these engagements a positive vision is in the process of developing, which both documents and attempts to plot an ideal system of transnational governance and public communication. Held (2002, 2003), Keane (2001) and Slaughter (2000) document the formal, international political architecture developing. Elsewhere, an accompanying vision of 'global civil society' is emerging (Anheier et al., 2001, Kaldor, 2003, Albrow and Glasius, 2008). This extends the Gramscian notion of civil society to the global level. It thus observes positive developments coming out of 'progressive' NGOs, social movements and citizen initiatives acting in the space between states, international institutions and the global market. It also emphasises public participation and deliberation drawing on a line of thinking from Dewey (1927), via early Habermas (1989 [1962]) to Dryzak (2002, 2006). As Albrow and Glasius (2008: 10) state: 'Most authors in this volume treat both global civil society and the global public sphere either as an existing reality, or at the least as an achievable ideal.'

Most of the literature on global civil society says little about media and ICTs but, of course, is fundamentally reliant on their existence. However, in parallel, there has been a spate of work linking old and new media to the perceived emergence of transnational (or regional) public spheres (Robinson, 1999, Volkmer, 1999, 2005, McNair, 2006, Albrow and Glasius, 2008, Price, 2008, Deane, 2008). Volkmer (1999, 2005) was amongst the first to argue for the emergence of a global public sphere, based on her initial insights into CNNI and its successful expansion in the 1990s. McNair (2006) and Chalaby (2009) note that, despite Anglo-American dominance of international news agencies and broadcasters, a number of more powerful national and regional players have emerged (Al Jazeera, Xinhua, Euro News, Russia Today, France 24). Chalaby's (2009) detailed study charts how significant changes in technology, the structure of the advertising industry, and European harmonisation policy, all enabled a pan-European television communicative infrastructure to fully develop from the early 1990s onwards. By 2006, 279 million people in thirty-two European countries had access to such channels. Estimated advertising income had reached 672 million Euros annually (Chalaby, 2009: 63, 85). Clearly, an international communications architecture is developing in tandem with transnational political and civil society structures. Alongside this work has come a series of studies focusing on those INGOs, social movements and deliberative forums which make up global civil society and utilise the internet (Naughton, 2001, Sparks, 2001, Gillmor, 2004, Pickerill, 2004, Cammaerts and Audenhove, 2005, Dahlgren, 2005, Kavada, 2005, Dean et al., 2006). Where mass media may potentially speak to a global citizenry, new media provides the platforms and connections for more intense forms of deliberation, exchange and organisation. Media technologies have caught up with McLuhan's original 'Global Village' (1962) account, thus producing the infrastructure for the emerging global public sphere.

Accordingly, such mass media and digital platforms are contributing to a sense of 'cosmopolitan identity' and impacting on international political affairs. Several studies of the perceived European Public Sphere have emerged (Schlesinger, 1999, Trenz, 2004, Gripsrud, 2007). These have attempted to gauge to what degree different national publics share similar international 'media events' (Dayan and Katz, 1992), international news content and interpretive frames (Trenz, 2004), and whether such news encourages a sense of shared European or 'cosmopolitan identity' (Beck, 2006). Gripsrud (2007) perceives something more preliminary evolving: namely 'a European layer' being added 'to the identities of Europeans'. There are now a number of documented examples of the 'CNN effect' (Robinson, 1999, Volkmer, 1999, see also Soroka, 2003) or 'the boomerang effect' (Keck and Sikkink, 1998). In the former, international coverage of wars and disasters pushes politicians to increase military or international aid spending, or intervene in conflicts abroad such as Somalia, Iraq and Rwanda in the 1990s. In the latter, nation-based protests gain international coverage, so forcing domestic governments to make responses they would not otherwise have contemplated. Media-driven international outcries have pushed public and political responses on: extra-judicial killing of street children in Brazil (Serra, 2000), the treatment of peasant communities in Southern Mexico (Knudsen, 1998), environmental degradation caused by energy firms (Anderson, 1997, de Jong, 2005), human suffering and global poverty (Boltanski, 1999, Sireau, 2009). Similarly, mobile and internet technologies have proved instrumental in the organisation and publicity surrounding anti-globalisation and anti-war protests in Western countries, and in popular challenges to transitional and authoritarian regimes in Burma, Iran and Thailand (Downing, 2001, Keane, 2001, McNair, 2006).

Global public sphere or the partially-sighted vision of a bourgeois cosmocracy

Arguably, there are a great many flaws in the global civil society/public sphere vision. The international political architecture currently remains very distant from any conventional conception of democracy linked to public 'opinion- and will-formation'. As Dahl (1999) points out there is a fundamental paradox of democracy which means it cannot be extended to the global level. The larger the demos, the more complex and representative it becomes. For Dahl, even though national democracies fall short of their 'ideal' images, any form of international democracy inevitably falls 'below any reasonable threshold of democracy'. Habermas (1999) is equally pessimistic about the prospects for nation-state democracy at this level. Fraser (2007) offers normative values but, as yet, no workable model. INGOs, despite their association with public and progressive causes, are not democratic organisations, and may be even less connected to public opinion and local publics than NGOs. Kaldor (2003) in fact refers to them as 'tamed social movements' and 'like quasi-governmental institutions'. Anderson and Reiff (2005) note that many of them represent reactionary movements and associations. All, reactionary or progressive, are self-appointed, pursue their own interests, and are not accountable or electable.

It also appears increasingly difficult to sustain the argument that elected governments have the power to control their economies. Regardless of whether international CEOs, fund managers and financial institutions apply overt pressure to politicians (they do!), the level of financial capital controlled in the financial sector far exceeds that of nation states. That is very significant for several writers (Ohmae, 1990, 1995, Strange, 1996, 1998, Hardt and Negri, 2000). In 2003, UK-based fund managers alone controlled approximately £2.2 trillion worth of funds (IMA, 2003). The largest of these, Barclays, managed £530 billion. In 2007 over £3 trillion worth of currency was traded on international exchanges on a daily basis (Steger, 2009: 49). To get this in proportion, the UK government's annual income and expenditure in 2004 was £430 billion. The ability of governments to thus regulate and manage their economies becomes increasingly difficult (see also Reich, 1991, Rosenau, 1997). Such mismatches prevented the UK's entry into the ERM in 1992. They were linked to a series of financial crises in the 1990s, and were at the heart of the near collapse of the global financial system and subsequent recession (2007–). Banks, corporations and investment funds around the world were able to trade financially engineered products worth many trillions; far in excess of either their asset bases or government balance sheets. Countries such as Iceland, the UK and US, with oversized financial sectors, have suffered most amongst the OECD nations. Their national economies will struggle under the huge debts, incurred by multiple bank rescues and fiscal stimulus packages, for many years. But barely any international economy, however prudent and regulated, has remained unaffected.

Neither does the existing transnational communicative architecture of the global public sphere resemble anything close to its idealised conception. In the twenty-first century, international media and culture, more than ever, are dominated by a few, mostly Western-based TNCs. Of the top ten media TNCs, by sales, seven are American, two are Japanese, and one is French (Albrow et al., 2008: 277). Reuters and Associated Press have consolidated their dominance of the wholesale international news supplier market. Of the six truly transnational news companies in operation, five are English-language, US and UK enterprises (CNNI, BBC World, CNBC, News Corporation, Bloomberg) and one (Al Jazeera) is not. Under such circumstances it may be argued that corporate Anglo-American media has been instrumental in globally promoting an Anglo-American form of neo-liberal market capitalism and 'Occidental' discourse (Said, 1978).

Despite the spread of transnational news operations, actual national news operations and patterns of consumption suggest that there is little in the way of a shared global or regional public sphere. First, the large majority of news consumption is of a national or local nature with the actual viewing figures for international news media relatively tiny (Curran, 2002, Sparks, 2005). International news on national news outlets, even of shared events, is repackaged, framed and addressed to national audiences (Clausen, 2004, Downey and Koenig, 2006, Eide et al., 2008). Coverage of 9/11 and the Iraq invasion in 2003 (Beringer, 2003), and the responses to the publishing of the Prophet Mohammed cartoons in 2005 (Eide et al., 2008), varied considerably across nations and continents. As Cottle and Rai (2008: 175) discovered, only 6.3 per cent of international news reporting of CNNI, BBC World, Fox News and Sky can be considered 'depth', contextualised or investigative reporting. Norris's (2000: ch. 9) study of news coverage of the European Union found that there was very limited coverage of EU political institutions. Her (Norris, 2003: 291) analysis of the World Values Survey of 70 nations found a distinct lack of 'cosmopolitan identity'. Strong doubts are also cast on the 'CNN effect'. As Foyle (1997) and Jakobson (2000) argue, politicians are rarely interested in public opinion on international affairs as it is hardly considered to be a significant voting issue. Media coverage of conflicts abroad is highly selective, out of step with decision-making, and is only encouraged by politicians when promoting previously-made decisions.

Such findings demonstrate that what exists falls far short of even being a 'fledgling public sphere' on the global scale. Nation states may be more integrated into transnational political, economic, environmental and cultural systems. Transnational organisations, and international systems of governance, trade, travel and communication, may have developed extensively. There may be a heightened awareness of global cultures and events and a sense of cosmopolitan identity. However, democratic political and media systems remain largely nation-state entities. Many of the 'ideals' of a global public sphere, including access, inclusiveness and deliberation, will never be achieved through existing global political and media institutions and structures. As Schlesinger (1999) and Baisnee (2007) conclude, what does exist of a European Public Sphere, is that experienced and promoted by elite political and corporate groups. It is those regular participants of the 'bourgeois cosmocracy' (Keane, 2001), relatively tiny in number, who are most positive about their global vision.

From transnational public spheres to cosmopolitan elite networks and communication

International political communication and cosmopolitan elite networks

Where does this leave us? Is there such a thing as international political communication? If so, what form does it take currently and how should it be observed?

What does currently exist, at the centre of these varied global institutions and systems, according to many of the above authors, is a set of 'cosmopolitan elite networks' and spaces. Castells (1996, 2001), in particular, has attempted to conceptualise such networks as drivers of social, economic and political change on a global level. He describes a restructuring of global capitalism, facilitated by new ICTs, new divisions of labour, post-Fordist production processes, and decentralised government and corporate bureaucracies. The new cosmopolitan elite networks that emerge from such configurations move between 'global cities' and other 'hubs' (technological, corporate, institutional). Holton, building on Castells and Thompson (2003), defines international networks:

> as forms of multi-centred social organisation that are distinct from two other major organisational types, namely markets and hierarchies. Networks involve more enduring forms of social commitment and trust than markets but are more flexible and less centralised than hierarchies.
>
> (Holton, 2008: 4)

Transnational elite networks emerge from several professional occupations. One network type commonly described is corporate and/or financial, referred to by some as the 'transnational capitalist class' (Sklair, 2001, see also Reich, 1991, Keane, 2001). Equally common are those made up of international institutional and transgovernmental technocrats and government ministers (Dahl, 1999, Slaughter, 2000, Richards and Smith, 2002, Held, 2003). There are also 'policy networks' and 'policy entrepreneurs', scientific and 'knowledge networks' (Marsh and Rhodes, 1992, Haas, 1992, Rhodes, 1997, Cerny et al., 2005, Kogut and MacPherson, 2008), as well as INGO networks (Keck and Sikkink, 1998, Kaldor, 2003, Anderson and Reiff, 2005). In these accounts it is the inhabitants of these transnational elite networks who have the greatest sense of cosmopolitan identity. They move across the globe with frequency, are comparatively well educated and wealthy. Those who inhabit the international levels primarily operate with minimal 'normative legitimacy', transparency, or accountability to national publics. Their experiences, knowledges and concerns are many steps removed from the publics of economically advanced nations let alone those billions living on less than a dollar a day.

What also seems clear is that it is the members of these networks who make most consistent use of the kind of international news media and ICTs described in the global public sphere literature (Castells, 1996, 2001, Schlesinger, 1999, 2007, Held, 2003, Sparks, 2005). Norris's (2003) analysis notes 'cosmopolitan identity' is more prevalent in those who are young, well educated, urban dwelling, English-speaking and post-materialist. Chalaby's (2009) research reveals that the success of transnational news channels in Europe is based on their ability to attract advertising focused on the high income of their viewers. Similarly, it is a predominantly wealthy elite which consumes international newspapers (the *Financial Times, Wall Street Journal, International Herald Tribune*) and weekly periodicals (*Time*, the *Economist*) (see Kantola, 2006, Durham, 2007). The dominant demographic for international online news consumption, as on the national basis, is also male, Western-based, English-speaking, well-educated and comparatively wealthy. Albrow et al. (2008: 280, 286) noted that internet penetration in 2005 had reached 70 per cent in North America but was as low as 11 per cent in Asia and 4 per cent in Africa. Political bloggers were predominantly male (72 per cent), older, and educated to degree level (78 per cent, 36 per cent to postgraduate level). Curran and Witschge's (2009: 110–11) study of the international online magazine, *OpenDemocracy*, found that 71 per cent of contributors, and 83 per cent of visitors, came from North America and Europe. Authors were also mostly male and from highly-educated professions such as academia and journalism. Thus it may be concluded it is such cosmopolitan elite networks that make most use of international media and new ICTs.

All of which suggests that if one wants to investigate the ways media and communication influence nation-state politics or transnational governance, one should focus on such transnational elite networks. One might speculate that the communicative architecture linking such networks operates on several mediated and media-oriented levels. At one level, those involved in a professional network may all automatically access the same specialist (electronic, print) sources of information. Thus, Knorr Cetina and Bruegger (2002) and Davis (2005) record the significance of shared, international electronic information flows for financial traders. There is also a series of specialist publications, such as reports and journals, produced by 'expert' and authoritative institutions, and in common circulation within international policy networks (Haas, 1992, Simmons et al., 2008). Lastly, there is the international media which is most consumed by, and influential amongst, cosmopolitan elite networks (Sparks, 2005, Schlesinger, 2007). As Chalaby notes (2009: 187), with reference to European opinion leader surveys, BBC World and CNN 'are considered influential because they know how to speak to influential people: they command the attention of an elite audience that is elusive, exclusive and difficult to impress'.

Taking in a broader interpretation of communication one should also look at the cultures, beliefs, discourses and practices of elite networks. Here the concern is with personal communication, micro-level contacts and exchanges, in person or via ICTs. This takes us into the territory of international sociology, anthropology, psychology and foreign policy analysis (FPA, see Hudson, 2005). Holton (2008) calls for 'charting and understanding the importance of active human agency' within international networks, advocating cultural and social-level investigation using 'multi-sited ethnography' (Marcus, 1995). In such a vein, Mintz (2004) has focused on the decision-making practices of leaders. Janis (1982) has revealed how the dynamics of small groups, or 'Groupthink', strongly influences and constrains policy debates and outcomes. Elsewhere, Haas (1992) has noted the increasing reliance of 'non-expert' political leaders on international 'networks of knowledge-based experts', or 'epistemic communities', for the identification of international risks and possible solutions. He describes the twentieth-century proliferation of such experts, both within governments and international institutions, on a range of technical subjects. Stone (1996), Mintram and Vergari (1998), Cerny et al. (2005), Kogut and MacPherson (2008) each focus on the rise of 'think tanks' and international 'policy entrepreneurs', their role in transmitting new ideas between networks, and encouraging their adoption through personal contacts with central decision-makers.

Each of these forms of communication helps to embed actors culturally, cognitively and behaviourally into cosmopolitan elite networks. They circulate norms, values and interpretive frameworks. They spread a sense of shared identity, highlight common problems, agendas and lines of consensus. In effect they make up the communicative architecture through which international policy communities form, and develop recognised discourses and practices. Within such an analytical framework, the concern then moves towards identifying and tracing the roots of certain dominant ideas, discourses, 'doxa' or 'episteme' that frame international policy choices. For example, Cerny et al. (2005) and Simmons et al. (2008) have sought to trace the social, cultural and communicative means by which neo-liberal economic policy has been disseminated globally.

Simmons et al. (2008: 47) found that 'simple coercion is seldom the main process underlying policy diffusion'. National policy elites also adopt changes because of a belief in the need to compete globally ('competition') or because they observe instances of success in other nations ('learning' and 'emulation').

Arguably, the international news media have played a significant part in terms of the global diffusion of dominant economic thinking through non-coercive mechanisms. Parsons (1989) considered their outputs as vital, both for the adoption of Keynesian and later Monetarism in both the UK and US. Kantola's studies, of the role of the *Financial Times* (2006, 2009) in global economic elite discourse, are telling. The paper's coverage of some thirty-two elections between 2000 and 2005 regularly backed candidates which supported pro-market reforms, and were critical of democracies, publics and leaders which did not. She also argues, in her analysis of coverage of Finland, that its evaluative discourse of nations actively encourages steps towards economic globalisation. Thus the international financial media, from the *Economist* to the *Wall Street Journal*, further 'disciplines' its cosmopolitan elite networks.

It might thus be concluded that by a variety of means of communication, national and international elite networks can become physically, culturally, cognitively and discursively 'disembedded' from other national elites and national publics (see Chapter 9). How actors in international elite networks and institutions perceive and respond to international issues may be quite different from those primarily inhabiting national elite spheres, and more different still from national publics. In the US, Kull and Ramsey's (2000) study of members of the elite 'foreign policy community' in Washington found that their foreign policy views were entirely at odds with the public, and also misinterpreted public opinion, on a range of foreign affairs issues. Three-quarters of the policy community believed that the public wanted international disengagement, were hostile to the UN and were against US troops being used in international peace-keeping missions. In each case, a clear majority of the public had the opposite view. The study also found that most of the community did not regard public opinion on foreign affairs as significant and gauged their views through personal contacts and 'vocal publics' (organised interests, think tanks, etc., see also Powlick, 1995, Herbst, 1998).

Communicative and cultural disengagements between UK national publics and cosmopolitan elites

The disparities between transnational foreign policy networks, national political networks, and publics did indeed emerge when interviewing political actors operating around the UK Parliament. It slowly became clear that there were significant informational and discursive differences between senior government politicians and civil servants, ordinary MPs and officials, and the wider public, on foreign affairs generally, and Europe in particular.

On the one hand it is apperent that there are clear differences between the information circulated within senior ministerial and civil servant circles, and the equivalent within the parliamentary sphere. Such a conclusion is deduced from studies of UK foreign policy networks and several insider accounts of the Foreign Office and Ministry of Defence (Marsh et al., 2001, Richards and Smith, 2002, Dickie, 2004, Meyer, 2005, Short, 2005). It was further supported in several interviews with former ministers and civil servants. Cabinet ministers and senior civil servants have access to specialist briefing and intelligence material from the Foreign Office (FCO), Ministry of Defence (MoD) and Joint Intelligence Services. As interviewees explained, the MoD and FCO are very restricted in both their gathering and dissemination of information and analysis. Some results go only to the Prime Minister's office and a select group of Cabinet Ministers and civil servants. As one civil servant relayed:

> a lot of our [source] material is internally generated, a rather hierarchical process ... a very narrow, almost totally internally driven process, with the other stakeholders being in other Government departments ... And the briefings and recommendations go up to the Cabinet Office, to NSID. In a sense it's Cabinet Office, NSID with, yes, say the Foreign Office. And if you're dealing with military allies well then it's a mixture of political liaison and also military to military ...
>
> (David Stevens, civil servant)

As these documented and interviewee accounts also stated (see Dickie, 2004, in particular), external sources of foreign affairs expertise, such as defence think tanks and correspondents, are usually kept relatively distanced from both information collection and dissemination. Unlike many other government departments, there are no regular briefings, meetings and other outputs for journalists from the FCO and MoD. Consequently there are now only a handful of UK diplomatic correspondents.

However, when ordinary MPs were asked about their information sources, they turned to the House of Commons Library and those very think tanks and journalists excluded from government policy networks. This included those with an occupational interest such as shadow ministers and select committee MPs and clerks covering foreign affairs and defence. In fact, those with a specialist interest often expressed frustration at their lack of access to significant government information:

> With Defence there were specialist publishers like Jane's. Then institutes like ... Chatham House. In terms of strategic studies, those sort of people put out stuff, which is quite useful. But I think that the insights came from talking to people who were involved, actually involved, you know, the soldiers ... because the higher up you get, and the closer to Whitehall you get, the more constrained people are about what they'll say to you.
>
> (John Maples, former Shadow Defence Minister)

MPs, in turn, are rather more knowledgeable about, and focused on, international affairs than their constituents. A large proportion of UK legislation is initiated by the European Union. Many policy areas, be it on the national or local constituency level, have an international dimension. There are 140–50 registered all-party parliamentary groups, each with a minimum of 20 listed members, focused on individual nations and regions. A large majority of MPs interviewed in the research period were indeed widely read on international affairs and had strong views on a number of policy areas. At the same time, many were concerned at the news media's lack of reporting of international affairs generally, and the European Union specifically. Indeed, the issue most MP and journalist interviewees listed as being excluded from media coverage and public debate, was European affairs and the activities of EU legislators and administrators.

Norris's (2000) survey of EU news coverage found it to be 'minimal' and usually 'given a negative-leaning' slant. In Curran et al.'s (2009) comparative survey of UK news content 29 per cent of broadcast news and 17 per cent of print news were classed as 'international'. However, a large majority of this was focused on either 'soft' news topics, such as celebrities, or conflict in Iraq and Afghanistan. So just 8 per cent of UK international news, or 2.3 per cent of broadcast and 1.3 per cent of print news overall, covers Europe. In one survey of MPs (Baker et al., 1999) the clear view was that there has been a 'paucity of debate' on Europe, both in the media (80 per cent Lab, 76 per cent Con, 84 per cent Lib Dem) and amongst the electorate (88 per cent Lab, 88 per cent Con, 100 per cent Lib Dem):

> on the issue of the European Union, which I'm very concerned about, and I was spokesman for the party … the media view of the situation is that institutional reform in the European Union is a dull issue now because they don't see it as being part of the agenda. And it's very difficult to get past that blockage, if you like.
>
> (Lord Robert Maclennan)

> Very few journalists understand European affairs, and that pool of journalists is ever reducing. Previously you used to have correspondents in Brussels. They would change around and come back … and be able to share their knowledge, their information, their understanding. I think that has declined markedly. There isn't a single Scottish print journalist based in Brussels … the domestic media has no contact with MEPs, they wouldn't know who to talk to.
>
> (Angus Robertson MP, former journalist)

Unsurprisingly, the disparity between parliamentarians and the wider public, in terms of information availability, interest and knowledge of foreign affairs, particularly regarding Europe, is reflected in several surveys. According to Ipsos-MORI

(1997–2009) 'Defence, Foreign Affairs, International Terrorism' has rarely been considered one of the top five 'most important issues facing Britain' by the public under Labour. This is in spite of being involved in several conflicts (Iraq, Afghanistan, Somalia, Kosovo and East Timor) in that time. It has been a negligible electoral issue, barely registering in four of the last five elections and, even in the wake of the Iraq Conflict (2003–), was still only considered the fifth most important issue in the 2005 election. In 2004 a majority of the public acknowledged that it was an area they knew little about (YouGov, May 2004). Asked 'How much do you think you know about the powers and responsibilities of the European Parliament?', 71 per cent answered 'not much' or 'nothing at all'.

There are also strong, contrasting views on European issues. Amongst parliamentarians, Labour and Liberal Democrat MPs, as well as civil servants, are generally in favour of greater integration with Europe. Conservative MPs and the public are generally against. In 1991 (Sanders and Edwards, 1992), before Britain's failed attempt to enter the ERM, 100 per cent of the 190 'foreign policy elite' interviewees agreed that 'The "EC Connection" is crucial or very important to Britain's International Role and Interests'. In 2005 (Smith, 2006) 80.3 per cent of civil servants, and 87.7 per cent of Labour MPs, agreed that 'For Britain the benefits of European integration outweigh the costs'. Public opinion throughout this period has remained fairly sceptical. From 1990 up to the present, support for the Single Currency has wavered between 22 and 33 per cent; opposition has moved between 50 and 60 per cent (Ipsos-MORI, 1990–2008). In one survey (YouGov, June 2005) 10 per cent said they wanted closer political integration with the European Union and 80 per cent less.

Conclusion

As discussed here nation-state politics and economics are becoming more international in orientation. International systems, networks and organisations are rapidly multiplying in response. Whether these processes are global or regional, real or imaginary, determined by coercion or emulation, national political actors are professionally more attuned to global matters. Likewise, transnational systems of media, communication and culture continue to spread swiftly. An accompanying sense of global connectedness is also to be found in most wealthy and medium-sized economies.

However, a closer look at the developing political, economic and media infrastructures reveals very uneven patterns of development. The relevant transnational architectures are not facilitating the emergence of global civil society or a transnational public sphere that involves national publics and forms of democratic accountability. Instead they are proving most useful to the functioning of cosmopolitan elite networks and transnational organisations and institutions. Such elite participants regularly move in international circles, have the greatest sense of cosmopolitan identity, are best placed to take advantage of international travel and communication, and are the most consistent users of transnational media and online professional exchanges. Conversely, nationally-based media reporting of foreign affairs, outside of conflicts and natural disasters, is declining and foreign bureaux being scaled back. National political bodies and publics are becoming further distanced (physically, socially, culturally and communicatively) from these networks and institutions. This suggests that vital political and economic policy agendas, issue priorities, and decision-making processes may be too.

Chapter 9

Foreign policy-making, war and the disembedding of cosmopolitan elite networks

The case of Iraq 2003

Introduction

This chapter focuses on the media and communication surrounding foreign policy-making and war. In contrast to the usual territory covered here, the concern is with how political leaders develop alternative interpretive frameworks to the public on foreign affairs and conflict. It thus investigates the role of media and communication in separating elite foreign and military policy-making networks from national parliaments and general publics.

After a limited review of the literature on war reporting, the chapter sketches out a basic theory of political cultural 'embedding' and 'disembedding'. It is argued that social and communicative differences create 'layers of cultural embedding and disembedding' as political actors step between the local, national and international spheres. This encourages globally-linked, political elite networks to become radically 'disentangled', first from wider publics, but also from nationally-based political networks. The discussion is followed by an extended case study, illustrating these ideas, and focusing on the US and UK in the lead up to the invasion of Iraq in 2003. This attempts to explain the large disparities in opinion and understanding that occurred between transnational political and diplomatic networks, state parliamentary spheres, and wider national publics. As argued, at each of these levels, the audiences involved were informed by quite different information systems and social relations and, accordingly, had quite distinct understandings of and responses to the issues.

The media politics of war and the separation of elites and masses

How are politicians and citizens separated or reconciled during national conflicts? Clearly, war can unite or divide political leaders from their publics as much as any issue. War is also a time when news reporters become most professionally conflicted between the requirements of the state and the public. Fourth estate media principles, including free speech, public accountability and transparency, are often wilfully abandoned, ironically, all in the cause of preserving democratic ideals. These themes, of conflict and difference between leaders, journalists and publics, are common in accounts of modern war report-ing. In many respects, the literature here is depressingly consistent in its record-ing of democratic government attempts to restrict information, manage reporters, and use propaganda to persuade citizens. Accounts only vary in the degree to which media passively support or question decision-makers, and on whether or not publics are persuaded to support military action.

For many, state propaganda and media management strategies are all too often successful as reporters and publics come to support their national leaders during conflicts (Mowlana et al., 1992, Miller, 1994, Philo, 1995, Herman and Chomsky, 2002, Stauber and Rampton, 2003, Thussu and Freedman, 2003, Knightley, 2004, Philo and Berry, 2004). Governments rapidly expand their propaganda structures and communicat budgets to manage the media. At such times, journalists are most restricted in their movements, are particularly dependent on political and military leaders granting them access, and suffer from political 'flak' and physical threats. At the same time, reporters often take a partisan, patriotic stance in support of their governments, self-censor and willingly accept access conditions. Consequently international conflicts often provide the strongest case examples of the 'propaganda model' (Herman and Chomsky, 2002) in action.

For others, interest lies more in establishing under what conditions journalists and publics come to question and challenge government military interventions (Hallin, 1994, Bennett and Paletz, 1994, Wolfsfeld, 1997, Entman, 2004, Tumber and Palmer, 2004). These studies emphasise the divisions and points of contention in journalism and, more significantly, within political elite circles. These variously theorise how divisions amongst political elites come to be reflected in news media frames. Entman's (2004) 'cascading activation' model, building on Bennett's (1990) and Hallin's (1994) earlier work, is the most com-plex account. This observes a series of ever-larger spheres, moving from gov-ernment to other political elites, then via media producers and news frames to the public; identifying a number of conditions which then determine whether the spheres become aligned or not.

Each of these lines of work clearly separates groups of actors and social spheres, from government leaders down to citizens. Each also conveys a sense of top-down information persuasion in which those networks above influence, to a greater or lesser degree, the larger audience below and, on rare occasions, transmit opinion back up. The additional question, explored in this chapter, is how are such spheres of peoples distanced from each other in the first place? Why should governments, legislatures, media and publics come to have contrasting initial outlooks?

Embedding and disembedding of elite foreign policy networks

The theme of cultural and cognitive separation of elites from publics has been touched upon in several earlier chapters. Chapters 2, 3, and 8 have all suggested that politicians (and civil servants) are likely to become more disengaged from publics the higher they progress, first in national, and then international political hierarchies. Information sources, social relations, discourses and practices all change and accordingly guide political elites. To more fully conceptualise these findings and patterns the chapter, drawing on work in economic sociology, now develops a theory of cultural 'embedding' and 'disembedding', and reorients it to the political sphere.

Two contrasting descriptions of these concepts have emerged within the literature. For Polanyi, in *The Great Transformation* (1944), modern market exchange was but one form of economic organisation that was 'embedded' in (but has become more disembedded from) social organisation generally. Markets emerge as socially embedded phenomena but evolve in ways that make them autonomous from society and, thus, disembedded from the social. This was a cause of crisis for Polanyi (1944: 57) because increasingly powerful, socially dis-embedded and unregulated market systems then imposed their logics on society and citizens: 'it means no less than the running of society as an adjunct to the market. Instead of economy being embedded in social relations, social relations are embedded in the economic system.'

When Mark Grannovetter later took up the theme of embedding ([1992]1985), he referred to economic actors and actions within defined market spheres, as being internally socially embedded. In attempting to avoid the extremes of ato-mised agency and social determination, he argued that the rules, regulations and norms of markets were established through the ongoing social interaction of rational agents. In other words, markets are not simply mechanistic systems which disembed themselves from societies. They also involve individuals who then become further embedded in the social aspects of those markets. Michel Callon (1998a, 1998b), too, argued, with reference to markets, that economic actors change as they enter the market sphere itself. Market actors become entangled in the social structures of their markets as they take on the norms, values and discursive practices of those markets. Thus, within the market, the 'homo economicus' of classical economic theory 'really does exist' but is also 'formatted, framed and equipped with prostheses which help him make calcula-tions and which are, for the most part, produced by economics' (Callon, 1998a: 51). Putting these concepts together it might be argued that actors are socially embedded in wider society but, upon entering into developed markets, become both further embedded in those markets socially, but also disembedded from wider society. This very process encourages the disembedding of a market from society.

These concepts may also be applied to political actors and bureaucrats who move between the local, national and transnational spheres. On the one hand, they have a role representing local populations but, on the other, also come to be entangled in the social and communicative elements, first of national parlia-ments and bureaucracies, and second, of the transnational policy networks they join. For high level politicians and civil servants there is, to use another Polanyi term, a political 'double movement' in play. They seek to be elected and/or represent their citizens; to be embedded in the social relations of their national citizenry. But they also want to debate and participate in the national, and then transnational, governance and regulatory spaces they enter into; which necessitates degrees of disembedding from other levels. In each case, political actors (politicians and civil servants) operate as 'network intermediaries', moving between the cultures, social structures and levels of power their social relations permit. But, as they progress upwards they become more embedded in those networks while also becoming more disembedded from the larger social networks or spheres below. The logics of those disembedded political elite networks then come to be imposed on wider social publics, just as Polanyi argued that disembedded markets impose themselves on societies.

The following case study, focusing on the varied information environments and decision-making levels in the lead up to the war in Iraq in 2003, illustrates this embedding/disembedding paradigm perspective.

The case of Iraq 2003 and the disembedding of cosmopolitan foreign policy networks

On 20th March 2003 a predominantly US and UK military coalition attacked Iraq, officially to uphold a series of seventeen breached UN resolutions dating back to 1991. Ostensibly, the invasion was justified by George Bush and Tony Blair as the only means of removing Iraq's 'weapons of mass destruction' (WMD) and halting its support for international terrorism. Military resistance was subdued and the war was over in six weeks (1st May). The invasion has turned out to be a foreign policy mistake of grand proportions and with tragic consequences. Following the invasion and removal of Saddam Hussein and his Ba'ath Party ruling structure, Iraq quickly degenerated into a state of violent anarchy. At least 100,000 civilians have died violently (rather more in several estimates), over four thousand occupying troops have been killed, several million refugees have been displaced, and basic infrastructures destroyed. WMD have never been found. The policy also severely tarnished the reputations of Blair, Bush and other political leaders who supported them. This leaves several questions: Why did the Bush and Blair administrations proceed without full UN support, without conclusive evidence and (debatably) contrary to international law? Why, at the height of their popularity, were they prepared to dismiss public opinion and take such political risks? Why were they decisively backed by their respective executives, legislative assemblies and national media in these decisions? And, what part did media and communication play?

In trying to investigate these questions evidence was gathered from a number of alternative spheres, including those of: the public, journalists, parliament and MPs, the government and specific foreign policy networks. These were gained from a mixture of existing polling data, academic studies of reporting and news content, official reports, (auto) biographies and personal interviewees. In total, the subject of Iraq was discussed with some thirty-seven MPs, journalists and civil servants, usually on the basis of their close professional interest in the case. Several declined to comment in any detail as, even some years later, it is still a sensitive subject. Indeed, another official enquiry began in late 2009.

The critical narrative

For many critics and sceptics of the war some strong arguments are put forward. For liberal and conservative commentators, at a minimum, the public was deceived and Iraq has further encouraged distrust of the media and political institutions. For critical scholars, the case is a classic example of political elites abusing their power, using extensive propaganda to manage the media and public opinion, and thus neutralising opposition. Either way, the narrative describes a situation where small elite networks, at the top of the US and UK political and bureaucratic hierarchies, for ulterior motives, persuaded those below them to support a problematic military action abroad. In turn, each set of actors persuaded those further down the pyramid of public opinion. The component parts and sources of this narrative are as follows: one, Iraq's WMD capability was very limited and US and UK leaders knew that it was not an imminent threat (Kampfner, 2004, Short, 2005, US Senate, 2008). The country's WMD capability had been largely contained and dismantled since the first Gulf War in 1991. Two, regime change in Iraq was a long-term objective of US foreign policy (Mazarr, 2007, Khong, 2008). For several reasons (political, military, economic) a small group of 'neocon' White House appointees and advisers had long since decided that it was in the national interest that the Iraqi Government be overthrown. The events of 11th September ('9/11') 2001 were politically expedient for the neocons and ultimately enabled them to push the Bush Administration to move forward on their long-term goal of 'regime change'.

Three, Tony Blair supported the US action to gain leverage for other policies, such as the resolution of the Israel–Palestine conflict (Meyer, 2005, Seldon, 2005, Dunne, 2008). Blair's foreign policy, since coming to power in 1997, had been tightly linked to successive US administrations (Clinton then Bush). This continued with greater intensity following the attack on the Twin Towers. Four, the US and UK administrations decided on invading Iraq early, somewhere between September 2001 and April 2002; i.e., at least eleven months before the actual invasion (Woodward, 2004, Clarke, 2004, Kampfner, 2004, Short, 2005, Dunne, 2008). Five, both sets of leaders and their inner circles put pressure on their respective intelligence services to find evidence of Iraqi WMD as well as links to al-Qaeda and other terrorist groups (HoC, July 2003, Butler, 2004, US Senate, 2004, 2005, 2008, Oborne, 2007). Both took a selective view of the existing intelligence, frequently ignoring its weaknesses, stated caveats, and contradictory findings. Six, both networks side-stepped traditional Cabinet, bureaucratic and parliamentary procedures, committees and systems of checks and balances (Woodward, 2004, Butler, 2004, Seldon, 2005, Short, 2005, Meyer, 2005, US Senate, 2008).

Seven, both sides developed extensive propaganda operations to 'sell' the war, to their own political supporters, their parliaments, other national leaders, and to media and citizens at home and abroad (Brown, 2003, Stauber and Rampton, 2003, Kull et al., 2004, Miller, 2004, Snow, 2003). The White House went further and on several occasions suggested that Saddam Hussein was linked to al-Qaeda, the '9/11' attacks, and was arming international terrorists. They deliberately misled all these audiences (Brown, 2003, Stauber and Rampton, 2003, Kull et al., 2004, Miller, 2004, Snow, 2003, and US Senate, 2008) with a series of public statements and official (or 'dodgy') dossiers of evidence. Eight, their respective parliaments, main opposition parties, and national media were too uncritical of what was happening until after the initial invasion and occupation (Thussu and Freedman, 2003, Lewis, 2004, Miller, 2004, Entman, 2004). Most of those interviewed, whether they supported the attack on Iraq at the time or not, concurred with several or all parts of this narrative.

Many of the component parts of the critical narrative are partially or entirely correct and now appear supported by substantial documented evidence, official and otherwise. For example, it now seems fairly certain that small circles of advisers around Blair and Bush had too much control over events, by-passed conventional systems of governance, and over-played the intelligence about the Iraqi threat. It is also now clear that there was no significant WMD programme in Iraq, not of the scale that could threaten Western powers, and nor was the Hussein regime likely to have had any links to al-Qaeda or the 9/11 attacks. On such a basis all official US and UK reports have been critical of the intelligence findings. It is also undeniable that extensive media and information operations were rolled out to promote the case for war, and misleading information was deliberately presented to both sets of parliaments and publics.

However, other parts of the narrative remain in doubt or offer a rather vague explanation of events and decision-making. What did the inner circles actually believe in relation to Iraq and for how long? Why did Blair support the US attack and when exactly was the decision made to invade Iraq? Why did clear majorities from the leading parties in the UK and US, despite concerns and questionable public support, fall into line and give their public backing? Why did the media fail to look sufficiently critically at the arguments being made? Similarly, why did a host of other political administrations from Europe and elsewhere defy public opinion to give political, if not military, support to the attack? Falling back on explanations of mass conspiracy, manipulation and/or mass gullibility to explain all these questions seems a little too simplistic.

Without contradicting the critical narrative, this chapter instead develops an alternative media- and communication-based account of events; one that fits in with the cultural embedding/disembedding paradigm described above. In the case of Iraq, a process of disembedding is described, in which each level or network of decision-makers became separated from its lower, larger level. The foreign 'policy communities', in which Blair and Bush moved, became disembedded from their wider government and parliamentary (including journalists) social spheres and these, in turn, became disembedded from their wider citizen bases.

The embedding and disembedding of elite foreign policy networks in the UK and US

The embedding/disembedding of elite foreign policy network(s) from national governments and parliaments

What is argued here is that Tony Blair came to inhabit an exclusive, socially-embedded, elite foreign policy network, well in advance of '9/11'. The participants of this network had long-term concerns about WMD, international terrorism and Iraq. This network and its concerns then directed his understanding of, and response to, US plans to invade Iraq. At the same time, this network had become disembedded from the Cabinet, the civil service and parliament.

Like Bush, Blair was very much a foreign affairs novice when he came to power in 1997. Like Bush, he increasingly turned away from the domestic policy agenda and towards foreign affairs (see Seldon, 2005, Short, 2005, Dunne, 2008). Partly as a result of his personal leadership style, he worked through select groups of loyal, personally-appointed advisers (Butler, 2004, Dickie, 2004, Seldon, 2005, Short, 2005, Campbell, 2007). This modus operandi, as well as a foreign affairs policy of 'humanitarian interventionism', became consolidated through peace negotiations in Northern Ireland, the bombing of Iraq in 1998 and intervention in Kosovo in 1999. By the time of September 11th, Blair had his trusted inner circle of people, a mix of personal political advisers and defence staff.[1] This group met regularly, and always in advance of the larger, official 'War Cabinet'. Others, such as Jack Straw (Foreign Secretary), Geoff Hoon (Defence Secretary) and Christopher Meyer (British Ambassador to the United States) were in frequent direct contact. The picture that emerges is that, by September 11th, Blair inhabited a very exclusive policy network or 'epistemic community' on international affairs.

In several accounts, too, it becomes clear that the views of Blair and his inner circle, on Iraq, international terrorism and WMD, were forming as far back as 1997 (Meyer, 2005, Seldon, 2005). According to Seldon (2005) and Short (2005), Bill Clinton had then impressed on Blair the problem of Iraq and WMD. In fact, just before the bombing of Iraq in 1998 ('Operation Desert Fox'), Blair had made a speech and prepared a document for MPs on 'Iraq's Weapons of Mass Destruction'. Campbell's (2007) diary makes many references to Blair's discussions and concerns on these issues over a lengthy period. In these same accounts, Blair is depicted as being more focused on Iraq than Bush, at least up until April 2002.

A parallel policy network had clearly evolved around George Bush in the White House (see accounts in Clarke, 2004, Woodward, 2004, Mazarr, 2007,

Khong, 2008) guided by the long-term ideological position of the neocons or 'vulcans' (Dick Cheney, Donald Rumsfeld, Paul Wolfowitz, Douglas Feith, Lewis Libby). This network too had been voicing its concerns about Iraq since Gulf War I.

Following the '9/11' attack both networks became further consolidated and intense. They also increased their exchanges significantly. According to Dickie (2004: 104), after '9/11' the JIC daily summary of intelligence became 'top priority reading' for Blair. Blair and Bush were, at times, in daily telephone contact, as were other members of Blair's select group with Condoleeza Rice, Colin Powell and others. Military intelligence and plans were regularly shared. Both elite networks not only acted as 'epistemic communities', they were subject to 'groupthink' (Janis, 1982). Both groups were increasingly self-guiding and reinforcing of their beliefs and concerns over several years. Such certainties were relayed down to the various intelligence services who, in the wake of '9/11', were clearly under institutional pressure to uncover any further potential threats, no matter how tenuous the information.

Through all the documented accounts and personal interviews there were clear points of disagreement. For example, the issue of when exactly Blair agreed to join the US attack, regardless of whether his conditions were met, remains disputed. However, it does seem clear now that Blair, Alistair Campbell and his inner circle very much overplayed and exaggerated the existing WMD threats (HoC, July 2003, Butler, 2004). They then, most probably, covered up their role in the producing of those intelligence dossiers (Short, 2005, Oborne, 2007, and several interviewees):

> On a personal level I want to know who and how we were lied to, or misled, and it's just unacceptable ... somebody, somewhere told us that there were weapons of mass destruction that were an immediate threat, and I want to know how such a cock-up came about or if it was deliberately set out to mislead.
>
> (Andrew MacKinlay MP, member of Foreign Affairs Select Committee 1997–)

At the same time, no-one suggested that Blair and his aides had lied about the WMD argument, or the nature of the Iraq regime and its potential to cause problems beyond its borders. Several interviewees said they had had personal exchanges with Blair and believed him to be genuine in his beliefs. Short (2005) described his actions as being 'an honourable deception'. Meyer (2005: 282–84) said that, at the time, he – Meyer – and all those connected, believed that WMD did exist, there was no early decision to go to war, and opposes the notion of a Bush and Blair 'conspiracy'. Seldon (2005: 583–84) also cites several insiders who support each of these points (see also Kearney, 2003, Campbell, 2007). Three official UK enquiries, albeit limited or compromised in various ways (HoC, July 2003, Butler, 2004, Hutton, 2004), conclude that the broader statements in the September 2002 'dodgy' dossier were reasonable, on the basis of existing intelligence, even if misleadingly presented in parts (although the latest 2010 inquiry may find otherwise). Peter Oborne, who has written an entire book on the 'lies' of New Labour (2007), said in interview:

> I knew he [Blair] had a record of not knowing what he was doing, a record of naivety and deceit ... I never believe anything a minister ever says, but I mean even I believed there were WMD ... my impression that what they [those on the inside] all say, and I don't disbelieve them, believed in the existence of WMD.

The US case remains more cloudy in terms of whether the neocon foreign policy network really believed in WMD and the wider Iraqi threat or not. Several accounts (Woodward, 2004, Clarke, 2004, US Senate, 2008) certainly argue that many basic claims put by the Bush administration, such as the al-Qaeda connection and Iraq's purchase of uranium in Niger, were indeed manufactured and known to be so. It also seems clear that Iraq was a likely target very early on, and that the neocon network had been 'fixated' on the Iraq threat for years. So, like the UK case, it could be argued that the 'epistemic community' of neocons did sincerely believe in the Iraqi threat but, also, that it had decided to invade early on and then engineered an extensive propaganda operation to push the case.

Just as Blair and his foreign policy network became socially embedded, internally and with its parallel US network, so they became culturally disembedded from the UK Cabinet, civil service and parliament. As several accounts note, Blair came to bypass traditional FCO (Foreign and Commonwealth Office) channels and the Cabinet (when in operation), while also becoming increasingly focused on his regular JIC briefing (Joint Intelligence Committee) and US networks. Blair's network had exclusive access to intelligence information and foreign contacts. In contrast, those parts of the governance system which could call Blair to account, the Cabinet and senior civil service ranks, were very much excluded from such information inputs and discussions.

Dickie's (2004) insider FCO account makes clear that much intelligence on Iraq bypassed the Cabinet and senior civil servants. Butler (2004) found that detailed briefing material was prepared for Cabinet discussion but never actually circulated. Short (2005) states that most of the Cabinet never saw the majority of the relevant material and that, those select few who did had limited access. In her accounts (2005, and interview) Blair, in effect, strongly managed and directed his Cabinet on the issue, while also pushing the 'collective cabinet responsibility' line. 'Groupthink' thus played a part at this level. Many voiced reservations in the September (2002) Cabinet meeting; the only one, according to Short, in which an open debate took place. However, almost all agreed to support Blair's policy and took his word about the military threat. As Estelle

Morris, a former Cabinet Minister, recounted: 'I was there for the September Cabinet meeting ... There was a sensible discussion but at that time most people in the room did believe there were weapons of mass destruction, and that, for me, was the key thing.' In Clare Short's recollection:

> There were no [Cabinet] papers ... it all fits with what I'm saying about Blair's policy-making structures, the less information others have the better because then he can control the decision-making ... in the big chunk of time, all through the summer when the whole atmosphere's building up, House of Commons isn't meeting, Cabinet doesn't meet, so everyone's getting their information from the media or whatever they get in their departments ... but no Cabinet. And so there would be bits of discussions before ... it's fair amounts of Tony saying 'Right Jack, could you just say about your visit to Colin Powell' ... then as Blair managed it week in, week out, it sort of becomes clear they're [Cabinet Ministers] not invited to that table.
>
> (Clare Short MP, former Secretary of State for Development)

Like many Cabinet Ministers, ordinary MPs, be they back-benchers or senior opposition party members, were further separated from the Government in terms of the information made available to them. They did not have access to the daily briefings produced by the extensive networks of the Foreign Office, Ministry of Defence and Joint Intelligence Services. As Dickie (2004) points out (and also, Richards and Smith, 2002, Meyer, 2005, Short, 2005, Chapter 8), the gathering and circulation of intelligence, FCO and Defence material generally was very insular and restricted. Ordinary MPs, even senior opposition ones, could not gain access to it. External sources of expertise, such as foreign affairs and defence think tanks and journalists, were also kept relatively distanced from this.

However, when MPs with a specific interest on such issues were asked about their information sources, they relied very heavily on the published outputs of those same foreign affairs think tanks and journalists. This included those opposition ministers and select committee MPs and clerks covering foreign affairs and defence. Several explained that they never had access to the vital documents necessary for evaluating government decisions. In fact, a key complaint of MPs who wanted to investigate government policy here was the lack of access to the actual intelligence reports, most specifically those on Iraq:

> we knew that much of the material would have been denied to us, and therefore we were groping in the dark ... [we] raised it frequently with the Liaison Committee, on shifting the balance, a series of reports on relations with the Executive, and we did a special report to the House complaining about the lack of cooperation on intelligence.
>
> (Lord Donald Anderson, Chair Foreign Affairs Committee, 1997–2005)

The embedding/disembedding of state parliaments from national publics

At the same time, the parliamentary sphere became both internally socially embedded and also disembedded from external national publics. Its information inputs, social exchanges and political considerations differed considerably from ordinary citizens. As stated (Chapter 8), MPs generally have a greater professional interest in international affairs than the general public and also much better access to information here. Clearly, by the time of the parliamentary vote on support for military action in Iraq (18th March, 2003), MPs had been fairly focused on the issue for much of the previous twelve months. Between February 2002 and the start of the war, in March 2003, there were six debates in the House of Commons on Iraq and a further three on closely related matters that included Iraq. In addition, Tony Blair made three statements to the House on Iraq plus two on related matters. Geoff Hoon made another four statements on Iraq, and one related, and Jack Straw three statements on Iraq (all figs. in HoC, 2009). Two select committee reports were circulated and the Commons Library produced several research papers summarising events, arguments and policy choices (e.g., HoC, September 2002, March 2003). MPs also received their own party briefing documents, gathered their own 'intelligence' and talked with colleagues frequently about the issue.

Several MPs were asked why the majority had backed the vote, when evidence seemed lacking, and in the face of strong public and international unease. The most frequent answer given was a genuine belief, at the time, in the potential military threat of the Iraqi regime. As several put it, even taking into account the notion that the threat was exaggerated, none believed that Blair and the intelligence would be entirely wrong. The second most common response was that the Hussein regime had a long record of committing human rights atrocities and defying UN resolutions and, officially, the war was to uphold UN resolutions. Several also believed that, as in earlier conflicts (Iraq, 1991, Kosovo, 1999), the war would be relatively quick, and peace and stability restored fairly easily:

> [we supported the Government] on the information available at the time, a large proportion of which obviously came from the Prime Minister. He felt it was the responsible thing to do ... and the intelligence services in countries like Germany, France, Britain and America, all believed that there were weapons of mass destruction, and it would be difficult to stand up and say 'I don't know but I think the intelligence services are wrong'. Take a brave man to do that.
>
> (Michael Ancram, Deputy Leader of Conservative Party, Shadow Secretary of State for Foreign Affairs, 2001–5)

The views and responses of MPs were also influenced by a number of internal party-political considerations. Many interviewees indicated that such factors played a large part in MP decisions. By all accounts Labour MPs were subject to some concerted lobbying by Blair, Cabinet Ministers and the party whips (Seldon, 2005, Short, 2005, Campbell, 2007). The stakes also appeared high for the Parliamentary Labour Party. It was widely propagated that Blair would resign, if he did not get at least a Labour majority, and a general election could potentially result. For others, it was simply a matter of being loyal to one's party and voting accordingly. Since it was clear that the Government were likely to win, because of solid Conservative support, so the personal risks of rebellion seemed high. According to some interviewees, those with doubts about Iraq felt they were outweighed by the personal political risk of rebellion, especially for those in the government. So ministers, whips and loyal MPs were further motivated to join the lobbying of doubters:

> not only would he [Tony Blair] have had to resign ... they [the Labour Government] would have been humiliated internationally, shown to be unfit to govern because they tried to do something. Then they couldn't do it. It's the ERM times ten, Suez revisited. It would have been cataclysmic. And in the end that's what people like Gordon Brown realised. And they knew they had to come out and put their shoulders to the wheel, whatever they thought in private.
>
> (Gary Gibbon political editor)

Ultimately, 139 out of 410 Labour MPs rebelled in the largest party revolt against a UK Government in the modern parliamentary era. They were joined by the Liberal Democrats. Three ministers, including Robin Cook, the former Foreign Secretary, resigned from the Government, as did Elizabeth Wilmshurst, the Deputy Legal Adviser in the Foreign Office. Clare Short resigned two months later. However, the Government was supported by the majority of Labour MPs as well as the Conservative Party, and won a clear victory. The Government won the cross-party support of 396 MPs against 217 opposition votes.

The Parliamentary sphere was, in turn, disembedded from wider public opinion, where opposition was confused but instinctively stronger. From an information source perspective most ordinary citizens had neither the specialist, inside intelligence information nor the detailed House of Commons information supplied to MPs. They were not encumbered by any personal and professional career concerns. They were almost entirely dependent on the mainstream media to inform them. But, in many accounts, the UK and US media proved to be all too vague and unquestioning of government foreign and military policy in the wake of the 11th of September attack (see collections in Greenberg, 2002, Zelizer and Allan, 2002, Stauber and Rampton, 2003, Thussu and Freedman, 2003, Entman, 2004, Kull et al., 2004, Lewis, 2004, Miller, 2004).

One explanation for this is that, almost immediately in the aftermath of '9/11', government and military sources came to dominate news coverage and continued until after the six-week war in Spring 2003 (Greenberg, 2002, Lewis, 2004). Significantly, the major opposition parties of both parliaments (Conservative Party and Democrats) gave strong support to their governments. In effect, despite many public protests from fringe politicians and journalists, mainstream political and media opinion found a consensus. As earlier studies of foreign affairs reporting demonstrate, journalists are unlikely to report disunity, go to outside sources, or act critically of government, if there is broad political elite consensus (Bennett, 1990, Hallin, 1994, Entman, 2004). So it was in the period between '9/11' and 'Operation Iraqi Freedom'. Several UK journalists interviewed defended their role at the time, saying they were not sufficiently expert enough to determine the veracity of the claims supporting war, and simply reported the views of the leaderships of the main political parties:

> we weren't experts. We did not know the scale to which the Government perhaps had exaggerated things on the dossier … we were reporters who were reporting what was going on in Parliament, in Government. Our views were not particularly of interest. We were just reflecting what MPs and politicians thought.
>
> (Ben Brogan, political editor)

Another reason for the news media's weakness was the fact that, during this period, the US and UK established the largest propaganda operations since World War Two. The US spent billions of dollars in its promotional efforts while the UK spent hundreds of millions (see accounts in Brown, 2003, Stauber and Rampton, 2003, Miller, 2004, Snow, 2003). Large-scale communication operations were set up, including the Pentagon's Office of Strategic Influence, the White House's Office of Global Communication, and the Civil Contingencies Secretariat in Downing Street. All fed continuous and coordinated information to reporters at different sites while also using strong-arm tactics. As one Labour MP remarked (Jeremy Corbyn MP): 'over the Iraq war the pressures put on the media were absolutely extraordinary, by the Ministry of Defence and Downing Street'. In the US, the Bush administration went further, presenting a series of unopposed but misleading statements about the reasons for war. These included the arguments that Iraq had WMD, was linked to al-Qaeda and 9/11, and that world public opinion supported US actions (Kull et al., 2004, US Senate, 2008).

Accordingly, this meant that news reporting rarely questioned the WMD thesis until too late. Lewis's (2004) survey of UK media content found that news coverage continued to reproduce claims of the 'possible' or 'likely' existence of WMD in Iraq. 89 per cent of references to the subject 'assumed their probable existence'. War reporting itself focused almost entirely on fighting and strategy. A pro-war bias was more detectable still in the US media (Entman, 2004, Kull et al., 2004). According to Kull et al.'s (2004) revealing study, a majority of viewers of Fox News, CBS, ABC, CNN and NBC television channels believed in one or more of the 'misperceptions' disseminated by the Bush regime. In January 2003, 68 per cent of the US public in fact believed that Iraq had had a role in '9/11'.

Actual UK and US public opinion polls reflected the confusion propagated by political leaders and transmitted by mainstream media but, when given the facts, were fairly critical of the war. Polls of the time are actually quite variable, confused and contradictory, mainly because the survey questionnaires reflected the doubts and misperceptions of media reports. Such ambiguities enabled several politicians and journalists to assume, erroneously, that a majority of the US and UK publics supported the attack on Iraq. Interestingly, there was a general perception amongst many interviewees (journalists and politicians) that a majority of the public had indeed supported the war prior to its commencement. Several interviewees mentioned this factor when explaining why they and others supported the Blair government. The February 2003 protest march across London, while being the largest in British history – figures vary between three quarters of a million and two million – was not considered politically significant. Former Cabinet Ministers played down its importance. Clare Short (interview) said it was never discussed in the Cabinet. As Estelle Morris recounted:

> I think people forget this. All the polls at the time of the invasion of Iraq were for the Prime Minister's action. Even if two million marched on London, there's a population of well over 56 million, and I think if you actually look at the polling data, I think it was in favour of the Prime Minister's action.

However, it seems more sensible to conclude that public opinion was actually unsure and uncommitted but, when presented with clear information, was largely at odds with political elite opinion. In the case of the UK, the evidence suggests that public support for action was conditional on WMD existing and UN approval. For example, in January 2003, 61 per cent of the public stated their support for Britain joining the American-led action against Iraq 'with UN approval'. However, 77 per cent opposed such action 'without' it (MORI, Jan. 2003). In general, support for Tony Blair personally and action in Iraq steadily declined through 2002. By March 2003, only 30 per cent 'approved' of his 'handling' of Iraq and 54 per cent disapproved (MORI, March 2003). Faith in the UN was rather higher than in either the Blair or Bush administrations. Once war began a majority of the public (56 per cent) came out 'in support of their troops' but, some months after the initial invasion, opponents of the war were again in the majority (see Lewis, 2004). They have continued to remain so since.

In the US, approval of George Bush was clearer but support for action in Iraq was also linked to particular conditions. In September 2002, 67 per cent of the public 'approved' of Bush's job performance, although only 52 per cent said he had explained the case for war clearly. By January 2003, 76 per cent favoured military action but this dropped to 28 per cent if no proof of WMD was found.

It dropped to 26 per cent if the US acted unilaterally and 21 per cent if significant US casualties were to result. Under such conditions 48 per cent opposed action (Pew, Jan. 2003). By February, following Hans Blix's UN report of no further WMD being found, 58 per cent said the US did not have enough international support to proceed and a new UN resolution was necessary (Pew, Feb. 2003). Clearly, US public support was dependent on certain conditions being met and many falsely believed that some of these conditions had indeed been met (see Kull et al., 2004).

The disembedding of political and foreign policy elite networks from national publics was not just confined to the US and UK nations. Public opinion elsewhere was largely opposed to military action and extremely hostile across most of the Middle East (Berenger, 2003, Hawley, 2003, Pew, March 2004, Schuster and Maier, 2006). Yet many governments supported the action, politically if not militarily. In fact, fifteen European nations supported the action in Iraq in spite of public opposition. Just five European governments, notably France and Germany, reflected the opposition of their citizens. Some Middle-Eastern and African nations also supported the action in spite of strong public opposition. Huge protest marches were staged, often in the hundreds of thousands, in many countries. The three largest were in Barcelona (1.3 million), Rome (3 million) and London (1–2 million). However, the UK, Spanish and Italian Governments all defied the polls and marches to back the action in Iraq.

Note

1 David Manning (Chief Foreign Policy Adviser), Jonathan Powell (Chief of Staff), John Scarlett (Chair of the JIC), Sally Morgan (Director of Political and Government Relations), Michael Boyce (Chief of the Defence Staff), Richard Dearlove (Head of MI6), and Alistair Campbell (Chief Press Secretary and PM's Spokesman).

Chapter 10

The 'crisis' of politics and communication in ageing democracies

Introduction

This chapter looks at the varied debates on the crisis of politics and public engagement in mature democracies. For almost all concerned there is, at the minimum, a perception of political crisis. This is recorded in the views and behaviours of general publics in regard to political institutions and politicians. By the end of the twentieth century, electoral turnout was dropping, party memberships had sharply declined, and trust in political institutions was extremely low. These trends are to be found in a majority of established democracies across the globe, despite differences of political system and culture (see Norris, 2000, Pharr and Putnam, 2000, Dalton and Wattenberg, 2002, Putnam, 2002, see figs. in Chapter 1). This perception of crisis, in itself, is damaging for the health and stability of democracy. In addition, at the end of the first decade of the twenty-first century, the crisis of politics and public engagement seems to be more than one of mere perception. The global economy is struggling to come out of a deep depression that will burden many nations for years to come. Democracies everywhere are failing to confront other major problems, including: global warming, energy dependence on declining fossil fuels, drastic forthcoming global water and food shortages, growing trade and production imbalances, rising inequality and exclusion, and an ageing and increasingly unhealthy population. The current model of capitalist democracy looks financially and environmentally unsustainable in the long-term.

The questions are: are we observing a substantive, long-term crisis of democracy, or simply a series of relatively minor and cyclical phenomena? If there is a real crisis what are its root causes and are they treatable? The chapter begins with a discussion of the relevant crisis literature. Within this section are inserted summaries of the views of many of those interviewed for this project. It then highlights and synthesises some of the crisis themes as they appear through the chapters of the book.

The causes of crisis

The causes of 'crisis' literature are spread across politics, sociology and media, and have many over-lapping strands. Much of it is directed by the discipline and object of study, the methods used, and the countries and time periods selected. Thus answers and explanations vary considerably, even when using similar data sets. Broadly, they fit into one of five categories: the public and political culture, alternative politics linked to globalisation and interest groups, the political system, parties and politicians, and the media and journalists. During the interview process, seventy-one of the interviewees offered their own opinions on the causes of the 'crisis' of politics and public engagement in the UK. The responses covered all the main themes of the crisis literature and are summarised accordingly in Table 10.1. Certain issues feature more heavily in one group than another.

The public, political culture and social modernisation

The most common focus of crisis literature is that which looks at the public and political culture. A tradition, traced from Almond and Verba (1963), up to recent authors as diverse as Putnam, Inglehart and Norris, each chooses to look at citizens. If the crisis is one of citizens' perceptions and beliefs changing then what is it about citizens that may have changed? As Hay (2007) notes, the crisis question, by default, then becomes discussed as a 'demand-side' (public) rather than a 'supply-side' (institutions) problem.

A proportion of this work is in fact fairly critical of citizens themselves and casts doubt on the crisis notion altogether. Inglehart's long-developed thesis (1977, 1990, 1997, 1999) is, in effect, a statement that 'we never had it so good'. The political crisis literature of the 1970s (e.g., Crozier et al., 1975, Habermas, 1977) was essentially driven by the real economic crisis of the time. However, by the late 1990s, when the question of crisis re-emerged, capitalist democracies were relatively stable. As Inglehart argues, when democracies mature, and economic and physical security is achieved, wealthier and more literate citizens adopt 'postmaterialist' values. They are more critical, demanding, less deferential towards authority, and come to have unreasonable expectations of the state and politicians. In fact, for Inglehart, there is no crisis to speak of. Having independent, critical citizens is actually positive for democracy. A public, with postmaterialist values, is a contented, more secure public that values democracy per se.

Table 10.1 Interviewee opinions on the perceived causes of political crisis and public disengagement from institutional politics

	Politicians (41)	Journalists (15)	Officials (15)	Total (71)
Journalists/media	26 (1)	10 (2)	8 (1)	44
Parties/politicians	21 (2)	11 (1)	4 (3)	36
Public/society	15 (3)	10 (2)	2 (6)	27
Alternate politics	14 (5)	4 (5)	8 (1)	26
Political system	15 (3)	5 (4)	4 (3)	24
No crisis	4 (6)	3 (6)	4 (3)	11

Crises are cyclical, rather than long-term. Ultimately, what counts is that governments and parties improve the well-being of their publics, not that they are poorly regarded in 'soft' measures of opinion.

The theme of a well-off, overly-critical, but also ignorant and inactive, public reappears in several guises both old and new. There are strong echoes here of the 'overloaded state' thesis developed in the 1970s (see Crozier et al., 1975, Buchanen and Wagner, 1977). That essentially argued that the state had been extended too far in the post-war period and this increased public expectations beyond what was practicable. More recently, both Dalton (2004) and Norris (1999b, 2000, 2002) are in broad agreement with Inglehart's assessment. Survey evidence offers some support here. As the Hansard Society's political audits (2009: 6) show, UK citizens are interested in politics and opinionated but only a small minority are willing to become active. They 'want influence over outcomes, but not involvement in the process'. Hibbings and Theiss-Morse (2002) reveal similar findings in regard to US citizens. These works (see also Webb, 2007) each argue that the general public simply does not understand the practice and process of politics and is unaware of the difficulties and complexities of the modern 'multi-dimensional policy space'.

Amongst those interviewed (see Table 10.1) one in seven stated that there was no crisis. Almost two-fifths, in the 'public/society' category, made comments that focused on the public themselves as a causal explanation. Half of these stated that the public had much higher living standards and were better educated, making them more 'content' and 'critical'. Others blamed the public for being too 'cynical', 'busy', 'ignorant' or 'apathetic' to vote. Some interviewees were in fact overtly critical of voters who 'had never had it so good'.

There is an alternative, more sympathetic body of work that focuses on issues of citizenship and incentives for participation. Key amongst these is the work of Putnam (1993, 1995, 2000, 2002). Putnam's studies of civic society, in Italy and the US, link declining levels of trust in political institutions to a decline of 'social capital'. For a range of reasons, citizens have less social capital because they are joining and participating less in local associations, be they political, civil or merely social. This reduces 'trust' in others and in political and state institutions. The reasons given by Putnam for this state of affairs are connected to 'generational change' brought by modernisation, including suburbanisation and electronic entertainment. It is a pattern that reoccurs in many countries (although see dissent in the UK case in Hall, 1999). The most comprehensive study of citizenship views and participation in the UK has been produced by Pattie et al. (2003, 2004). This tested the links between public engagement and a number of social factors, including social capital, civic volunteerism, rational choice and their preferred theory of 'general incentives'. They conclude that it is the range of citizen incentives which do most to encourage or discourage citizen participation.

Interestingly, despite their differences, all these studies also reveal that those who are most engaged are also better educated, wealthier, and have higher status occupations. Most also reveal that high engagers have more associational memberships (social capital), are more knowledgeable about politics, are more confident of their knowledge, and are more likely to read broadsheet newspapers. These things all suggest that there is a growing gap in democracies between those who participate and benefit, and those who do not.

Looking beyond institutional politics: globalisation and interest groups

Other work relates the crisis to wider processes and external organisations that compete with traditional political institutions. One development is the impressive expansion of interest groups and social movements in the last decades of the twentieth century. This rise in alternative politics is widely documented beyond the crisis literature (e.g., Castells, 1997, Della Porta and Diani, 1999, Downing, 2001, Albrow et al., 2008). Within the crisis literature, Inglehart (1990, 1997) and Norris (1999, 2002) are particularly enthusiastic about such developments. As they point out (see also Power Report, 2006), citizens have not lost interest in politics but have simply redirected it. 'Progressive' interest groups accommodate a wider range of citizens and issues, offer more forms of participation, and are less hierarchical and exclusive than parties. In effect, politics and participation, in Norris's estimation (2002), are simply being reborn, phoenix-like, for the twenty-first century.

However, others are rather more sceptical here. As Putnam (1995) argues, paid membership of such groups may be growing impressively but paying annual dues does not in itself constitute participation. As others point out (Kaldor, 2003, Anderson and Reiff, 2005, Kavada, 2005), established interest groups, 'progressive' or not, are not particularly democratic, accountable, or transparent in their practices. Their leaders are not elected. Lastly, many campaign groups, associations and lobbies represent 'reactionary' or corporate interests. Indeed the economic and professional resources at the disposal of such organisations are significantly higher than those of grass roots and public interest movements (Ewen, 1996, Mitchell, 1997, Davis, 2002, Dinan and Miller, 2007).

This introduces the other external cause of political crisis: the forces of globalisation (see Chapter 8). In many accounts (Reich, 1991, Strange, 1996, Crouch, 2004, Cerny et al., 2005) the international organisations and markets of 'turbo capitalism' have come to control or influence capital flows that are far in excess of those managed by nations. Similarly, it seems clear that an increasing amount of state politics is bound up with inter-governmental and transgovernmental institutions. At a minimum, state politics is now increasingly embedded in international, multi-layered political, industrial and financial systems (Slaughter, 2000, Held, 2002). Alternatively (Strange, 1996, Habermas, 1999, Hardt and Negri, 2000, Beck, 2006), such developments are severely eroding national sovereignty. It thus becomes clear, to publics as well as politicians, that casting votes for national parties may have little impact when it comes to influencing global warming or international financial markets.

A fifth of interviewees (but no journalists) gave answers that fitted into this 'alternate politics' category. In contrast to the 'public/society' responses, they believed that the public were as interested in politics as ever but were more attracted to single-issue interest groups and local campaigns. A smaller group stated that the public were increasingly aware that politicians and national governments were less able to influence the big political issues of the day.

The political system

The explanations so far each seem to indicate that the problems of state politics are inexorable and beyond the state's making. 'Generational change', 'post-materialism', 'modernisation', 'capitalism' and 'globalisation' are unalterable forces that will erode democracy. As Crouch declares (2004: 29): 'Entropy of maximal democracy has to be expected.' However, other literature has focused more directly on those institutions and actors that operate at the centres of national political power suggesting, in effect, that some problems are treatable.

Most obvious amongst these is the literature comparing political systems (for example, Lijphart, 1984, 1999, Hague and Harrop, 2007, LeDuc et al., 2009). The indication is that some types of system may be more immune to crisis than others. At a system level the discussion ranges over several issues (see Chapter 1). These include: the balance of power between the executive, legislature and judiciary, and between central and local government; the representativeness of electoral systems (majoritarian or proportional representation); the strengths and weaknesses of two-party or multi-party legislatures, and unitary or coalition governments. At another level the concern is whether a democratic political system encourages more 'minimal', 'representative' or 'maximal' and 'direct' forms of participation (Crouch, 2004). In theory, changes may improve citizen engagement, reduce political instability, achieve a more inclusive society, reduce inequality, and so on. Although, as several crisis authors point out, significant problems have been documented across many system types, albeit at different times and rates (Pharr and Putnam, 2000, Dalton, 2004, Hay, 2007).

There is an alternative system-based thesis which points out that the govern-ance strategies of many democracies are a significant causal factor of crisis. A convincing argument, put forward most clearly by Hay (2007), and supported by others (Rhodes, 1997, Burnham, 2001, Buller and Flinders, 2005), argues that British politics has contributed to its own 'depoliticisation'. Since the 1970s crisis, both public discourse (political, academic, institutional) and political practices, have encouraged politicians to cede power to others. Public choice theory, free-market economists, advocates of the 'overloaded state' thesis, and global institutions such as the IMF and World Bank, all encouraged the same things: smaller, less-influential government, an end to Keynesian economics, technocratic rather than ideological politics, and the handing over of power to 'non-political' institutions and experts. Consequently, many of the levers of state power and resource management have been steadily handed to organisations that operate with little transparency, public accountability, or engagement with ordinary citizens. Democratic politics, linking governance to public 'opinion- and will-formation', has suffered.

Parties and politicians

Crisis literature has also highlighted the part played by modern political parties and politicians. For a variety of reasons, beyond their control, parties have had to adapt (Dalton and Wattenberg, 2002, Gunther et al., 2002, Dalton, 2004). Increased mobility, and changes in class, religion and ethnicity, have eroded the traditional regional and ideological links between parties and voters. The arrival of mass broadcast media, has also had a significant impact on the way parties communicate with their members and voters (Hallin, 1994, Maarek, 1995, Blumler and Kavanagh, 1999, Wring, 2005). By all accounts parties have rein-vented themselves, becoming more professional and employing a range of experts from marketing, business, public relations and media. For some, the changes have been more positive than negative in terms of party–public engagement (Scammell, 1995, Newman, 1999, Norris, 2000, Lees-Marshment, 2001/2008). Parties are now less dogmatically-ideological, and better at con-sulting and communicating with citizens.

However, for a large group of critics the transformation of parties has had a corrosive effect on politician–citizen engagement. First, the main political parties have converged, pushing left-leaning parties, such as Labour and the Democrats, considerably closer to the political centre/right and free-market consensus (Entman, 1989, Heath et al., 2001, Wring, 2005). Second, as outside experts and corporate funders have become more important to party leaderships, so the views and efforts of ordinary, local party organisations and members have been marginalised (Swanson and Mancini, 1996, Heffernan, 2003, Crouch, 2004). Third, professional campaigning is increasingly focused on a small group of 'swing voters' and marginal constituencies. This encourages parties to narrow their policy agendas and campaign foci on the few (Lilleker, 2005, Savigny, 2005). Fourth, professional campaign strategies, rather than communicating policies well, use negative attacks, spin, symbolic and pseudo politics, because they are effective (Boorstin, 1962, Wernick, 1991, Hall Jamieson, 1996, Herman and Chomsky, 2002, Franklin, 2004). In effect, 'electoral-professional' or 'modern cadre' party leaderships have become distanced, physically and com-municatively, from ordinary members and voters. Citizens feel ignored, ignorant of the policy debates, and unaware of the differences between parties. Therefore, parties themselves are responsible for eroding the 'general incentives' (Pattie et al., 2004) that propel voters to participate.

The second most common answer, when interviewees were asked about crisis causes, fell into this 'parties/politicians' category (Table 10.1). Two arguments were typically put forward. The first was that parties had become less ideologi-cal, leaving voters unclear about the differences between parties or the utility of their vote. The second was that party political 'spin', 'lies' and media management trivialised politics and put a disenchanted public off politics. In both cases, a quarter of all interviewees mentioned each of these factors. The power of parties over individual MPs, political 'sleaze' and the 'calibre' of current politicians were also mentioned as causes by several respondents.

Despite these criticisms of parties this does not necessarily mean that the political profession, as opinion surveys (Ipsos-MORI, 1983–2009, World Values Survey, 2005–8) suggest, is more greedy, 'sleazy', or incompetent than before. There seems little if any evidence of this. Several scholars and reports (Cowley, 2002, 2005, Power Report, 2006, Webb, 2007, Hay, 2007) argue that UK politicians are as 'hard-working', 'professional' and 'accessible' as ever, and, that the public have little idea about real politicians. Interestingly, the Power Inquiry (2006) survey also found that the public were far more inclined to be 'satisfied' with their own MP than the general class of MPs as observed only in media (see also Healey et al., 2005). Of note, a fifth of all interviewees (higher amongst journalists), across each of the three occupational categories, unprompted, declared that politicians were indeed unfairly portrayed. Terms such as 'honest', 'hard-working', 'well-meaning' and 'committed to constituents' came up often. Ultimately, politicians, as members of parties and governments, have contributed to the faults of the political system. At the same time, it would be difficult to demonstrate that their morals and technical deficiencies are to blame.

The media and journalists

In much of the crisis literature the media is hardly mentioned or dismissed altogether as a contributory factor. Of all the authors, Putnam (1995, 2000: 283) makes the clearest association, guestimating that up to 25 per cent of the decline in civic engagement is down to 'the effect of electronic entertainment – above all television … and the "TV generation"'. Others either implicate the media without further discussion, ignore it, or discount it entirely. Norris (2000, 2004, and also Norris et al., 1999), in fact goes to great lengths to exonerate the media and to disprove the 'media malaise' thesis. She argues that democracies and free media systems develop hand in hand, media 'effects' on audiences are 'minimal', and that those most engaged with politics are also greater news consumers. Thus she concludes, largely on the basis of simple correlations rather than causal links (an important point) that media is positively associated with democracy and public engagement. Her studies are particularly significant as they are often given undue prominence by other authors in the crisis literature.

There are a range of studies within media and political communication which also discount the media's negative impact on citizens. Those who look at news production admit that news can never fully fulfil its professional, 'ideal' remit but, on balance, it is pluralistic, diverse, accessible and critical enough to serve democratic polities well (Lichtenberg, 2000, McNair, 2003, 2006, Schudson, 2003, 2006, Zelizer, 2004). At the same time, a long history of work on media effects and audience studies (Lazarsfeld et al., 1944, Blumler and Katz, 1974, Morley, 1980, Ang, 1985, Norris et al., 1999) has argued that media does not have a powerful effect on personal cognitions and behaviours. The best that can be said is that there are 'minimal' effects or that audiences use media for their own purposes such as to reinforce existing beliefs.

However, there is also a sizeable literature which does pinpoint the media as a major source of crisis. News fails democratic publics because it is dominated by powerful and well-resourced sources and advertisers, guided down narrow avenues by journalist practices and cost questions, and altered by government and corporate pressures (McChesney, 1999, Herman and Chomsky, 2002, Curran and Seaton, 2003, Bagdikian, 2004, Davies, 2008). Political coverage, whether directed by party campaigns or media logic, is full of 'soundbites', 'horse-race' stories, negative and confrontational reporting, political personalities and scandal (Hallin, 1994, Hall Jamieson, 1996, Delli Carpini and Williams, 2001, Franklin, 2004, Esser, 2008). Since the large majority of people learn about politics through the mass media, rather than personal experience (see above), political understanding is likely to be fairly affected. Indeed, there are a number of more sophisticated studies which demonstrate that media has a series of minor effects that, in aggregate, have a significant influence. Agenda-setting, framing, priming, demobilisation, and partisan reinforcement, each affect how people make sense of media (Gerbner et al., 1984, Iyengar and Kinder, 1987, Jhally and Lewis, 1992, Ansolabehere and Iyengar, 1995, Capella and Hall Jamieson, 1997).

In the case of the UK, all these negative trends have been recorded. Deacon et al.'s (2005) study of the last (2005) general election found, that in the best-selling tabloid press the three party leaders alone accounted for 60 per cent of direct quotations. They also found that 44 per cent of coverage focused on the electoral process itself ('horse race' issues) and 8 per cent on 'political propriety'. The most important electoral issues, according to voters (Ipsos-MORI, 1997–2009), such as health and taxation, each appeared in only 3 to 4 per cent of stories. Unsurprisingly the UK public do not have much faith in news coverage. Between 1983 and 2009, Ipsos-MORI found that 'trust' in journalists moved between 10 and 22 per cent. The last World Values Survey (2005–8) reveals that the UK comes 56th out of 57 countries in terms of public levels of trust in the press. In 2007, Ofcom (2007) noted that 55 per cent of people said that 'much of the news on TV was not relevant to them' (see also Pew, 2009, for similar findings in the US).

Overall, the 'journalists/media' crisis explanation was the one that came up most consistently with interviewees; although, the nature of the research project may well have directed responses here. Within this category a fairly common response related to the levels of political 'cynicism' and 'trivial' coverage in political reporting. Half of the journalists and a third of the MPs gave such an answer. Many, including journalists, described coverage as being driven by personalities, scandal and conflicts, rather than policy or investigation. At the same time many responses, in each sector, looked to the larger media system. Such explanations referred to the fragmentation, competition and pace of the modern twenty-four-hour news environment and how that restricted journalists. Others mentioned the inadvertent biases of news frames, directed by the focus on government over parliament, or the limited movements of political lobby reporters.

Crisis: book themes and findings

The political 'crisis' theme is touched upon throughout the book. Many of the chapters explored how the varied communicative processes involved in politics might be either feeding or ameliorating such crisis tendencies. Since these focused on the institutions and actors at the centre of UK politics it is these 'supply-side' causes which are delved into here. The themes discussed focus on social contexts, institutions and systems. This is because potential change is more possible here than when one simply attributes decline to 'the public', specific political leaders, or the inexorable path of modernity. They are as follows:

The political system, representation, checks and balances

One repeated theme centres on the UK's system of citizen representation, as that feeds into the cognitions, deliberations and behaviours of politicians in regard to 'public opinion- and will-formation'. On the positive side, as Chapter 2 showed, the system does encourage most MPs to regularly engage with their constituents and feel accountable to them. The Westminster Parliament operates as a well-organised public sphere, in terms of its structures, deliberative processes, cultural norms, and links to 'public opinion- and will-formation'. Personally, my experience of extensive visits and interviews over the years leads me to agree with Cowley, Webb and others; i.e., that politicians generally are 'hard-working', 'professional', 'accessible', and 'well-intentioned'. I maintain these views in spite of the 2009 MPs' expenses scandal, my opposition to many political views and legislative outcomes, and the risk of being labelled a 'captured observer'. There is also much evidence to support the notion that the public are neither knowledgeable enough about, nor willing to 'participate' in, many policy discussions. A much higher level of participation is neither demanded by most citizens nor practical in large, complex democracies.

However, none of these observations and arguments ameliorates the need for extensive reform of UK politics. Chapter 1 identified particular aspects of the UK political system and, arguably, such system elements are a contributory factor to crisis. There has been much criticism of the inequities of the ageing 'Westminster model' of democracy (Lijphart, 1999, Brazier et al., 2005, Cook and Maclennan, 2005, Power Report, 2006). There are a series of power imbalances between: Prime Ministers and senior officials over Cabinets, executives over legislatures and judiciaries, party leaderships over MPs and members, and central over local government. The majoritarian electoral system results in politically-unrepresentative parliaments, penalises smaller parties, and results in aggressive two-party politics. Despite recent devolution and sets of reforms of the civil service and Westminster (Commons and Lords), too many fundamentals remain unchanged. In effect, the UK political system is unbalanced and does not encourage consensual, representative and participatory forms of democracy.

Such arguments found support across many of the chapters. Chapters 2 and 9 suggested that such imbalances are significant because political and bureaucratic elites become more culturally and socially disembedded as they move up the political structure. The UK Executive (government and civil service) is less linked to the outside public and also cancels out the public sphere qualities of the Legislature. Chapter 3 showed that the 'electoral-professional' transformation of political parties made them more centralised and hierarchical, and prioritised electoral success over engagement and consultation with ordinary members. Although front-rank politicians are as educated and professionally able to deal with the policy process as ever before, their social and experiential links to society are weaker. They are less likely to have had a career outside politics, worked as a local councillor, or have exchanges with ordinary party members. Chapter 8 showed that such tendencies are further exacerbated by globalisation. As political leaders are increasingly drawn into a series of unaccountable and opaque transnational corporate and governance structures and networks, so parliaments are further bypassed and national policy agendas constrained. Chapter 9 demonstrated how simply the existing sets of institutional checks and balances could be by-passed by a Prime Minister and an elite cosmopolitan policy network determined to go to war.

Mediation and media fragmentation

Another recurrent theme focuses on news media's contribution to crisis. While public service broadcasting, in the shape of the BBC, retains a significant audience share, the longer-term trend for UK media has been one of increased marketisation. Independent broadcast channels, the free press and online sites have flourished, and regulation has eased or failed to be applied to new media formats. In many ways it could be argued that such developments have been positive for the UK democratic process. News is more critical and less deferential towards politicians, more independent of government, pluralistic, accessible, and enabling of alternative voices. Markets and new communication technologies have contributed.

However, as many chapters argued, market-led news journalism is both a contributor to the UK's political crisis and is itself now in crisis. As Chapter 4 showed news audiences have been steadily declining and fragmenting for several decades. The pressures on journalists to be more efficient and productive, and to maintain profits amid falling revenues, have encouraged them to cut further corners. They now rely more on PR handouts, newswires, and cut and pasting from other journalists' copy. They leave their desks less, engage less directly and less often with news sources, and investigate less. Chapters 4 and 7 indicated that digital media had aided journalists but also exacerbated these trends. Journalists had greater access to information online but also had to produce more outputs and for more media platforms. Advertising is shifting rapidly away from traditional print and broadcast media but is not being redirected to digital news formats. Online, free newspaper and citizen journalism alternatives are not adequate replacements for conventional news. They are poorly-resourced, almost entirely dependent on traditional news outputs, and are far more likely to entice the already engaged rather than widen the news consumption net. If news does survive the collapse of its business model, many providers will no longer be producing what we have come to identify as 'news'.

As several other chapters also argued, news is contributing in several ways to the disengagement of citizens. Chapter 2 revealed that news fails to report the everyday parliamentary business of public debates, and policy deliberations, instead being oriented around inter- and intra-party competition. As Chapters 4 and 6 argued, extreme competition for consumers has led to a focus on personalities, political conflict, sound-bites and scandal. All of which, as other studies point out, means that news fails to properly inform people about policy matters and points of party difference. Of equal significance is the key point that news media fundamentally misrepresents the nature of the UK political process. Parties and leaders, rather than institutions and processes, are news. Political and economic power has seeped away from politicians, towards quangos, state institutions, civil servants, transnational bodies, financial markets and multi-national corporations. However, the media spotlight rarely attempts to follow these alternative, but undemocratic, forms of governance and power. As Chapter 6 suggested, the mismatch between 'media capital' and 'meta-capital', or perceived and actual power, in turn encourages greater public expectations of, and cynicism towards, politicians, political institutions, and journalism. Surveys also show a general crisis of faith and trust in news as bad as that noted in formal politics (see above).

The working conditions and influences of late modernity: capitalism, bureaucracy and mediation

One regular theme of the book is its observation of political actors – MPs, ministers, journalists, officials – as being influenced by the social conditions of their occupations. In part, these are linked to the general trends of modernity, bureaucracy, capitalism and media technologies. Each affects the daily working practices, comprehensions and behaviours of political actors, just as they do the rest of society. But, in this case, the consequences ripple out far beyond the political centre. As Chapters 2, 3 and 4 showed, politicians move between multiple, conflicted roles, as public representatives, party members, parliamentary participants and government employees. They lack the operational resources for keeping up with constituency work and developing depth policy knowledge.

They suffer from information overload and a barrage of human/information exchanges. Many corners have to be cut in the effort to appear 'more productive' and fulfil unrealistic demands and expectations. Being successful, and becoming a party leader, no longer depends on greater societal experience, local contact, or specific policy knowledge. Instead, it requires adaptability, generating peripheral knowledge on a range of subjects fast, an ability to shift quickly between audiences and demands. Thus, political knowledge and public engagement are becoming more 'pseudo' and 'symbolic' than 'substantive', and based on 'thin' rather than 'thick' communicative links.

Media contributes to each of these trends. As Chapter 4 indicated, politicians have more media outlets to respond to than ever and these operate twenty-four hours per day, are updated quicker, and operate across multiple formats. Chapter 7 showed that new media, while being a wonderful resource for politicians, also means that they are being overwhelmed with information and constituency email exchanges. As Chapter 5 revealed, the heightened presence of journalists and media in politics means 'media logic' increasingly influences politics itself. Oppositions and governments are more prone to make policy statements, push legislation and select party leaders, to gain media attention and to be seen to act publicly. Chapter 6 indicated that the growing importance of 'media capital' in politics has had a destabilising impact on the profession. Compared to other capital forms, 'media capital' is rather more volatile, artificial and insecure and, consequently, may be suddenly lost, bringing down good careers in the process. Similarly, the ability of contemporary politicians to accumulate media and symbolic capital, in greater quantities than their actual political or meta-capital, means that far more is expected of them than they can deliver.

In effect, market competition, bureaucratic control and encroaching mediation produce politicians who are increasingly stretched and conflicted, detached and insecure, focused on elections, and dependent on external experts, corporate funders, reporters and cosmopolitan elite networks. On the one hand, all of these things appear to be related to the common trends and problems of late modernity. There is a sense that nothing much is to be done to prevent the onward marches of capitalism, globalisation, the administrative iron cage and new communication technologies. What can be done about the growing level of complexity and risks associated with contemporary societies? What can nation-state politics do about the organisation and policies of international institutions and multi-national corporations abroad? On the other hand, many aspects of work, industry, finance and media, are regulated. Why cannot similar sets of regulations also be applied to the working conditions of those involved in parties, parliaments and governments?

Two propositions are suggested here as starting principles for reform. First, politics, finance and media are too often allowed to investigate themselves and self-regulate in ways that other occupations cannot. Commissions and enquiries are, almost always, led by those very participants and experts from within the sector. They take place within the discourses and remits of the professions themselves. Conclusions and reforms are usually limited and do not fundamentally challenge the system. It seems evident that this needs to be challenged. Second, any truly independent commissions need to look closely at the elements of personal accountability, resources, status goals, and risk–reward balances of elites. Politicians, CEOs and political editors may hold great power and/or gain substantial monetary and status rewards. However, their careers also carry large risks and insecurities, are often relatively brief, and encourage short-term thinking and reward seeking. As Sennett asks (1998: 10): 'How can long-term goals be pursued in an economy devoted to the short-term? How can mutual loyalties be sustained in institutions which are constantly breaking apart or continually being redesigned?' Is it then any wonder that CEOs and fund managers are driven by quarterly results and annual bonuses, or politicians motivated by policies that will win the next election, or editors by recent ratings figures? Such short-term risk–reward balances do not encourage decision-making on long-term, chronic issues, such as global warming, energy management, financial stability, and so on.

Of course not all the causal factors of crisis are simply addressed. However, a number of measures, large and small, can be introduced to reform the UK's ageing political, media and financial systems. Changing an outdated and corrupted electoral system, and the strengthening of parliament, are very achievable. Making powerful political and economic institutions more accountable and transparent is realistic. Enabling a variety of forms of public opinion aggregation, and practical, limited forms of participation at local and national levels, is technically possible. UK media reforms are also more realisable and necessary than many claim as the current market model is not going to support the production of quality news as we know it. Public service models, remits and regulations can be extended beyond the broadcasting format to sustain other news formats, including print. They can also direct and legally empower coverage towards reporting the many less-visible centres of political and economic power. The occupations of politics and journalism can be made into carefully regulated 'professions', and the working practices and conditions altered in the way medicine or law are. Is change that simple and achievable? Despite the many objections of those involved, yes, actually it is.

List of interviewees

105 interviews took place and 101 interviewees are listed here. Four individuals, including two civil servants and two bloggers, are not. The majority of interviews took place 'on-the-record' and most citations are referenced. However, four interviewees, as well as particular parts of on-the-record interviews, were recorded 'off-the-record'. The titles and position of the interviewers listed were those given at the date of the interviews.Many have since changed.

Diane Abbott, Labour MP for Hackney North and Stoke Newington, 24th April 2006.

Danny Alexander, Liberal Democrat MP for Nairn, Badenoch and Strathspey, 28th February 2006.

Michael Ancram, Conservative MP for Devizes, government minister 1983–87, 1993–97, Party Chairman 1998–2001, Deputy Leader and shadow minister 2001–5, 20th March 2007.

Lord Donald Anderson, Labour MP for Swansea East Manmouth 1966–70, 1974–2005, 31st January 2007.

Lord Kenneth Baker of Dorking, Conservative Cabinet Minister 1985–92, 2nd March 2006.

Rt Hon David Blunkett, Labour MP for Sheffield Brightside, Shadow Cabinet Minister 1992–97, Cabinet Minister 1997–2004, 20th March 2006.

Adam Boulton, Political Editor for *Sky News*, 31st January 2007.

Tom Bradby, Political Editor for *ITN*, 9th October 2008.

Graham Brady, Conservative MP for Altrincham and Sale West, 8th December 2005.

Ben Brogan, Political Editor of the *Daily Mail*, 26th April 2007.

Colin Brown, Deputy Political Editor of the *Independent*, 1st August 2006.

Lyn Brown, Labour MP for West Ham, 1st March 2006.

Chris Bryant, Labour MP for Rhondda, 12th December 2005.

Greg Clark, Conservative MP for Tunbridge Wells, adviser and Director of Conservative Policy Unit, 25th April 2006.

Nick Clegg, Liberal Democrat MP for Sheffield Hallam, Shadow Home Secretary, 14th March 2006.

Rob Clements, Director of Research, House of Commons, 18th April 2006.

Sam Coates, Political Correspondent for *The Times*, 29th January 2007.

Jeremy Corbyn, Labour MP for Islington North, 24th April 2006.

Iain Dale, Conservative political blogger, author, publisher, television and radio presenter, 22nd March 2007.

Wayne David, Labour MP for Caerphilly, 10th January 2006.

Yasmin Diamond, Head of Communication at Department for Environment, Food and Rural Affairs, 18th May 2007.

Rt Hon Frank Dobson, Labour MP for Holborn and St Pancras, shadow minister and Cabinet Minister 1983–97, Cabinet Minister 1997–99, 29th March 2006.

Frank Doran, Labour MP for Aberdeen North, shadow minister, 1988–92, Select Committee Chair, 2005–, 15th May 2006.

Rt Hon Iain Duncan Smith, Conservative MP for Chingford and Woodford Green, Shadow Cabinet Minister 1997–2001, Party Leader 2001–3, 25th April 2006.

Gwyneth Dunwoody, Labour MP for Crewe and Nantwich, Chair of Select Committees 1997–, 8th May 2006.

Clare Ettinghausen, Chief Executive Officer of Hansard Society, 9th May 2006.

Rt Hon Frank Field, Labour MP for Birkenhead, government minister 1997–99, Chair of Select Committees 1987–97, 19th April 2006.

Lord Norman Fowler, Conservative Cabinet Minister 1981–90, 8th Feb 2006.

Neil Gerrard, Labour MP for Walthamstow, 10th May 2006.

Gary Gibbon, Political Editor for *Channel Four News*, 25th January 2007.

Paul Goodman, Conservative MP for Wycombe, shadow minister 2003–, 27th March 2006.

Chris Grayling, Conservative MP for Epsom and Ewell, Shadow Secretary of State for Transport, 14th June 2006.

Damien Green, Conservative MP for Ashford, Shadow Minister for Immigration, shadow minister 2001–, 14th August 2006.

Elizabeth Hallam-Smith, Director of Information Services and Library, House of Lords, 10th May 2006.

Simon Heffer, Political Columnist and Associate Editor of the *Daily Telegraph*, 30th August 2006.

Philippa Helm, Clerk of the Defence Committee, 21st September 2006.

Alex Hilton, Labour political blogger, 10th May 2007.

Matthew Hilton, Director of Strategy and Communication at the Department of Trade and Industry, 15th May 2007.

Lucien Hudson, recent Head of Communication at the Foreign and Commonwealth Office, on secondment to the Department of Justice, 29th January 2009.

Simon Hughes, Liberal Democrat MP for North Southwark and Bermondsey, party leadership contender 1999, 2006, Party President and Shadow Secretary for Constitutional Affairs and Attorney General, 4th July 2006.

Chris Huhne, Liberal Democrat MP for Eastleigh, MEP 1999–2004, Shadow Cabinet 2005–, party leadership contender 2006, 9th August 2006.

Rt Hon Michael Jack, Conservative MP for Fylde, government minister 1992–97, shadow minister, 1997–98, Select Committee Chair 2002–, 12th June 2006.

Glenda Jackson, Labour MP for Hampstead and Highgate, government minister 1997–99, 17th January 2007.

Howell James, Permanent Secretary, Government Communication, the Cabinet Office, 14th May 2007.

Adrian Jenner, Clerk on Defence Committee, 21st September 2006.

Kevan Jones, Labour MP for North Durham, 8th February 2006.

Gerald Kaufman, Labour MP for Manchester Gorton, government minister 1974–79, Shadow Cabinet Minister 1980–92, Select Committee Chair 1997–2005, 29th January 2007.

Martha Kearney, Political Editor *Newsnight*, 25th April 2007.

Fraser Kemp, Labour MP for Houghton and Washington East, assistant whip 2001–5, 30th January 2007.

Sadiq Khan, Labour MP for Tooting, 1st March 2006.

Peter Kilfoyle, Labour MP for Liverpool Walton, opposition whip and spokesperson 1992–94, parliamentary secretary 1997–2000, 20th March 2007.

Lord Neil Kinnock, Shadow Cabinet Minister and Leader of the Labour Party 1983–92, EU Commissioner 1995–2004, 4th May 2006.

Julie Kirkbride, Conservative MP for Bromsgrove, shadow minister 2003–4, political journalist, 3rd February 2006.

Michael Lea, Political Correspondent for the *Sun*, 14th May 2007.

Martin Linton, Labour MP for Battersea, 24th February 2006.

Peter Luff, Conservative MP for Mid-Worcestershire, Assistant Chief Whip 2002–5, Chair of Select Committees 1997–2000, 2005–, 29th March 2006.

Andrew MacKinlay, Labour MP for Thurrock, opposition whip 1993–94, 20th March 2007.

Lord Robert Maclennan of Rogart, Labour government minister 1974–79, leader of Social Democratic Party 1987–88, Liberal Democrat Shadow Cabinet Minister 1988–98, 8th February 2006.

John Maples, Conservative MP for Stratford on Avon, Deputy Chairman 1994–95, Shadow Cabinet Minister 1997–2000, 28th March 2006.

Daisy McAndrew, Political Editor for ITN, 30th January 2007.

Christine McCafferty, Labour MP for Calder Valley, 3rd May 2006.

Austin Mitchell, Labour MP for Great Grimsby, former journalist,15th February 2006.

Mary Morgan, Director of Public Information, House of Lords, 15th February 2006.

Estelle Morris, Cabinet Minister 2001–2, government minister 2003–5, 8th March 2007.

Joe Murphy, Political Editor of the *Evening Standard*, 11th April 2007.

David Normington, Permanent Secretary at the Home Office, 9th July 2007.

Peter Oborne, Political Columnist for the *Daily Mail*, Contributing Editor for *The Spectator*, political journalist and commentator, 19th March 2007.

Lord Cecil Parkinson, government minister 1981–83, Cabinet Minister 1983, 1987–90, Chair of Conservative Party 1981–83, 1997–98, 30th January 2007.

John Pullinger, Head Librarian, House of Commons Library, 29th March 2006.

John Quinn, Chief Knowledge Officer, Department of Children, Schools and Families, 24th March 2009.

Rt Hon Nick Raynsford, Labour MP for Greenwich and Woolwich, shadow minister 1993–97, government minister 1997–2005, 2nd May 2006.

Rt Hon John Redwood, Conservative MP for Wokingham, Cabinet Minister 1990–95, shadow minister 1997–2000, 2004–5, party leadership candidate 1995, 1997, 20th February 2006.

Peter Riddell, Chief Political Commentator for *The Times*, 30th August 2006.

Angus Robertson, Scottish National Party MP for Moray, journalist, 17th January 2006.

Nick Robinson, Political Editor at the BBC, 27th February 2007.

David Rowlands, Permanent Secretary at the Department of Transport, 11th April 2007.

Chris Shaw, Clerk of the Science and Technology Committee, 20th September 2006.

Clare Short, Labour MP for Ladywood, opposition spokesperson 1985–96, shadow minister 1996–97, Cabinet Minister 1997–2003, 18th January 2007.

John Sills, Director of Communication at the Department of Constitutional Affairs, 22nd May 2007.

Sion Simon, Labour MP for Birmingham Erdington, journalist, 31st January 2007.

Dennis Skinner, Labour MP for Bolsover, member of Labour NEC 1978–92, 1994–98, 1999–, Vice Chairman and Chairman of Labour Party 1987–89, 19th March 2007.

Lord Chris Smith of Finsbury, Labour MP, shadow minister 1992–97, government minister 1997–2001, 6th February 2006.

John Smith, Political Editor of Associated Press, 6th August 2007.

Paul Staines (AKA Guido Fawkes), Conservative political blogger, 29th March 2007.

Phyllis Starkey, Labour MP for Milton Keynes South West, Select Committee Chair 2005–, 16th May 2006.

David Stevens, Iraq and Special Projects, Ministry of Defence, 16th March 2009.

Jo Swinson, Liberal Democrat MP for East Dunbartonshire, Shadow Secretary of State for Scotland, 21st March 2006.

Hugh Taylor, Permanent Secretary at the Department of Health, 16th May 2007.

Lord John Thurso, Liberal Democrat MP for Caithness, Sutherland and Easter Ross, shadow minister 2003–, 7th December 2005.

Polly Toynbee, Political Columnist for the *Guardian*, 25th August 2006.

Lord Paul Tyler, former Liberal Democrat MP, Chief Whip and shadow minister 1997–2005, 2nd March 2006.

Lord John Wakeham, Conservative government minister 1983–87, Cabinet Minister 1987–92, Leader of the House of Lords 1992–94, 23rd January 2007.

Angela Watkinson, Conservative MP for Upminster, whip 2002–4, 2005–, shadow minister 2003–6, 13th June 2006.

Philip Webster, Political Editor of the *Times*, 9th August 2006.

Michael White, Political Editor of the *Guardian*, 1st August 2006.

John Whittingdale, Conservative MP for Malden and East Chelmsford, shadow minister 2001–4, Select Committee Chair 2005–, 28th February 2006.

Rt Hon Ann Widdecombe, Conservative MP for Maidstone and the Weald, government minister 1994–97, Shadow Cabinet Minister 1997–2001, 9th March 2006.

Carole Willis, Director of Research, Department of Children, Schools and Families, 24th March 2009.

Robert Wilson, Principal Clerk of Select Committees, 3rd May 2006.

Caroline Wright, Director of Communication, Department of Children, Schools and Families, 24th March 2009.

Tony Wright, Labour MP for Cannock Chase, Chair of Select Committee 1999–, 15th March, 2006.

Derek Wyatt, Labour MP for Sittingbourne and Sheppey, 23rd May 2006.

Bibliography

Aaronovitch, D. (04.10.05) 'Passionate, Personable, Dynamic and in Touch, I Know Who I'd Vote For' in *The Times*, London: News Group Newspapers.

Advertising Association (2007) *The Advertising Statistics Yearbook*, London: Warc.

Alberoni, F. (2006 [1972]) 'The Powerless Elite: Theory and Sociological Research on the Phenomenon of the Stars' in Marshall, P. (ed.) *The Celebrity Culture Reader*, London: Routledge.

Albrow, M. and Glasius, M. (2008) 'Introduction: Democracy and the Possibility of a Global Public Sphere' in Albrow, M., Anheier, H., Glasius, M., Price, M. and Kaldor, M. (eds) *Global Civil Society 2007/08: Communicative Power and Democracy*, London: Sage.

Albrow, M., Anheier, H., Glasius, M., Price, M. and Kaldor, M., eds (2008) *Global Civil Society 2007/08: Communicative Power and Democracy*, London: Sage.

Allan, S. (2006) *Online News: Journalism and the Internet*, Maidenhead: Open University Press.

Almond, G. and Verba, S. (1963) *The Civic Culture: Political Attitudes and Democracy in Five Nations*, Princeton, New Jersey: Princeton University Press.

Altheide, D. and Snow, R. (1979) *Media Logic*, Beverly Hills, CA: Sage.

Anderson, A. (1997) *Media, Culture and the Environment*, London: UCL Press.

Anderson, K. and Reiff, D. (2005) '"Global Civil Society": A Sceptical View' in Anheier, H., Glasius, M. and Kaldor, M. (eds) *Global Civil Society Yearbook 2004/05*, London: Sage.

Ang, I. (1985) *Watching Dallas*, London: Methuen.

Anheier, H., Glasius, M. and Kaldor, M. (2001) Introduction in Anheier, H., Glasius, M. and Kaldor, M. (eds) *Global Civil Society Yearbook 2001*, Oxford: Oxford University Press.

Ankersmit, F. (1997) *Aesthetic Politics: Political Philosophy Beyond Fact and Value*, Palo Alto, CA: Stanford University Press.

Ansolabehere, S. and Iyengar, S. (1995) *Going Negative: How Political Advertisements Shrink and Polarize the Electorate*, New York: The Free Press.

Anstead, N. (2009) *A Comparative Study of Factors Influencing the Adoption and Impact of E-Campaigning in the United States and the United Kingdom*. Unpublished PhD Thesis, London: Royal Holloway, University of London.

Atton, C. (2004) *An Alternative Internet*, Edinburgh: Edinburgh University Press.

Bagdikian, B. (2004) *The Media Monopoly*, 7th edn, Boston: Beacon Press.

Baisnee, O. (2007) 'The European Public Sphere Does Not Exist (At Least it's Worth Wondering …)' in *European Journal of Communication*, Vol. 22, No. 4, pp. 493–503.

Baker, D., Gamble, A. and Seawright, D. (July, 1999) *Mapping Changes in British Parliamentarians' Attitudes to European Integration*, Colchester, Essex: UK Data Archive.

Barnett, S. and Gaber, I. (2001) *Westminster Tales: the Twenty First Century Crisis in Political Journalism*, London: Continuum.

Bauman, Z. (2000) *Liquid Modernity*, Cambridge: Polity Press.

Baumgartner, F. R. and Jones, B. D. (1993) *Agendas and Instability in American Politics*, Chicago: University of Chicago Press.

Beck, U. (1994) 'The Reinvention of Politics: Towards a Theory of Reflexive Modernization' in Beck, U., Giddens, A. and Lash, S. *Reflexive Modernization: Politics, Tradition and Aesthetics in the Modern Social Order*, Cambridge Polity: Preas.

——(2006) *Cosmopolitan Vision*, Cambridge: Polity Press.

Becker, H. (1963) *Outsiders: Studies in the Sociology of Deviance*, New York: Free Press.

Benavides, J. (2000) 'Gacetilla: A Key Word for a Revisionist Approach to the Political Economy of Mexico's Print News Media' in *Media, Culture and Society*, Vol. 22, No. 1, pp. 85–104.

Bennett, W. L. (1990) 'Towards a Theory of Press–State Relations in the United States' in *Journal of Communication*, Vol. 40, No. 2, pp. 103–25.

——(2003) *News: The Politics of Illusion*, 5th edn, Addison Wesley, Longman Inc.

Bennett, W. L. and Paletz, D. L. (1994) *Taken By Storm: The Media, Public Opinion, and U.S. Foreign Policy in the Gulf War*, Chicago: University of Chicago Press.

Benson, R. (1998) 'Field Theory in Comparative Context: A New Paradigm for Media Studies' in *Theory and Society*, Vol. 28, No. 3, pp. 463–98.

——(May, 2008) *Public Relations in the Public Sphere: Habermas, Bourdieu and the Question of Power*, Montreal: International Communication Association.

Benson, R. and Hallin, D. (2007) 'How States, Markets and Globalization Shape the News: The French and US National Press, 1965–97' in *European Journal of Communication*, Vol. 22, No. 1, pp. 27–48.

Benson, R. and Neveu, E. (2005) 'Introduction: Field Theory as a Work in Progress' in Benson, R. and Neveu, E. (eds) *Bourdieu and the Journalistic Field*, Cambridge: Polity Press.

Berenger, R., ed. (2003) *Global Media Go to War: Role of News and Entertainment Media During the 2003 Iraq War*, Spokane, WA: Marquette Books.

Bimber, B. (2003) *Information and American Democracy: Technology in the Evolution of Political Power*, Cambridge: Cambridge University Press.

Blumler, H. (1971) 'Social Problems as Collective Behaviour' in *Social Problems*, Vol. 18, pp. 298–306.

Blumler, J. and Katz, E., eds (1974) *The Uses of Communications*, Beverly Hills, California: Sage.

Blumler, J. and Kavanagh, D. (1999) 'The Third Age of Political Communication: Influences and Features' in *Political Communication*, Vol. 16, No. 3, pp. 209–30.

Blumler, J. G. and Gurevitch, M. (1995) *The Crisis of Public Communication*, London: Routledge.

Bohman, J. (1996) *Public Deliberation: Pluralism, Complexity, and Democracy*, Cambridge, MA: MIT Press.

Boltanski, L. (1999) *Distant Suffering: Morality, Media and Politics*, Cambridge: Cambridge University Press.

Boltanski, L. and Chiapello, E. (2007) *The New Spirit of Capitalism*, London: Verso.

Bonfadelli, H. (2002) 'The Internet and Knowledge Gaps: A Theoretical and Empirical Investigation' in *European Journal of Communication*, Vol. 17, No. 1, pp. 65–84.

Boorstin, D. (1962) *The Image*, London: Weidenfeld and Nicolson.

Bourdieu, P. (1984) *Distinction: A Social Critique of the Judgement of Taste*, London: Routledge.
——(1986) 'The Forms of Capital' in Richardson, J. (ed.) *Handbook of Theory and Research for the Sociology of Education*, New York: Greenwood Press.
——(1991) *Language and Symbolic Power*, ed./introduction by Thompson, J., Cambridge, Mass: Harvard University Press.
——(1993) *The Field of Cultural Production: Essays on Art and Literature*, ed. Johnson, R., Cambridge: Polity Press.
——(1996) *The State Nobility: Elite Schools in the Field of Power*, Palo Alto, CA: Stanford University Press.
——(1998a) *On Television and Journalism*, London: Pluto Press.
——(1998b) *Practical Reason: On the Theory of Action*, Cambridge: Polity.
——(2005) 'The Political Field, the Social Science Field, and the Journalistic Field' in Benson, R. and Neveu, E. (eds) *Bourdieu and the Journalistic Field*, Cambridge: Polity Press.
——(2008) *Political Interventions: Social Science and Political Action*, London: Verso.
Bourdieu, P. et al. (1999) *The Weight of the World: Social Suffering in Contemporary Society*, Cambridge: Polity Press.
Boyd-Barrett, O. and Rantanen, T. (1998) 'The Globalization of News' in Boyd-Barrett, O. and Rantanen, T. (eds) *The Globalization of News*, London: Sage.
Brandenberg, H. (2006) 'Pathologies of the Virtual Public Sphere' in Oates, S., Owen, D. and Gibson, R. (eds) *The Internet and Politics: Citizens, Voters and Activists*, London: Routledge.
Brazier, A., Flinders, M. and McHugh, D. (2005) *New Politics, New Parliament? A Review of Parliamentary Modernization Since 1998*, London: Hansard.
Brown, R. (2003) 'Spinning the War: Political Communications, Information Operations and Public Diplomacy in the War on Terrorism' in Thussu, D. and Freedman, D. (eds) *War and the Media: Reporting Conflict 24/7*, London: Sage.
Buchanen, J. and Wagner, R. (1977) *Democracy in Deficit*, New York: Basic Books.
Buller, J. and Flinders, M. (2005) 'The Domestic Origins of Depoliticization in the Area of British Economic Policy' in the *British Journal of Politics and International Relations*, Vol. 7, No. 4, pp. 526–43.
Burnham, P. (2001) 'New Labour and the Politics of Depoliticization' in the *British Journal of Politics and International Relations*, Vol. 3, No. 2, pp. 127–49.
Butler, F. (2004) *The Butler Report/Review of Intelligence on Weapons of Mass Destruction*, HC 898, London: HMSO.
Butsch, R., ed. (2007) *Media and Public Spheres*, Basingstoke, Hampshire: Palgrave Macmillan.
Calhoun, C. (1988) 'Populist Politics, Communication Media and Large Scale Societal Integration' in *Sociological Theory*, Vol. 6, pp. 219–41.
Calhoun, C., ed. (1992) 'Introduction' in *Habermas and the Public Sphere*, Cambridge, Mass: MIT Press.
Callon, M. (1998a) 'The Embeddedness of Economic Markets in Economics' in Callon, M. ed. *The Laws of the Markets*, Oxford: Blackwell.
——(1998b) 'An Essay on Framing and Overflowing: Economic Externalities Revisited by Sociology' in Callon, M. (ed.) *The Laws of the Markets*, Oxford: Blackwell.
Cammaerts, B. and Audenhove, L. (2005) 'Online Political Debate, Unbounded Citizenship and the Problematic Nature of a Transnational Public Sphere' in *Political Communications* Vol. 22, No. 2, pp. 179–96.

Campbell, A. (2007) *The Blair Years: The Alistair Campbell Diaries*, London: Hutchinson.

Capella, J. and Hall Jamieson, K. (1997) *Spiral of Cynicism: The Press and the Public Good*, Oxford: Oxford University Press.

Carlson, M. (2007) 'Blogs and Journalistic Authority: The Role of Blogs in US Election Day 2004 Coverage' in *Journalism Studies*, Vol. 8, No. 2, pp 264–79.

Castells, M. (1996) *The Rise of the Network Society*, Oxford: Blackwell.

——(1997) *The Power of Identity*, Oxford: Blackwell.

——(2001) *The Internet Galaxy: Reflections on the Internet, Business and Society*, Oxford: Oxford University Press.

Cerny, P., Menz, G. and Soderberg, S. (2005) 'Different Roads to Globalization: Neo-Liberalism, the Competition State, and Politics in a More Open World' in Soderberg, S., Menz, G.and Cerny, P. (eds) *Internalizing Globalization: The Rise of Neo-Liberalism and the Decline of National Varieties of Capitalism*, Houndmills, Basingstoke: Palgrave Macmillan.

Chadwick, A. (2006) *Internet Politics: States, Citizens and New Communication Technologies*, Oxford: Oxford University Press.

Chalaby, J. (1996) 'Journalism as an Anglo-American Invention' in the *European Journal of Communication*, Vol. 11, No. 3 pp. 303–26.

——(1998) *The Invention of Journalism*, London: Macmillan.

——(2005) 'French Political Communication in a Comparative Perspective: The Media and the Issue of Freedom' in *Modern and Contemporary France*, Vol. 13, No. 3, pp. 273–90.

——(2009) *Transnational Television in Europe: Reconfiguring Global Communications Networks*, London: IB Tauris.

Champagne, P. (1991) *Faire L'Opinion*, Paris: Ed. de Minuit.

——(2005) 'The "Double Dependency": The Journalistic Field Between Politics and Markets' in Benson, R. and Neveu, E. (eds) *Bourdieu and the Journalistic Field*, Cambridge: Polity Press.

Childs, S., Lovenduski, J. and Campbell, R. (2005) *British Representation Study?*

CIA (July 2009) Central Intelligence Agency World Fact Book, https://www.cia.gov, accessed October 2009.

Clarke, R. (2004) *Against all Enemies: Inside America's War on Terror*, London: Free Press.

Clausen, L. (2004) 'Localizing the Global: "Domestication" Processes in International News Production' in *Media, Culture and Society*, Vol. 26, No. 1, pp. 25–44.

Cohen, E. (2002) 'Online Journalism as Market-Driven Journalism' in *Journal of Broadcasting and Electronic Media*, Vol. 46, No. 4, pp. 532–48.

COI (2006) 'The IPO Directory: Information and Press Officers in Government Departments and Public Corporations', London: Central Office of Information.

Coleman, J. (1988) 'Social Capital in the Creation of Human Capital' in the *American Journal of Sociology*, Vol. 94, Supplement, pp. 95–120.

Coleman, S. (2004) 'Connecting Parliament to the Public via the Internet: Two Case Studies of Online Consultations' in *Information, Communication & Society*, Vol. 7, No. 1, pp.1–22.

——(2005) 'New Mediation and Direct Representation: Reconceptualising Representation in the Digital Age' in *New Media and Society*, Vol. 7, No. 2, pp. 177–98.

Coleman, S. and Gotze, J. (2001) *Bowling Together: Online Public Engagement in Policy Deliberation*, London: Hansard Society.

Cook, F. L., Tylor, T. R., Goetz, E. E., Gordon, M. T., Protess, D., Leff, D. R. and Molotoch, H. L. (1983) 'Media and Agenda Setting: Effects on the Public, Interest Group Leaders, Policy Makers and Policy' in *Public Opinion Quarterly*, Vol. 47, No. 1, pp. 16–35.

Cook, R. and Maclennan, R. (2005) *Looking Back, Looking Forward. The Cook–Maclennan Agreement, Eight Years On*, London: New Politics Network.

Cook, T. (1998) *Governing with the News: The News Media as a Political Institution*, Chicago: University of Chicago Press.

Corner, J. (2003) 'Mediated Persona and Political Culture' in Corner, J. and Pels, D. (eds) *Media and the Restyling of Politics*, London: Sage.

Corner, J. and Pels, D. (2003) 'Introduction: the Restyling of Politics' in Corner, J. and Pels, D. (eds) *Media and the Restyling of Politics*, London: Sage.

——(2003) *Media and the Restyling of Politics*, London: Sage.

Cottle, S., ed. (2003) 'Introduction' in *News, Public Relations and Power*, London: Sage.

Cottle, S. and Rai, M. (2008) 'News Providers: Emissaries of Global Dominance or Global Public Sphere' in *Global Media and Communication*, Vol. 4, No. 2, pp. 157–81.

Couldry, N. (2003) 'Media Meta-Capital: Extending the Range of Bourdieu's Field Theory' in *Theory and Society*, Vol. 32, pp. 653–77.

——(2009) 'New Online News Sources and Writer-Gatherers' in Fenton, N. (ed.) *New Media, Old News: Journalism and Democracy in a Digital Age*, London: Sage.

Cowley, P. (2002) *Revolts and Rebellions: Parliamentary Voting Under Blair*, London: Politicos.

——(2005) *The Rebels: How Blair Mislaid His Majority*, London: Politicos.

Cracknell, J. (1993) 'Issue Arenas, Pressure Groups and Environmental Issues' in Hansen, (ed.) *The Mass Media and Environmental Issues*, Leicester: Leicester University Press.

Criddle, B. (1984) 'Candidates' in Butler, D. and Kavanagh, D. (eds) *The British General Election of 1983*, Basingstoke: Palgrave Macmillan.

Crossley, N. and Roberts, J. M., eds (2004) *New Perspectives on the Public Sphere*, Oxford: Blackwell Publishing.

Crouch, C. (2004) *Post-Democracy*, Cambridge: Polity.

Crozier, M., Huntingdon, S. and Watanuki, J. (1975) *The Crisis of Democracy: Report on the Governability of Democracies in the Trilateral Commission*, New York: New York University Press.

Curran, J. (2002) *Media and Power*, London: Routledge.

Curran, J. and Park, M., eds (2000a) *De-Westernizing Media Studies*, London: Routledge.

——(2000b) 'Beyond Globalization Theory' in Curran, J. and Park, M. (eds) (2000a) *De-Westernizing Media Studies*, London: Routledge.

Curran, J. and Seaton, J. (2003) *Power Without Responsibility*, 6th edn, London: Routledge.

Curran, J. and Witschge, T. (2009) 'Liberal Dreams and the Internet' in Fenton, N. (ed.) *New Media, Old News: Journalism and Democracy in a Digital Age*, London: Sage.

Curran, J., Iyengar, S., Lund, A. and Salovaara-Moring, I. (2009) 'Media Systems, Public Knowledge and Democracy' in *European Journal of Communication*, Vol. 24, No. 1, pp. 5–26.

Curtice, J. (2005) 'Turnout: Electors Stay Home Again' in Norris, P. and Wlezien, C. (eds) *Britain Votes 2005*, Oxford: Oxford University Press.

Dahl, R. (1961) *Who Governs? Democracy and Power in an American City*, New Haven, CT: Yale University Press.

——(1971) *Polyarchy, Participation and Opposition*, New Haven, CT: Yale University Press.

——(1989) *Democracy and its Critics*, New Haven, CT: Yale University Press.

——(1999) 'Can International Organisations Be Democratic?: A Skeptic's View' in Shapiro, I. and Hacker-Cordon, C. (eds) *Democracy's Edges*, Cambridge: Cambridge University Press.

Dahl, R. and Lindblom, C. (1953) *Politics, Economics and Welfare: Planning and Politico-Economic Systems Resolved into Basic Social Processes*, New York: Harper and Row.

Dahlberg, L. (2001) 'The Internet and Democratic Discourse: Exploring the Prospects of Online Deliberative Forums Extending the Public Sphere' in *Information, Communication and Society*, Vol. 4, No. 4, pp. 615–33.

——(2007) 'Rethinking the Fragmentation of the Cyberpublic: From Consensus to Contestation' in *New Media and Society*, Vol. 9, No. 5, pp. 827–47.

Dahlgren, P. (1995) *Television and the Public Sphere: Citizenship, Democracy and the Media*, London: Sage.

——(2005) 'The Internet and the Public Sphere' in *Political Communication*, Vol. 22, No. 2, pp. 147–62.

Dahlgren, P. and Sparks, C. (1992) *Communication and Citizenship: Journalism and the Public Sphere*, London: Routledge.

Dalton, R. (2004) *Democratic Challenges, Democratic Choices: The Erosion of Political Support in Advanced Industrial Democracies*, Oxford: Oxford University Press.

Dalton, R. and Wattenberg, M., eds (2002) *Parties Without Partisans: Political Change in Advanced Industrial Democracies*, Oxford: Oxford University Press.

Darras, E. (2005) 'Media Consecration of the Political Order' in Benson, R. and Neveu, E. (eds) *Bourdieu and the Journalistic Field*, Cambridge: Polity Press.

Davies, N. (2008) *Flat Earth News*, London: Chatto and Windus.

Davis, A. (2002) *Public Relations Democracy: Public Relations, Politics and the Mass Media in Britain*, Manchester: Manchester University Press.

——(2003) 'Whither Mass Media and Power? Evidence for a Critical Elite Theory Alternative' in *Media, Culture and Society*, Vol. 25, No. 5, pp. 669–90.

——(2005) 'Media Effects and the Active Elite Audience: A Study of Media in Financial Markets' in *European Journal of Communications*, Vol. 20, No. 3, pp. 303–26.

——(2007) *The Mediation of Power: A Critical Introduction*, London: Routledge.

Davis, R. (2005) *Politics Online: Blogs, Chatrooms, and Discussion Groups in American Democracy*, New York: Routledge.

Dayan, D. and Katz, E. (1992) *Media Events*, Cambridge, MA: Harvard University Press.

de Jong, W. (2005) 'The Power and Limits of Media Based Opposition Politics – a Case Study: the Brent Spar Conflict' in de Jong, W., Shaw, M. and Stammers, N. (eds) *Global Activism Global Media*, London: Pluto Press.

Deacon, D. and Golding, P. (1994) *Taxation and Representation*, London, John Libby Press.

Deacon, D., Wring, D., Billig, M., Downey, J., Golding, P., and Davidson, S. (2005) *Reporting the 2005 General Election*, Loughborough University, Loughborough Communication Research Centre.

Dean, J., Anderson, J. and Lovinck, G., eds (2006) *Reformatting Politics: Information Technology and Global Civil Society*, London: Routledge.

Deane, J. (2008) 'Democratic Advance or Retreat? Communicative Power and Current Media Developments' in Albrow, M., Anheier, H., Glasius, M., Price, M. and Kaldor, M. (eds) *Global Civil Society 2007/08: Communicative Power and Democracy*, London: Sage.

Della Porta, D. and Diani, M. (1999) *Social Movements: an Introduction*, Oxford: Blackwell.

Delli Carpini, M. and Keeter, S. (1996) *What Americans Know About Politics and Why It Matters*, New Haven, CT: Yale University Press.

Delli Carpini, M. S. and Williams, B. A. (2001) 'Let Us Infotain You: Politics in the New Media Environment' in Bennett, W. L. and Entman, R. M. (eds) *Mediated Politics: Communication in the Future of Democracy*, Cambridge: Cambridge University Press.

Dewey, J. (1927) *The Public and Its Problems*, New York: Henry Holt.

Dickie, J. (2004) *The New Mandarins: How British Foreign Policy Works*, New York: IB Tauris.

Dinan, W. and Miller, D. (2007) *Thinker, Faker, Spinner, Spy: Corporate PR and the Assault on Democracy*, London: Pluto.

Domhoff, W. (2005) *Who Rules America? Power, Politics and Social Change*, 5th edn, New York: McGraw-Hill.

Donsbach, W. and Patterson, T. (2004) 'Political News Journalists: Partisanship, Professionalism, and Political Roles in Five Countries' in Esser, F. and Pfetsch, B. (eds) *Comparing Political Communication: Theories, Cases and Challenges*, Cambridge: Cambridge University Press.

Downey, J. and Koenig, J. (2006) 'Is There a European Public Sphere? The Berlusconi–Schulz Case' in the *European Journal of Communication*, Vol. 21, No. 2, pp. 165–87.

Downing, J. (2001) *Radical Media: Rebellious Communication and Social Movements*, London: Sage.

Downs, A. (1957) *An Economic Theory of Democracy*, New York: Harper and Row.

Dryzak, J. (2002) *Deliberative Democracy and Beyond: Liberals, Critics, Contestations*, Oxford: Oxford University Press.

——(2006) *Deliberative Global Politics*, Cambridge: Polity.

Duffy, B. and Rowden, L. (April, 2005) *You Are What You Read?* London: MORI.

Dunne, T. (2008) 'Britain and the Gathering Storm Over Iraq' in Smith, S., Hadfield, A. and Dunne, T., (eds) *Foreign Policy: Theories, Actors, Cases*, Oxford: Oxford University Press.

Durham, F. (2007) 'Framing the State in Globalisation: The *Financial Times*' Coverage of the 1997 Thai Currency Crisis' in *Critical Studies in Media Communication*, Vol. 24, No. 1, pp. 57–76.

EarthTrends (2009) World Resources Institute http://earthtrends.wri.org, accessed October 2009.

Edelman, M. (1964) *The Symbolic Uses of Politics*, Urbana: University of Illinois Press.

Eide, E., Kunelius, R. and Phillips, A., eds (2008) *Transnational Media Events: The Mohammed Cartoons and the Imagined Clash of Civilisations*, Goteborg: Nordicom.

Elliott, F. and Hanning, J. (2007) *Cameron: The Rise of the New Conservative*, London: Fourth Estate.

Ely, G. (1992) 'Nations, Publics and Political Cultures: Placing Habermas in the Nineteenth Century' in Calhoun, C. (ed.) *Habermas and the Public Sphere*, Cambridge, Mass: MIT Press.

Entman, R. (1989) *Democracy Without Citizens: Media and the Decay of American Politics*, Oxford: Oxford University Press.

——(2004) *Projections of Power: Framing News, Public Opinion, and US Foreign Policy*, Chicago: University of Chicago Press.

——(2005) 'Media and Democracy Without Party Competition' in Curran, J. and Gurevitch, M. (eds) *Mass Media and Society*, 4th edn. London: Arnold.

Ericson, R. V., Baranek, P. M. and Chan, J. B. L. (1989) *Negotiating Control: a Study of News Sources*, Milton Keynes: Open University Press.

Esser, F. (2008) 'Dimensions of Political News Cultures: Sound Bite and Image Bite News in France, Germany, Great Britain, and the United States' in the *Harvard International Journal of Press/Politics*, Vol. 13, No. 4, pp. 401–28.

Evans, J. and Hesmondhalgh, D. (2005) *Understanding Media: Inside Celebrity*, Maidenhead: Open University Press.

Ewen, S. (1996) *PR! A Social History of Spin*, New York: Basic Books.

Farrell, D., Kolodny, R. and Medvic, S. (2001) 'Parties and Campaign Professionals in a Digital Age. Political Consultants in the United States and Their Counterparts Oversea', in the *Harvard International Journal of Press/Politics*, Vol. 6, No. 4, pp. 11–30.

Fenton, N., ed. (2009) *New Media, Old News: Journalism and Democracy in a Digital Age*, London: Sage.

Fishkin, J. (1992) *Democracy and Deliberation: New Directions for Democratic Reform*, New Haven, CT: Yale University Press.

Fishman, M. (1980) *Manufacturing the News*, Austin: University of Texas.

Flynn, K. (2006) 'Covert Disclosures: Unauthorized Leaking, Public Officials and the Public Sphere' in *Journalism Studies*, Vol. 7, No. 2, pp. 256–73.

Foucault, M. (1971) *Madness and Civilization: A History of Insanity in the Age of Reason*, London: Tavistock Publications.

——(1975) *Discipline and Punish: The Birth of the Prison* (trans. by Sheridan, A.), London: Penguin.

——(1980) *Power/Knowledge: Selected Interviews and Other Writings 1972–77* (Gordon, C. ed.), Hemel Hempstead, Herts.: Harvester Wheatsheaf.

——(1991) 'Governmentality' in Burchell, G., Gordon, C. and Miller, P. (eds) *The Foucault Effect: Studies in Governmentality*, Chicago: University of Chicago Press.

Foyle, D. (1997) 'Public Opinion and Foreign Policy: Elite Beliefs as a Mediating Variable' in *International Studies Quarterly*, Vol. 41, pp. 141–63.

Franklin, B. (1997) *Newzak and News Media*, London: Arnold.

——(2004) *Packaging Politics: Political Communications in Britain's Media Democracy*, 2nd edn, London: Arnold.

——(2005) 'McJournalism: The Local Press and the McDonaldization Thesis': in Allan, S. (eds) *Journalism: Critical Issues*, Maidenhead: Open University Press.

Fraser, N. (1992) 'Rethinking the Public Sphere: A Consideration of Actually Existing Democracy' in Calhoun, C. (ed.) *Habermas and the Public Sphere*, Cambridge, MA: MIT Press.

——(1997) 'Rethinking the Public Sphere: A Contribution to the Critique of Actually Existing Democracy' in *Justice Interruptus: Critical Reflections on the 'Postsocialist' Condition*, London: Routledge.

——(2007) 'Transnationalizing the Public Sphere: On the Legitimacy and Efficacy of Public Opinion in a Post-Westphalian World' in *Theory, Culture and Society*, Vol. 24, No. 7, pp. 7–30.

Freedman, D. (2008) *The Politics of Media Policy*, Cambridge: Polity Press.

——(2009) 'The Political Economy of the "New" News Environment' in Fenton, N. (ed.) *New Media, Old News: Journalism and Democracy in a Digital Age*, London: Sage.

Freedom House (2009) Freedom of the World Ratings, http://www.freedomhouse.org, accessed October 2009.

Gaber, I. (1998) 'The Media and Politics' in Briggs, A. and Cobley, P. (eds) *The Media: An Introduction*, Harlow, Essex: Longman.

Gandy, O. (1982) *Beyond Agenda Setting: Information Subsidies and Public Policy*, NJ: Ablex Publishing Corporation.

Gans, H. J. (1979) *Deciding What's News: A Study of CBS Evening News, NBC Nightly News, Newsweek and Time*, New York: Pantheon.

Garnham, N. (1992) 'The Media and the Public Sphere' in Calhoun, C. (ed.) *Habermas and the Public Sphere*, Cambridge, Mass: MIT Press.

——(2007) 'Habermas and the Public Sphere' in *Global Media and Communication*, Vol. 3, No. 2, pp. 201–14.

Gauntlett, D. (1998) 'Ten Things Wrong with the Effects Model' in Dickinson, R., Havindranath, R. and Linne, O. (eds) *Approaches to Audiences: A Reader*, London: Arnold.

Gerbner, G., Gross, L., Morgan, M. and Signorielli, N. (1984) 'Political Correlates of Television Viewing' in *Public Opinion Quarterly*, Vol. 48, No. 1, pp. 283–300.

Giddens, A. (1991) *Modernity and Self-Identity: Self and Society in the Late Modern Age*, Cambridge: Polity Press.

Gillmor, D. (2004) *We the Media: Grassroots Journalism by the People, for the People*, Sebastopol: O'Reilly Media.

Gilpin, R. (2001) *Global Political Economy: Understanding the International Economic Order*, Princeton, NJ: Princeton University Press.

Glasgow University Media Group (1976) *Bad News*, London: Routledge.

——(1980) *More Bad News*, London: Routledge.

GMMP (2005) *Global Media Monitoring Project*, London: World Association for Christian Communication, accessed December 2009.

Goldenberg, E. (1975) *Making the Papers: The Access of Resource-Poor Groups to the Metropolitan Press*, Lexington, Mass: D.C. Heath and Co.

Golding, P. and Murdock, G. (2000) 'Culture, Communications and Political Economy' in Curran, J. and Gurevitch, M. (eds) *Mass Media and Society*, 3rd edn, London: Arnold.

Goode,. L. (2005) *Jürgen Habermas: Democracy and the Public Sphere*, London: Pluto Press.

Grannovetter, M. (1992 [1985]) 'Economic Action and Social Structure: The Problem of Embeddedness' in Grannovetter, M. and Swedberg, R. (eds) *The Sociology of Economic Life*, Boulder: Westview Press.

Greenberg, B., ed. (2002) *Communication and Terrorism: Public and Media Responses to 9/11*, NJ: Hampton Press.

Gripsrud, J. (2007) 'Television and the European Public Sphere' in the *European Journal of Communication*, Vol. 22, No. 4, pp. 479–92.

Grunig, J., ed. (1992) *Excellence in Public Relations and Communication Management*, Hillsdale, NJ: Lawrence Erlbaum Associates.

Grunig, J. and Hunt, T. (1984) *Managing Public Relations*, New York: Holt, Rinehart and Winston.

Gulati, G. (2004) 'Members of Congress and Presentation of Self on the World Wide Web', *Harvard Journal of Press/Politics*, Vol. 9, No. 1, pp. 22–40.

Gunther, R. and Mughan, A. (2001a) *Democracy and the Media: A Comparative Perspective*, Cambridge: Cambridge University Press.

——(2001b) 'The Political Impact of the Media: A Reassessment' in Gunther, R. and Mughan, A. *Democracy and the Media: A Comparative Perspective*, Cambridge: Cambridge University Press.

Gunther, R., Mantero, J. and Linz, J. (2002) *Political Parties: Old Concepts and New Challenges*, Oxford: Oxford University Press.

Haas, P. (1992) 'Epistemic Communities and International Policy Coordination' in *International Organization*, Vol. 46, No. 1, pp. 1–35.

Habermas, J. (1977) *Legitimation Crisis*, Cambridge: Polity Press.

——(1987) *The Theory of Communicative Action*, Cambridge: Polity Press.

——(1989 [1962]) *The Structural Transformation of the Public Sphere: An Inquiry into a Category of Bourgeois Society* (trans. by Burger, T.), Cambridge: Polity Press.

——(1992) 'Further Reflections on the Public Sphere' (trans. by Burger, T.) in Calhoun, C. (ed.) *Habermas and the Public Sphere*, Cambridge, Mass: MIT Press.

——(1996) *Between Facts and Norms*, Cambridge: Polity Press.

——(1999) 'The European Nation State and the Pressures of Globalization' in *New Left Review*, Issue 235, pp. 425–36.

——(2001) *The Postnational Constellation: Political Essays*, Cambridge, Mass: MIT Press.

——(2002) 'A Conversation About Questions of Political Theory' in von Schomberg, R. and Baynes, K. (eds) *Essays on Habermas: Between Facts and Norms*, Albany, New York: State University of New York.

Hague, R. and Harrop, M. (2007) *Comparative Government and Politics*, 7th edn, Houndmills, Basingstoke: Palgrave Macmillan.

Hall, P. (1999) 'Social Capital in Britain' in the *British Journal of Politics*, Vol. 29, pp. 417–61.

Hall, S., Critcher, C., Jefferson, T., Clarke, J. and Roberts, B. (1978) *Policing the Crisis – Mugging, the State, and Law and Order*, London: Macmillan.

Hallin, D. (1994) *We Keep America on Top of the World – Television Journalism and the Public Sphere*, London: Routledge.

Hallin, D. and Mancini, P. (2004) *Comparing Media Systems: Three Models of Media and Politics*, Cambridge: Cambridge University Press.

Hall Jamieson, K. (1996) *Packaging the Presidency: A History and Criticism of Presidential Campaign Advertising*, 3rd edn, Oxford: Oxford University Press.

Hansard (2004) *An Audit of Political Engagement*, London: Hansard Society and Electoral Commission.

——(2005) *Members Only: Parliament in the Public Eye*, London: Hansard Society.

——(2009) *Audit of Political Engagement 6: The 2009 Report*, London: Hansard Society.

Hansen, A., ed. (1993) *The Mass Media and Environmental Issues*, Leicester: Leicester University Press.

Hardt, M. and Negri, A. (2000) *Empire*, Cambridge, MA.: Harvard University Press.

Hardy, J. (2008) *Western Media Systems*, London: Routledge.

Hawley, C. (2003) 'Confusion and Betrayal: An Arab Mosaic' in Beck, S. and Downey, M. (eds) *The Battle for Iraq: BBC News Correspondents on the War Against Saddam and a New World Agenda*, London: BBC Books.

Hay, C. (2007) *Why We Hate Politics*, Cambridge: Polity.

Healey, J., Gill, M. and McHugh, D. (2005) *MPs and Politics in Our Time*, London: MORI and Hansard Society.

Heath, A., Jowell, R. and Curtice, J. (2001) *The Rise of New Labour: Party Policies and Voter Choices*, Oxford: Oxford University Press.

Heffernan, R. (2003) 'Political Parties and the Party System' in Dunleavy, P., Gamble, A., Heffernan, R. and Peele, G. (eds) *Developments in British Politics 7*, Basingstoke: Palgrave Macmillan.

Held, D. (2002) 'Laws of States, Laws of Peoples' in *Legal Theory*, Vol. 8, pp. 1–44.

——(2003) 'Cosmopolitanism: Globalisation Tamed?' in *Review of International Studies*, Vol. 29, pp. 465–80.

Held, D. and McGrew, A. (2003) 'The Great Globalization Debate: An Introduction' in Held, D. and McGrew, A. (eds) *The Global Transformations Reader: An Introduction to the Globalization Debate*, Cambridge: Polity Press.

Herbst, S. (1998) *Reading Public Opinion: Political Actors View the Democratic Process*, Chicago: University of Chicago Press.

Herman, E. and Chomsky, N. (2002) *Manufacturing Consent*, 2nd edn, New York: Pantheon.

Herman, E. and McChesney, R. (1997) *The Global Media: The New Missionaries of Global Capitalism*, London: Cassell.

Hesmondhalgh, D. (2006) 'Bourdieu, the Media and Cultural Production' in *Media, Culture and Society*, Vol. 28, No. 2, pp. 211–31.

Hess, S. (1984) *The Government/Press Connection: Press Officers and Their Offices*, Washington, DC: Brookings Institute.

Hibbings, J. and Theiss-Morse, E. (2002) *Stealth Democracy: Americans' Beliefs About How Government Should Work*, Cambridge: Cambridge University Press.

Hilgartner, S. and Bosk, C. (1988) 'The Rise and Fall of Social Problems: A Public Arenas Model' in *American Journal of Sociology*, Vol. 94, No. 1, pp. 53–78.

Hindman, M. (2008) *The Myth of Digital Democracy*, Princeton: Princeton University Press.

Hirst, P. and Thompson, G. (1996) *Globalization in Question: The International Economy and the Possibilities of Governance*, Cambridge: Polity Press.

Holton, R. (2008) *Global Networks*, Houndsmill, Basingstoke: Palgrave Macmillan.

Hoogvelt, A. (1997) *Globalization and the Postcolonial World*, 2nd edn, Houndmills, Basingstoke: Palgrave.

Horkheimer, M. and Adorno, T. (1977) *The Frankfurt School: The Critical Theories of Max Horkheimer and Theodor Adorno*, ed. Tar, Z., London: Wiley.

Horton, D. and Wohl, R. (1993) 'Mass Communication and Para-Social Interaction' in Corner, J. and Hawthorn, J. (eds) *Communication Studies: An Introductory Reader*, 4th edn, London: Arnold.

House of Commons (HoC) Reports, London: HMSO.

—(July 2002) *Digital Technology: Working for Parliament*, London: House of Commons Information Committee.

—Research Paper 02/53 (September, 2002) *Iraq: the Debate on Policy Options*, House of Commons Library.

—Research Paper 03/22 (March 2003) *Iraq: Developments Since UN Security Council Resolution 1441*, House of Commons Library.

—Foreign Affairs Committee (July 2003) *The Decision to go to War in Iraq: Ninth Report of Session 2002–03*, HC 813–1.

—(June 2004) *Connecting Parliament with the Public: First Report of Session 2003–04*, Select Committee on Modernisation of the House of Commons.

—(2004) *House of Commons Liaison Committee: Annual Report for 2004*.

—(July 2005) *Twenty-Seventh Annual Report – Financial Year 2005/2006*, House of Commons Commission.

—(December 2005) *House of Commons Corporate Business Plan 2006*.

—(2007) *Twenty-Ninth Annual Report – Financial Year 2006–07*, House of Commons Commission.

—Library Standard Note (June 2009) *Timeline of House of Commons Responses to the War*, SN/PC/02941, House of Commons Library.

Hudson, V. (2005) 'Foreign Policy Analysis: Actor-Specific Theory and the Ground of International Relations' in *Foreign Policy Analysis*, Vol. 1, No. 1, pp. 1–30.

Hurst, G. (11.10.05) 'Leadership Contenders Set up Camp as Cameron Rides High' in *The Times*, London: News Group Newspapers.

Hutton, J. (2004) *The Hutton Inquiry/Report of the Inquiry into the Circumstances Surrounding the Death of David Kelly*, HC 247, London: HMSO.

Hutton, W. (1996) *The State We're In*, London: Vintage.

IDEA (2009) Institute for Democracy and Electoral Assistance, http://www.idea.int, accessed October 2009.

IMA (Investment Management Association) (2003) *Survey of Members*, London: IMA.

IMF (2008) International Monetary Fund, http://www.imf.org, accessed October 2009.

Inglehart, R. (1977) *The Silent Revolution: Changing Values and Political Styles Amongst Western Publics*, Princeton, New Jersey: Princeton University Press.

——(1990) *Culture Shift*, Princeton New Jersy: Princeton University Press.

——(1997) *Modernization and Postmodernization: Cultural, Economic and Political Change in 43 Countries*, Princeton, New Jersey: Princeton University Press.

——(1999) 'Postmodernization Erodes Respect for Authority, but Increases Support for Democracy' in Norris, P. (ed) *Critical Citizens: Global Support for Democratic Government*, Oxford: Oxford University Press.

Internet World Stats (2009), http://www.internetworldstats.com/, accessed October 2009.

Ipsos-MORI (1983–2009) *Trust in People*, London: Ipsos-MORI.

——(1990–2008) *British Public Opinion Newsletter*, London: Ipsos-MORI.

——(1997–2009) *Long Term Trends: The Most Important Issues Facing Britain*, London: Ipsos-MORI.

IPU (2009) Inter-Parliamentary Union, http://www.ipu.org, accessed October 2009.

Iyengar, S. and Kinder, D. (1987) *News that Matters*, Chicago: Chicago University Press.

Jackson, N. (April, 2003) 'Vote Winner or a Nuisance: Email and British MPs' Relationships with their Constituents', paper presented to Political Studies Association, Leicester.

Jackson, N. and Lilleker, D. (2004) 'Just Public Relations or an Attempt at Interaction? British MPs in the Press, On the Web and "In Your Face"' in *European Journal of Communication*, Vol. 19, No. 4, pp. 507–33.

Jakobson, P. (2000) 'Focus on the CNN Effect Misses the Point: the Real Media Impact on Conflict Managment is Invisible and Indirect' in the *Journal of Peace Research*, Vol. 37, No. 2, pp. 131–43.

Janis, I. (1982) *Groupthink*, Boston: Houghton-Mifflin.

Jensen, J. (2006) 'The Minnesota E-Democracy Project: Mobilising the Mobilised?' in Oates, S., Owen, D. and Gibson, R. (eds) *The Internet and Politics: Citizens, Voters and Activists*, London: Routledge.

Jhally, S. and Lewis, J. (1992) *Enlightened Racism: the Cosby Show, Audiences, and the Myth of the American Dream*, Boulder, Colorado, Oxford: Westview Press.

Jones, G. and Helm, T. (7.10.05) 'Davis Puts on a Brave Face After a Week that Turns to Disaster' in the *Daily Telegraph*, London: Telegraph Newspapers.

Jones, N. (1995) *Soundbites and Spin Doctors: How Politicians Manipulate the Media and Vice Versa*, London, Cassell.

——(2002) *The Control Freaks: How New Labour Gets its Own Way*, London: Politicos.

Kaldor, M. (2003) 'The Idea of Global Civil Society' in *International Affairs*, Vol. 79, No. 3, pp. 583–93.

Kampfner, J. (2004) *Blair's Wars*, London: Free Press.

Kantola, A. (2006) 'On the Dark Side of Democracy: The Global Imaginary of Financial Journalism' in Cammaerts, B. and Carpentier, N. (eds) *Reclaiming the Media: Communication, Rights and Democratic Media Roles*, Bristol: Intellect.

——(2009) 'The Disciplined Imaginary: The Nation Rejuvenated for the Global Condition' in Roosvall, A. and Salovaara-Moring, I. (eds) *Communicating the Nation*, Stockholm: Nordicom.

Kateb, G. (1992) *The Inner Ocean: Individualism and Democratic Culture*, New York: Cornell University Press.

Kauppi, N. (2003) 'Bourdieu's Political Sociology and the Politics of European Integration' in *Theory and Society*, Vol. 32, pp. 775–89.

Kavada, A. (2005) 'Civil Society Organisations and the Internet: the Case of Amnesty International, Oxfam and the World Development Movement' in de Jong, W., Shaw, M. and Stammers, N. (eds) *Global Activism Global Media*, London: Pluto Press.

Kavanagh, T. (28.05.05) 'David in Bullying Warning' in the *Sun*, London: News Group Newspapers.

Keane, J. (1991) *The Media and Democracy*, Cambridge: Polity Press.

——(2001) 'Global Civil Society?' in Anheier, H., Glasius, M. and Kaldor, M. (eds) *Global Civil Society Yearbook 2001*, Oxford: Oxford University Press.

Kearney, M. (2003) 'Blair's Gamble' in Beck, S. and Downey, M. (eds) *The Battle for Iraq: BBC News Correspondents on the War Against Saddam and a New World Agenda*, London: BBC Books.

Keck, M. and Sikkink, K. (1998) *Activists Beyond Borders: Advocacy Networks in International Politics*, Ithaca, New York: Cornell University Press.

Kellner, D. (2000) 'Habermas, the Public Sphere, and Democracy: A Critical Intervention' in Hahn, L. (ed.) *Perspectives on Habermas*, Chicago: Open Court Press.

Khong, Y. F. (2008) 'Neoconservativism and the Domestic Sources of American Foreign Policy: the Role of Ideas in Operation Iraqi Freedom' in Smith, S., Hadfield, A. and Dunne, T. (eds) *Foreign Policy: Theories, Actors, Cases*, Oxford: Oxford University Press.

Kircheimer, O. (1966) 'The Transformation of the Western European Party Systems' in Weiner, M. and LaPalombara, J. (eds) *Political Parties and Political Development*, Princeton, NJ: Princeton University Press.

Klein (1996), *Primary Colours: A Novel of Politics*, New York, Grand Central Publishing.

Knightley, P. (2004) *The First Casualty*, 3rd edn, London: André Deutsch.

Knorr Cetina, K. and Bruegger, U. (2002) 'Global Microstructures: the Virtual Societies of Financial Markets' in *American Journal of Sociology*, Vol. 107, No. 4, pp. 905–50.

Knuckey, J. and Lees-Marshment, J. (2005) 'American Political Marketing: George W. Bush and the Republican Party' in Lilleker, D. and Lees-Marshment, J. (eds) *Political Marketing: A Comparative Perspective*, Manchester: Manchester University Press.

Knudsen, J. (1998) 'Rebellion in Chiapas: Insurrection by Internet and Public Relations' in *Media, Culture and Society*,Vol. 20, No. 3, pp. 507–18.

Kogut, B. and MacPherson, J. (2008) 'The Decision to Privatize: Economists and the Construction of Ideas and Prices' in Simmons, B., Dobbin, F. and Garrett, G. (eds) *The Global Diffusion of Markets and Democracy*, Cambridge: Cambridge University Press.

Kull, S. and Ramsey, C. (2000) 'Elite Misperceptions of US Public Opinion and Foreign Policy' in Nacos, B., Shapiro, R. and Isernia, P. (eds) *Decisionmaking in a Glass House: Mass Media, Public Opinion, and American and European Foreign Policy in the 21st Century*, Lantham, Boulder: Rowman and Littlefield.

Kull, S., Ramsey, C. and Lewis, E. (2004) 'Misperceptions, the Media and the Iraq War' in *Political Science Quarterly*, Vol. 118, No. 4, pp. 569–98.

Kurtz, H. (1998) *Spin Cycle: Inside the Clinton Propaganda Machine*, Pan Books

Lazarsfeld, P., Berelson, B. and Gaudet, H. (1944) *The People's Choice*, New York: Duell, Sloan and Pearce.

LeDuc, L., Niemi, R. and Norris, P. eds (2009) *Comparing Democracies 3: Elections and Voting in the 21st Century*, London: Sage.

Lees, C. (2005) 'Political Marketing in Germany: The Campaigns of the Social Democratic Party' in Lilleker, D. and Lees-Marshment, J. (eds) *Political Marketing: A Comparative Perspective*, Manchester: Manchester University Press.

Lees-Marshment, J. (2001/2008) *Political Marketing and British Political Parties: The Party's Just Begun*, 1st/2nd edn, Manchester: Manchester University Press.

——(2004) *The Political Marketing Revolution: Transforming the Government of the UK*, Manchester: Manchester University Press.

Lewis, J. (2004) 'Television, Public Opinion and the War in Iraq: The Case of Britain' in *International Journal of Public Opinion Research*, Vol. 16, No. 3, pp. 295–310.

Lewis, J., Inthorn, S. and Wahl-Jorgensen, K. (2005) *Citizens or Consumers? What the Media Tell us About Political Participation*, Buckingham: Open University Press.

Lewis, J., Williams, A. and Franklin, B. (2008) 'A Compromised Fourth Estate? UK News Journalism, Public Relations and News Sources' in *Journalism Studies*, Vol. 9, No. 1, pp 1–20.

Leys, C. (2001) *Market Driven Politics*, London: Verso.

Lichtenberg, J. (2000) 'In Defence of Objectivity' in Curran, J. and Gurevitch, M. (eds) *Mass Media and Society*, 3rd edn, London: Arnold.

Liebes, T. and Katz, E. (1990) *The Export of Meaning: Cross Cultural Readings of Dallas*, Cambridge: Polity Press.

Lievrouw, L. and Livingstone, S. (2006) 'Introduction' in Lievrouw, L. and Livingstone, S. (eds) *The Handbook of New Media*, 2nd edn, London: Sage.

Lijphart, A. (1984) *Democracies: Patterns of Majoritarian and Consensus Government in Twenty-One Countries*, New Haven, CT: Yale University Press.

——(1999) *Patterns of Democracy: Government Forms and Performances in Thirty Six Countries*, New Haven, CT: Yale University Press.

Lilleker, D. (2005) 'The Impact of Political Marketing on Internal Party Democracy' in *Parliamentary Affairs*, Vol. 58, No. 3, pp. 570–84.

Lilleker, D. and Lees-Marshment, J. (2005) *Political Marketing: A Comparative Perspective*, Manchester: Manchester University Press.

Lindblom, C. (1977) *Politics and Markets: The World's Political Economic Systems*, New York: Basic Books.

Lippmann, W. (1925) *The Phantom Public*, New York: Harcourt Brace and Co.

Livingstone, S. (2003) 'On the Challenges of Cross-National Comparative Media Research' in *The European Journal of Communication*, Vol. 18, No. 4, pp. 477–500.

——(2005) 'Critical Debates in Internet Studies: Reflections on an Emerging Field' in Curran, J. and Gurevitch, M. (eds) *Mass Media and Society*, 4th edn, London: Hodder Arnold.

Lloyd, J. (2004) *What the Media Do to Our Politics*, London: Constable.

Lovink, G. (2007) *Zero Comments: Blogging and Critical Internet Culture*, New York: Routledge.

Lowrey, W. (2006) 'Mapping the Journalism-Blogging Relationship' in *Journalism: Theory, Criticism and Practice*, Vol. 7, No. 4, pp. 477–500.

Lull, J. (1995) *Media, Communication, Culture*, Cambridge: Cambridge University Press.

Lusoli, W. and Ward, S. (2003) 'Digital Rank-and-File: Party Activists' Perceptions and Use of the Internet', paper for the American Political Science Association Conference, Philadelphia, August.

Lusoli, W., Ward, S. and Gibson, R. (2006) '(Re)Connecting Politics? Parliament, the Public and the Internet' in *Parliamentary Affairs*, Vol. 59, No. 1, pp. 24–42.

Maarek, P. (1995) *Political Marketing and Communication*, Eastleigh: John Libby Press.

MacBride Report (1980) *Many Voices, One World: Communications and Society Today and Tomorrow*, International Commission for the Study of Communication Problems, Paris: UNESCO.

MacKenzie, D. and Wajcman, J., eds (1999) *The Social Shaping of Technology*, 2nd edn, Buckingham: Open University Press.

MacPherson, C. (1965) *The Real World of Democracy*, Toronto: Canadian Broadcasting Company.

Maltese, J. (1994) *Spin Control: The White House Office of Communications and the Management of Presidential News*, University of California Press.

Mancini, P. (1991) 'The Public Sphere and the Use of News in the "Coalition" System of Government' in Dahlgren, P. and Sparks, C. (eds) *Communication and Citizenship: Journalism and the Public Sphere*, London: Routledge.

Mann, M. (1997) 'Has Globalization Ended the Rise and Rise of the Nation State?' in *Review of International Political Economy*, Vol. 4, No. 3, pp. 472–96.

Manning, P. (2000) *News and News Sources*, London: Sage.

Marcus, G. (1995) 'Ethnography in/of World Systems: the Emergence of Multi-Sited Ethnography' in the *Annual Review of Anthropology*, Vol. 24, pp. 95–117.

Marsh, D. and Rhodes, R. (1992) *Policy Networks in British Government*, Oxford: Clarendon.

Marsh, D., Richards, D. and Smith, M. J. (2001) *Changing Patterns of Governance in the United Kingdom*, Houndmills, Basingstoke: Palgrave.

Mattelart, A., Delcourt, X. and Mattelart, M. (1984) *International Image Markets: In Search of an Alternative Perspective*, London: Comedia.

Mazarr, M. (2007) 'The Iraq War and Agenda Setting' in *Foreign Policy Analysis*, Vol. 3, No. 1, pp. 1–23.

McChesney, R. (1999) *Rich Media, Poor Democracy: Communication Politics in Dubious Times*, Urbana: University of Illinois Press.

McGrew, A. (2002) 'Models of Transnational Democracy' in Carter, A. and Stokes, G. (eds) *Democratic Theory Today*, Cambridge: Polity Press.

McLuhan, M. (1962) *The Gutenberg Galaxy: The Making of Typographic Man*, Toronto: University of Toronto Press.

McNair, B. (2000) *Journalism and Democracy: An Evaluation of the Public Sphere*, London: Routledge.

——(2003) *An Introduction to Political Communication*, 3rd edn, London: Routledge.

——(2006) *Cultural Chaos: Journalism, News and Power in a Globalised World*, London: Routledge.

Merrill, J. (1974) *The Imperatives of Freedom*, New York: Hastings House.

Meyer, C. (2005) *DC Confidential: The Controversial Memoirs of Britain's Ambassador to the United States at the Time of 9/11 and the Run-up to the Iraq War*, London: Phoenix.

Meyer, T. (2002) *Media Democracy: How the Media Colonize Politics*, Cambridge: Polity Press.

Michels, R. (1967 [1911]) *Political Parties*, New York: Free Press.

Miller, D. (1994) *Don't Mention the War: Northern Ireland, Propaganda and the Media*, London: Pluto Press.

——(2004) 'Introduction' in Miller, D. (ed.) *Tell Me Lies: Propaganda and Media Distortion in the Attack on Iraq*, London: Pluto Press.

Miller, D., Kitzenger, J., Williams, K. and Beharrell, P. (1998) *The Circuits of Mass Communication*, London: Sage.

Mills, C. Wright (1956) *The Power Elite*, Oxford: Oxford University Press.

Mintram, M. and Vergari, S. (1998) 'Policy Networks and Innovation Diffusion: The Case of State Education Reforms' in the *Journal of Politics*, Vol. 60, No. 1, pp. 126–48.

Mintz, A. (2004) 'How do Leaders Make Decisions? A Polyheuristic Perspective' in *Journal of Conflict Resolution*, Vol. 48, pp. 3–13.

Mitchell, N. (1997) *The Conspicuous Corporation – Business, Publicity, and Representative Democracy*, Ann Arbor: University of Michigan Press.

Monbiot, G. (2000) *Captive State: The Corporate Takeover of Britain*, Basingstoke: Pan.

Montgomery, T. (Dec, 2006) *How Cameron Won and Davis Lost*, on ConservativeHome.Com.

MORI (Jan, March 2003) *War with Iraq – Public View*, London: MORI.

Morley, D. (1980) *The Nationwide Audience*, London: BFI.

Morley, D. and Robins, K. (1995) *Spaces of Identity: Global Media, Electronic Landscapes and Cultural Boundaries*, London: Routledge.

Mosca, G. (1939) *The Ruling Class*, New York: McGraw-Hill.

Mosley, L. (2003) *Global Capital and National Governments*, Cambridge: Cambridge University Press.

Mowlana, H., Gerbner, G. and Schiller, H., eds (1992) *Triumph of the Image: The Media's War in the Persian Gulf*, Boulder: Westview Press.

Murshetz, P. (1998) 'State Support for the Daily Press in Europe: A Critical Appraisal – Austria, France, Norway and Sweden Compared' in *European Journal of Communication*, Vol. 13, No. 3, pp. 291–313.

Naughton, J. (2001) 'Contested Space: The Internet and Global Civil Society' in Anheier, H., Glasius, M. and Kaldor, M. (eds) *Global Civil Society Yearbook 2001*, Oxford: Oxford University Press.

Negrine, R. (1998) *Parliament and the Media: A Study of Britain, Germany and France*, London: Royal Institute of International Affairs.

Negroponte, N. (1995) *Being Digital*, London: Hodder and Stoughton.

Nelson, J. (1989) *Sultans of Sleaze: Public Relations and the Media*, Toronto: Between the Lines.

Nerone, J., ed. (1995) *Last Rights: Revisiting Four Theories of the Press*, Urbana, Illinois: University of Illinois Press.

Nessman, K. (1995) 'Public Relations in Europe: A Comparison with the United States' in *Public Relations Review*, 21, pp. 151–60.

Newman, B., ed. (1999) *The Handbook of Political Marketing*, Thousand Oaks, CA: Sage.

Nichols, J. and McChesney, R. (2009) 'The Death and Life of Great American Newspapers' in *The Nation* (April 6th 2009), New York.

Norris, P., ed. (1997) *Passages to Power: Legislative Recruitment in Advanced Democracies*, Cambridge: Cambridge University Press.

Norris, P. (1999a) 'Changes in Party Competition at Westminster' in Evans, G. and Norris, P. (eds) *Critical Elections: British Parties and Voters in Long-Term Perspective*, London: Sage.

Norris, P., ed. (1999b) *Critical Citizens: Global Support for Democratic Government*, Oxford: Oxford University Press.

Norris, P. (2000) *A Virtuous Circle: Political Communication in Postindustrial Societies*, Cambridge: Cambridge University Press.

——(2001) *Digital Divide: Civic Engagement, Information Poverty and the Internet Worldwide*, Cambridge: Cambridge University Press.

——(2002) *Democratic Phoenix: Political Activism World Wide*, New York: Cambridge University Press.

——(2003) 'Global Governance and Cosmopolitan Citizens' in Held, D. and McGrew, A. (eds) *The Global Transformations Reader*, Cambridge: Polity.

——(2004) 'Global Political Communication: Good Governance, Human Development, and Mass Communication' in Esser, F. and Pfetsch, B. (eds) *Comparing Political Communication: Theories, Cases and Challenges*, Cambridge: Cambridge University Press.

Norris, P. and Lovenduski, J. (1992) *British Candidate Study.*?

——(1997a) *British Representation Study.*?

——(1997b) 'United Kingdom' in Norris, P. (ed.) *Passages to Power: Legislative Recruitment in Advanced Democracies*, Cambridge: Cambridge University Press.

Norris, P., Curtice, J., Sanders, D., Scammell, M. and Semetko, H. (1999) *On Message: Communicating the Campaign*, London: Sage.

Norton, P. (2007) 'The House of Commons' in Jones, B., Kavanagh, D., Moran, M. and Norton, P. *Politics UK*, 6th edn, Harlow, Essex: Pearson.

NUJ (2006) *National Union of Journalists Survey of Members*, London: National Union of Journalists.

Oborne, P. (2007) *The Rise of Political Lying*, London: Simon and Schuster.

Ofcom (2007) *New News, Future News: The Challenges for Television News After Digital Switchover*, London: Ofcom.

Ohmae, K. (1990) *The Borderless World: Power and Strategy in the Interlinked Economy*, New York: HarperCollins.

——(1995) *The End of the Nation State*, New York: Free Press.

ONS (2007) *Civil Service Employment Q2 2007*, London: Office for National Statistics.

Palmer, J. (2000), *Spinning Into Control*, London: Continuum Books.

Pareto, V. (1935) *The Mind and Society*, New York: Dover.

Parsons, W. (1989) *The Power of the Financial Press: Journalism and Economic Opinion in Britain and America*, London: Edward Elgar.

Pateman, C. (1970) *Participation and Democratic Theory*, Cambridge: Cambridge University Press.

Patterson, T. (1994) *Out of Order*, Vintage Books.

Pattie, C., Seyd, P. and Whiteley, P. (2003) 'Citizenship and Civic Engagement: Attitudes and Behaviours in Britain' in *Political Studies*, Vol. 51, pp. 443–68.

——(2004) *Citizenship in Britain: Values, Participation and Democracy*, Cambridge: Cambridge University Press.

Pels, D. (2003) 'Aesthetic Representation and Political Style: Re-balancing Identity and Difference in Media Democracy' in Corner, J. and Pels, D. (eds) *Media and the Restyling of Politics*, London: Sage.

Pew (16th Jan 2003) 'Public Want Proof of Iraqi Weapons Programs', Washington, DC: Pew Research Centre.

Pew (20th Feb 2003) 'US Needs More International Backing', Washington, DC: Pew Research Centre.

Pew (16th March 2004) 'A Year After Iraq', *Pew Global Attitudes Report*, Washington, DC: Pew Research Centre.

Pew (2009) *The State of the News Media 2009*, Washington, DC: Pew/The Project for Excellence in Journalism.

Pharr, J. and Putnam, R., eds (2000) *Disaffected Democracies: What's Troubling the Trilateral Countries?* Princeton, New Jersey: Princeton University Press.

Philips, A. (2009) 'Old Sources, New Bottles' in Fenton, N. (ed.) *New Media, Old News: Journalism and Democracy in a Digital Age*, London: Sage.

Philo, G. (1995) *Glasgow Media Group Reader, Vol. 2: Industry, Economy, War and Politics*, London: Routledge.

Philo, G. and Berry, M. (2004) *Bad News from Israel*, London: Pluto Press.

Picard, R. (1985) *The Press and the Decline of Democracy*, Westport, CT: Greenwood Press.

Pickerill, J. (2004) 'Rethinking Political Participation: Experiments in Internet Activism in Australia and Britain' in Gibson, R., Roemmele, A. and Ward, S. (eds) *Electronic Democracy: Mobilisation, Organisation and Participation Via New ICTs*, London: Routledge.

——(2006) 'Radical Politics on the Net' in *Parliamentary Affairs*, Vol. 59, No. 2, pp. 266–82.

PICT (August 2006) Unpublished Internal House of Commons Statistics on Email Traffic, Produced by Parliamentary ICT Unit, London: House of Commons.

Piore, M. and Sabel, C. (1984) *The Second Industrial Divide*, New York: Basic Books.

Polanyi, K. (1944) *The Great Transformation*, Boston: Beacon Press.

Polat, R. (2005) 'The Internet and Political Participation' in *European Journal of Communication*, Vol. 20, No. 4, pp. 435–59.

Poulantzas, N. (1975) *Classes in Contemporary Capitalism*, London: New Left Books.

Power Report (2006) *Power to the People: An Independent Enquiry into Britain's Democracy*, York: Joseph Rowntree Trust.

Powlick, P. (1995) 'The Sources of Public Opinion for American Foreign Policy Officials' in *International Studies Quarterly*, Vol. 39, No. 4, pp. 427–51.

Price, L. (2005) *The Spin Doctor's Diary: Inside Number 10 with New Labour*, London: Hodder and Stoughton.

Price, V. (2008) 'Democracy, Global Publics and World Opinion' in Albrow, M., Anheier, H., Glasius, M., Price, M. and Kaldor, M. (eds) *Global Civil Society 2007/08: Communicative Power and Democracy*, London: Sage.

Protess, D., Cook, F. L., Doppelt, J. C., Ettema, J. S., Gordon, M. T., Leff, D. R. and Miller, P. (1991) *The Journalism of Outrage: Investigative Reporting and Agenda Building in America*, New York: The Guilford Press.

Przeworski, A. and Teune, H. (1970) *The Logic of Comparative Social Inquiry*, New York: Wiley.

Putnam, R. (1993) *Making Democracy Work: Civic Traditions in Modern Italy*, Princeton, New Jersey: Princeton University Press.

——(1995) 'Bowling Alone: America's Declining Social Capital' in *Journal of Democracy*, Vol. 6, No. 1, pp. 65–78.

——(2000) *Bowling Alone: The Collapse and Revival of American Community*, New York: Simon and Schuster.

Putnam, R., ed. (2002) *Democracies in Flux: The Evolution of Social Capital in Contemporary Societies*, Oxford: Oxford University Press.

Quandt, T., Loffelholz, M., Weaver, D., Hanitzsch, T. and Aitmeppen, K. (2006) 'American and German Online Journalists at the Beginning of the 21st Century: A Bi-National Survey' in *Journalism Studies*, Vol. 7, No. 2, pp. 171–86.

Rantanen, T. (2005) *The Media and Globalisation*, London: Sage.

Rash, W. (1997) *Politics on the Net*, New York: Freeman and Co.

Reese, S., Rutigliano, L., Hyun, K. and Jeong, J. (2007) 'Mapping the Blogosphere: Professional and Citizen-Based Media in the Global News Arena' in *Journalism: Theory, Criticism and Practice*, Vol. 8, No. 3, pp. 235–61.

Rees-Mogg, W. (02.10.05) 'The Tories' Future? It's Up To Gordon Brown' in the *Mail on Sunday*, London: Daily Mail and General Trust.

Rehg, W. and Bohman, J. (2002) 'Discourse and Democracy: The Formal and Informal Basis of Legitimacy in Between Facts and Norms' in von Schomberg, R. and Baynes, K. (eds) *Essays on Habermas: Between Facts and Norms*, Albany, New York: State University of New York.

Reich, R. (1991) *The Work of Nations*, New York: Simon and Schuster.

Reich, Z. (2006) 'The Process Model of News Initiative: Sources Lead, Reporters Thereafter' in *Journalism Studies*, Vol. 7, No. 4, pp. 497–514.

Reid, C. (2000) 'Whose Parliament? Political Oratory and Print Culture in the Later Eighteenth Century' in *Language and Literature*, Vol. 9, No. 2, pp. 122–34.

Rheingold, H. (2002) *Smart Mobs: The Next Social Revolution*, London: Perseus.

Rhodes, R. (1997) *Understanding Governance: Policy Networks, Governance, Reflexivity and Accountability*, Buckingham: Open University Press.

Richards, D. and Smith, M. (2002) *Governance and Public Policy in the UK*, Oxford: Oxford University Press.

Ritzer, G. (1998) *The McDonaldization Thesis*, London: Sage.

——(2004) *The McDonaldization of Society*, Thousand Oaks: Pine Forge Press.

Robinson, P. (1999) 'The CNN Effect: Can the News Media Drive Foreign Policy?' in *Review of International Studies*, Vol. 25, pp. 301–9.

Rommele, A. (2003) 'Political Parties, Party Communication and New Information and Communication Technologies' in *Party Politics*, Vol. 9, No. 1, pp. 7–20.

Rosenau, J. (1997) *Along the Domestic–Foreign Frontier*, Cambridge: Cambridge University Press.

Rosenbaum, M. (1997) *From Soapbox to Soundbite: Party Political Campaigning Since 1945*, Basingstoke, Hampshire: Macmillan.

Roudakova, N. (2008) 'Media-Political Clientalism: Lessons from Anthropology' in *Media, Culture and Society*, Vol. 30, No. 1, pp. 41–59.

Russell, M. (2005) *Must Politics Disappoint?* London: Fabian Society.

Said, E. (1978) *Orientalism*, London: Vintage Books.

Sanders, D. and Edwards, G. (1992) 'Consensus and Diversity in Elite Opinion: The Views of the British Foreign Policy Elite in the 1990s', Essex Papers in Politics and Government No. 92, Essex: University of Essex.

Sandford, J. (1997) 'Television in Germany' in Coleman, J. and Rollet, B. (eds) *Television in Europe*, Exeter: Intellect.

Savigny, H. (2005) 'Political Marketing and the 2005 Election: What's Ideology Got To Do With It?' in Lilleker, D., Jackson, N. and Scullion, R. (eds) (2006) *The Marketing of Political Parties: Political Marketing at the 2005 British General Election*, Manchester: Manchester University Press.

Scammell, M. (1995) *Designer Politics: How Elections are Won*, London: Macmillan.

——(1999) 'Political Marketing: Lessons for Political Science' in *Political Studies*, Vol. 47, No. 4, pp. 718–39.

——(2003) 'Citizen Consumers: Towards a New Marketing of Politics?' in Corner, J. and Pels, D. (eds) *Media and the Restyling of Politics: Consumerism, Celebrity and Cyncism*, London: Sage.

Scheuerman, W. (2002) 'Between Radicalism and Resignation: Democratic Theory in Habermas's *Between Facts and Norms*' in *Essays on Habermas: Between Facts and Norms*, Albany, New York: State University of New York.

Schiller, H. (1969) *Mass Communication and American Empire*, New York: Kelly.

——(1989) *Culture Inc: The Corporate Takeover of Public Expression*, Oxford: Oxford University Press.

——(1992) *Mass Communication and American Empire*, Boulder: Westview Press.

——(1996) *Information Inequality: The Deepening Social Crisis in America*, New York: Routledge.

Schlesinger, P. (1987) *Putting Reality Together*, 2nd edn, London: Methuen.

——(1999) 'Changing Spaces of Political Communication: The Case of the European Union' in *Political Communication*, Vol. 16, pp. 263–79.

——(2007) 'A Cosmopolitan Temptation' in the *European Journal of Communication*, Vol. 22, No. 4, pp. 413–26.

Schlesinger, P. and Tumber, H. (1994) *Reporting Crime: The Media Politics of Criminal Justice*, Oxford: Clarendon Press.

Scholte, J. (1997) 'Global Capitalism and the State' in *International Affairs*, Vol. 73, No. 3, pp. 427–52.

Schudson, M. (1995) *The Power of News*, Cambridge, Mass: Harvard University Press.

——(2003) *The Sociology of News*, New York: WW Norton and Co.

——(2006) *Why Democracies Need an Unlovable Press*, Cambridge: Polity Press.

Schumpeter, J. (1942) *Capitalism, Socialism and Democracy*, London: Unwin Books.

Schuster, J. and Maier, H. (2006) 'The Rift: Explaining Europe's Divergent Iraq Policies in the Run-Up to the American-Led War on Iraq' in *Foreign Policy Analysis*, No. 2, pp. 223–44.

Scott, B. (2005) 'A Contemporary History of Digital Journalism' in *Television and New Media*, Vol. 6, No. 1, pp. 84–126.

Seldon, A. (2005) *Blair*, London: Free Press.

Sennett, R. (1998) *The Corrosion of Character: The Personal Consequences of Work in the New Capitalism*, New York: Norton and Co.

——(2006) *The Culture of the New Capitalism*, New Haven: Yale University Press.

Sepstrup, P. (1989) 'Implications of Current Developments in Western European Broadcasting' in *Media, Culture and Society*, Vol. 11, No. 1, pp. 29–54.

Serra, S. (2000) 'The Killing of Brazilian Street Children and the Rise of the International Public Sphere' in Curran, J. (ed.), *Media Organisations in Society*, London: Arnold.

Short, C. (2005) *An Honourable Deception? New Labour, Iraq and the Misuse of Power*, London: Free Press.

Siebert, F., Peterson, T. and Schramm, W. (1956) *Four Theories of the Press*, Urbana: University of Illinois Press.

Sigal, L. V. (1973) *Reporters and Officials: The Organisation and Politics of Newsmaking*, Lexington, MA: Lexington Books.

Simmons, B., Dobbin, F. and Garrett, G. (2008) 'Introduction: the Diffusion of Liberalisation' in Simmons, B., Dobbin, F. and Garrett, G. (eds) *The Global Diffusion of Markets and Democracy*, Cambridge: Cambridge University Press.

Singer, J. (2003) 'Who Are These Guys? The Online Challenge to the Notion of Journalistic Professionalism' in *Journalism: Theory, Practice and Criticism*, Vol. 4, No. 2, pp. 139–68.

Sireau, N. (2009) *Make Poverty History: Political Communication in Action*, Houndmills, Basingstoke: Palgrave Macmillan.

Sklair, L. (2001) *The Transnational Capitalist Class*, Oxford: Blackwell.

Slaughter, A. (2000) 'Governing the Global Economy through Government Networks' in Byers, M. (ed.) *The Role of Law in International Politics*, Oxford: Oxford University Press.

Smith, M. (2003) 'The Core Executive and the Modernization of Central Government' in Dunleavy, P., Gamble, A., Heffernan, R. and Peele, G. (eds) *Developments in British Politics 7*, London: Palgrave Macmillan.

Smith, N. (July 2006) *Discourses of Globalisation and European Integration in the UK and Ireland, 2004–05*, Colchester, Essex: UK Data Archive.

Snow, N. (2003) 'Brainscrubbing: The Failures of US Public Diplomacy After 9/11' in Miller, D. (ed.) *Tell Me Lies: Propaganda and Media Distortion in the Attack on Iraq*, London: Pluto Press.

Soroka, S. (2003) 'Media, Public Opinion, and Foreign Policy' in *Harvard International Journal of Press/Politics*, Vol. 8, No. 1, pp. 27–48.

Sparks, C. (2001) 'The Internet and the Global Public Sphere' in Bennett, W. L. and Entman, R. (eds) *Mediated Politics: Communication in the Future of Democracy*, Cambridge: Cambridge University Press.

——(2005) 'Media and the Global Public Sphere: An Evaluative Approach' in de Jong, W., Shaw, M. and Stammers, N. (eds) *Global Activism Global Media*, London: Pluto Press.

Sparks, C. and Tulloch, J. (2000) *Tabloid Tales: Global Debates Over Media Standards*, Oxford: Rowman and Littlefield.

Sreberny-Mohammadi, A. (1996) 'The Global and the Local in International Communications' in Curran, J. and Gurevitch, M. (eds) *Mass Media and Society*, 2nd edn, London: Arnold.

Stammers, N. and Eschle, C. (2005) 'Social Movements and Global Activism' in de Jong, W., Shaw, M. and Stammers, N. (eds) *Global Activism Global Media*, London: Pluto Press.

Stanyer, J. and Wring, D. (2004) 'Public Images, Private Lives: An Introduction', Special Issue of *Parliamentary Affairs*, Vol. 57, No. 1, pp. 1–8.

Stauber, J. and Rampton, S. (2003) *Weapons of Mass Deception: The Uses of Propaganda in Bush's War on Iraq*, New York: Tarcher/Penguin.

Steger, M. (2009) *Globalization: A Very Short Introduction*, Oxford: Oxford University Press.

Stone, D. (1996) *Capturing the Political Imagination: Think Tanks and the Policy Process*, London: Frank Cass.

Strange, S. (1986) *Casino Capitalism*, Oxford: Blackwell.

——(1996) *The Retreat of the State: The Diffusion of Power in the World Economy*, Cambridge: Cambridge University Press.

——(1998) *Mad Money: When Markets Outgrow Governments*, Ann Arbor: University of Michigan Press.

Street, J. (1997) *Politics and Popular Culture*, Cambridge: Polity Press.

——(2003) 'The Celebrity Politician: Political Style and Popular Culture' in Corner, J. and Pels, D. (eds) *Media and the Restyling of Politics*, London: Sage.

Stromback, J. (2005) 'In Search of a Standard: Four Models of Democracy and their Normative Implications for Journalism' in *Journalism Studies*, Vol. 6, No. 3, pp. 331–45.

Stromback, J. and Nord, L. (2006) 'Do Politicians Lead the Tango? A Study of the Relationship Between Swedish Journalists and their Political Sources in the Context of Election Campaigns' in *European Journal of Communication*, Vol. 21, No. 2, pp. 147–64.

Sunstein, C. (2001) *Republic.Com*, Princeton: Princeton University Press.

Swank, D. (2002) *Global Capital, Political Institutions and Policy Change in Developed Welfare States*, Cambridge: Cambridge University Press.

Swanson, D. and Mancini, P., eds (1996) *Politics, Media and Modern Democracy: An International Study of Innovations in Electoral Campaigning and Their Consequences*, New York: Praeger Press.

Swartz, D. (2006) 'Pierre Bourdieu and North American Political Sociology: Why He Doesn't Fit But Should' in *French Politics*, Vol. 4, pp. 84–99.

Sylvester, R. (13.06.05) 'Blood and Feathers will Fly Before the Tories Pick a Leader' in the *Daily Telegraph*, London: Telegraph Newspapers.

Thompson, G. (2003) *Between Hierarchies and Markets: The Logic and Limits of Network Forms of Organization*, Oxford: Oxford University Press.

Thompson, J. (1995) *The Media and Modernity: A Social Theory of the Media*, Cambridge: Polity Press.

——(2000) *Political Scandal*, Cambridge: Polity Press.

Thussu, D., ed. (1998) *Electronic Empires: Global Media and Local Resistance*, London: Arnold.

——(2000) *International Communication: Continuity and Change*, London: Arnold.

——(2007) *Media on the Move: Global Flow and Contra-Flow*, London: Routledge.

——(2008) *News as Entertainment: The Rise of Global Infotainment*, London: Sage.

Thussu, D. and Freedman, D., eds (2003) *War and the Media: Reporting Conflict 24/7*, London: Sage.

Tiffen, R. (1989) *News and Power*, Sydney: Allen and Unwin.

——(1999) *Scandals: Media, Politics and Corruption in Contemporary Australia*, Sydney: UNSW Press.

Todd, M. and Taylor, G., eds (2004) *Democracy and Participation: Popular Protest and New Social Movements*, London: Merlin.

Tomlinson, J. (1999) *Globalization and Culture*, Cambridge: Polity Press.

Trenz, H. (2004) 'Media Coverage on European Governance: Exploring the European Public Sphere in National Quality Newspapers' in the *European Journal of Communication*, Vol. 19, No. 3, pp. 291–319.

Trippi, J. (2004) *The Revolution Will Not be Televised: Democracy, the Internet and the Overthrow of Everything*, Regan Books.

Tuchman, G. (1972) 'Objectivity as a Strategic Ritual: An Examination of Newsmen's Notion of Objectivity' in *American Journal of Sociology*, Vol. 77, No. 4, pp. 660–79.

Tumber, H. and Palmer, J. (2004) *Media at War: The Iraq Crisis*, London: Sage.

Tunstall, J. (1979) *The Media Are American*, London: Constable.

——(1996) *Newspaper Power: The National Press in Britain*, Oxford: Oxford University Press.

——(2007) *The Media Were American: US Mass Media in Decline*, Oxford: Oxford University Press.

Turner, G. (2004) *Understanding Celebrity*, London: Sage.

UNDP Human Development Index (2008) United Nations Development Programme, http://www.undp.org, accessed October 2009.

UNESCO (2004) United Nations Educational, Scientific and Cultural Organisation, http://portal.unesco.org, accessed October 2009.

US Senate (2004) *The Senate Report on Iraqi WMD Intelligence*, Washington: US Government Printing Office.

——(2005) *The Commission on the Intelligence Capabilities of the United States Regarding Weapons of Mass Destruction*, Washington: US Government Printing Office.

——(2008) *Report on Whether Public Statements Regarding Iraq by United States Government Officials Were Substantiated*, Washington: US Government Printing Office.

Varis, T. (1988) 'Trends in International Television Flow' in Schneider, C. and Wallis, B. (eds) *Global Television*, New York: Wedge.

Volkmer, I. (1999) *CNN News in the Global Sphere: A Study of CNN and its Impact on Global Communication*, Luton, Beds.: University of Luton Press.

——(2005) 'News in the Global Public Sphere' in Allan, S. (ed.) *Journalism: Critical Issues*, Maidenhead: Open University Press.

Von Schomberg, R. and Baynes, K., eds (2002) *Essays on Habermas: Between Facts and Norms*, Albany, New York: State University of New York.

Wacquant, L. (2004) 'Pointers on Pierre Bourdieu and Democratic Politics' in *Constellations*, Vol. 11, No. 1, pp. 3–15.

Walgrave, S. and van Aelst, P. (2006) 'The Contingency of the Mass Media's Political Agenda-Setting Power: Towards a Preliminary Theory' in *Journal of Communication*, Vol. 56, pp. 88–109.

Ward, S. and Gibson, R. (2000) 'The Politics of the Future? UK Parties and the Internet' in Coleman, S. (ed.) *Elections in the Age of the Internet: Lessons from the United States*, London: Hansard Society.

Ward, S., Gibson, R. and Lusoli, W. (2005) *The Promise and Perils of 'Virtual Representation': The Public's View*, London: NOP Opinion Survey.

Ward, S., Lusoli, W. and Gibson, R. (2002) 'Virtually Participating: A Survey of Online Party Members' in *Information Polity*, Vol. 7, No. 4, pp. 199–215.

Washbourne, N. (2005) *(Comprehensive) Political Marketing, Expertise and the Conditions for Democracy*, Reading: Paper Presentation PSA Conference.

Webb, P. (2000) *The Modern British Party System*, London: Sage.

——(2007) 'Political Parties and the Democratic Disconnect: A Call for Research' in Webb, P. *Democracy and Political Parties*, London: Hansard.

Webb, P. and Farrell, D. (1999) 'Party Members and Ideological Change' in Evans, G. and Norris, P. (eds) *Critical Elections: British Parties and Voters in Long-Term Perspective*, London: Sage.

Weber, M. (1948) *From Max Weber: Essays in Sociology*, Gerth, H. and Wright Mills, C. (eds), London: Routledge.

Webster, F. (2006) *Theories of the Information Society*, 3rd edn, London: Routledge.

Wernick, A. (1991) *Promotional Culture – Advertising, Ideology and Symbolic Expression*, London: Sage.

West, D. and Orman, J. (2003) *Celebrity Politics*, Upper Saddle River, NJ: Prentice-Hall.

Wikland, H. (2005) 'A Habermasian Analysis of the Deliberative Democratic Potential of ICT-Enabled Services in Swedish Municipalities' in *New Media and Society*, Vol. 7, No. 5, pp.701–23.

Willetts, P. (2008) 'Transnational Actors and International Organizations in Global Politics' in Baylis, J., Smith, S. and Owens, P. (eds) *The Globalization of World Politics: An Introduction to International Relations*, 2nd edn, Oxford: Oxford University Press.

Winston, B. (1998) *Media, Technology and Society: A History from the Telegraph to the Internet*, London: Routledge.

Wolfsfeld, G. (1997) *Media and Political Conflict: News from the Middle East*, Cambridge: Cambridge University Press.

Woodward, B. (2004) *Plan of Attack*, New York Pocket Books.

——(2006) *State of Denial: Bush at War, Part III*, New York: Simon and Schuster.

World Bank Group (2009) http://www.worldbank.org, accessed October 2009.

World Values Survey (2005–8) World Values Survey 5th Wave, http://www.worldvaluessurvey.org, accessed October 2009.

Wring, D. (2005) *The Politics of Marketing the Labour Party*, London: Palgrave.

YouGov Opinion Polls (25.05.04) *YouGov/Daily Telegraph Survey on the European and Local Elections*, London: YouGov.

YouGov Opinion Polls (June 2005) *YouGov/Sky News Survey on Britain, Europe and the G8*, London: YouGov.

Zelizer, B. (2004) *Taking Journalism Seriously: News and the Academy*, Thousand Oaks, California: Sage.

Zelizer, B. and Allan, S., eds (2002) *Journalism After September 11*, London: Sage.

Zhao, Y. and Hackett, R. (2005) 'Media Globalization, Media Democratization: Challenges, Issues, and Paradoxes' in Hackett, R. and Zhao, Y. (eds) *Democratizing Global Media: One World, Many Struggles*, Oxford: Rowman and Littlefield.

Index

News and Journalism in the UK
Fifth Edition

Brian McNair

Series: COMMUNICATION AND SOCIETY
Series editor: James Curran

News and Journalism in the UK is an accessible and comprehensive introduction to the political, economic and regulatory environments of press and broadcast journalism in Britain and Northern Ireland.

Surveying the industry in a period of radical economic and technological change, Brian McNair examines the main trends in journalistic media in the last two decades and assesses the challenges and future of the industry in the new millennium.

Integrating both academic and journalistic perspectives on journalism, topics addressed in this revised and updated edition include:

- The rise of online journalism and the impact of blogging on mainstream journalism
- The emergence of 24 hour news channels in the UK
- The role and impact of journalism, with reference to issues such as democracy, health scares and the war on terror
- Trends in media ownership and editorial allegiances
- 'Tabloidisation', Americanisation and the supposed 'dumbing down' of journalistic standards
- The implications of devolution for regional journalists.

ISBN 13: 978-0-415-41071-7 (hbk)
ISBN 13: 978-0-415-41072-4 (pbk)
ISBN 13: 978-0-203-88141-5 (ebk)